Waters of the Son

Baptists in Georgian Bath

Kerry J Birch

Kappa Beta Publications

Copyright © Kerry J Birch, 2009

First published in 2009 by Kappa Beta Publications

www.kappa-beta.org.uk

All rights reserved. No part of this publication may be reproduced, stored in a retrieval system, or transmitted in any form or by any means, electronic, mechanical, photocopying, recording or otherwise, without the prior permission of the publisher.

ISBN 978-0-9565066-0-3

AEEB

Table of Contents

Table of Contents v
List of Figures and Illustrations vii
Preface and Acknowledgements ix
Chapter 1: Introduction 1
   Matthew Arnold on Nonconformity 1
   The Long Eighteenth Century 3
   Local Baptist Histories 15
   Eighteenth Century Baptist Growth 33
Chapter 2: Origins and Overview 37
   Western Baptist Association 37
   Baptists at Haycombe 52
   The Presbyterian Connection 57
Chapter 3: Community and Minister 61
   Robert Parsons of Widcombe 61
   The Community and its Pastor 71
   The Community and its Covenant 76
   Propagation and Growth 87
   The First Burial Ground 92
Chapter 4: Challenge and Change 99
   Association and Gospel 99
   Education and Ministry 105
   Thomas Parsons 112
   An Uneasy Succession 119
   Parsons' Public Voice 126
Chapter 5: Growth and Fragmentation 131
   Gospel Propagation in Twerton 131
   John Paul Porter's Success 138
   Opie Smith 145
   The New Baptist Burial Ground 161
   Somerset Street in Trouble 168
Chapter 6: A New Community 177
   Twerton Separates 177
   Bath Baptists approaching 1837 218
Chapter 7: Conclusion 223
Bibliography 231

List of Figures and Illustrations

Figure 1. Manvers Street Baptist Church, 1902 13
Figure 2. Oldfield Park Baptist Church, 1928 14
Figure 3. Cadby House, Twerton 31
Figure 4. Bath Baptists in Published Lists, 1790-1835 35
Figure 5. Western Baptist Association, 1733-1823. 48
Figure 6. Western Baptist Association, 1733-1823 – Analysis. 49
Figure 7. Western Baptist Association Total Baptisms. 50
Figure 8. Western Baptist Association Average Baptisms. 50
Figure 9. Western Baptist Association Membership Increase. 51
Figure 10. The Parsons Vase at Stourhead 65
Figure 11. Possible site of Marchant's Passage Meeting House 70
Figure 12. The plaque from Marchant's Passage 71
Figure 13. The 1759 Garrard Street Communion Cup 75
Figure 14. The 1807 James Evill Communion Cup 76
Figure 15. The Somerset Street Covenant 79
Figure 16. An Account of Bath Baptist Strength, 1760 86
Figure 17. Former Somerset Street Chapel, 1912 90
Figure 18. Somerset Street Members, 1759-89. 91
Figure 19. Bladud by Thomas Parsons alongside its source 118
Figure 20. Opie Smith and Robert Goldstone sent to Twerton 132
Figure 21. Somerset Street Members, 1789-1837. 138
Figure 22. John Paul Porter's Baptism Record 139
Figure 23. John Paul Porter, Baptisms 1790-1828 140
Figure 24. Portrait of John Paul Porter 143
Figure 25. Westfield House 149
Figure 26. Southcot House 153
Figure 27. Stone Vase in front of Westfield House 160
Figure 28. Headstone of George Cox 165
Figure 29. Lyncombe Hill Baptist Burial Ground Restored 167
Figure 30. York Street Chapel, 1829 172
Figure 31. Members of Twerton Baptist Church. 186
Figure 32. Population of Twerton. 186
Figure 33. Baptist Members as % of Twerton Population 187
Figure 34. Twerton Baptist Chapel, c1900 206
Figure 35. Twerton Baptist Chapel, 1926 209

Figure 36. Thomas Street Chapel.. 220
Figure 37. Former Bethesda Chapel, York Street................................ 222
Figure 38. Somerset Street Members, 1759-1851. 223
Figure 39. Total Baptist Church Members in Bath, 1837-1851 224
Figure 40. Members of Baptist Churches in Bath. 225
Figure 41. Population of the City of Bath. 225
Figure 42. Baptist Members as % of Bath Population......................... 225
Figure 43. The Living Giants of Manvers Street, 1935........................ 229

Preface and Acknowledgements

This book has been a long time in the making. It began as a personal voyage of discovery in the 1980s, as a young man was exploring the history of the city he loved and the church where he grew up. Parts of it have subsequently appeared in talks given to members of the churches involved, in an historical exhibition at Manvers Street Baptist Church, in a report for the Bath Preservation Trust, in a Chapels Society study weekend in Bath, a walking tour around Bath, in a presentation to the History of Bath Research Group, in college essays, and finally in a study awarded an MLitt degree from the University of Bristol through Bristol Baptist College. This was titled *The Contribution of the Baptists of Bath to the Religious and Social History of the City (1714-1837) with Special Reference to Somerset Street and Twerton Baptist Churches*. It is the text of this study that appears in this book – although I do not consider it the final word that can be said or written on the subject. Rather, exploring the story of the early Baptists of Bath remains a work in progress, yet one which requires something appear in print at some point! Thank you to those who have encouraged me to do so, and have been patient in waiting for it to appear. If any reader has any further information or query related to the subject they may contact me via the publishers' web site given at the front of this book. I am currently working on fuller studies of Richard Gay at Haycombe, Opie Smith and his contribution to Baptist life, Rev Edward Clarke and his involvement in Education at Twerton, and the life and ministry of Rev Octavius Winslow – if you can help with any of these I shall be very pleased to hear from you.

This book is dedicated to the memory of my Mum, Anne Elizabeth Eyles Birch, who died just as the MLitt study was being completed. I also want to remember four other women: Faith A E Brettell, Joan Rusbridge, Cynthia Turner and Marjorie Reeves, who each in different ways inspired the young man in his quest to understand the history of his home city, church and faith. Finally I want to remember Twerton Baptist Church, a creative family of Christian people during my formative years, yet closed in 2004 after two hundred and fifty years of faithful witness. The Twerton Baptist legacy now resides in the Twerton Fellowship (Baptists and Methodists meeting together in Twerton Village Hall) and of course in the Baptist Church at Oldfield Park. I wish I could thank you all personally but, as I cannot, I gladly take this opportunity to thank you now. Thank you.

I acknowledge the patience and encouragement of everyone who has helped in the course of my researches, particularly Ruth Gouldbourne, John Briggs, Brian Haymes, Chris Ellis, and members and friends at Gas Green Baptist Church in Cheltenham and Rainbow Hill Baptist Church in Worcester where I have been minister over the past decade. I also gladly acknowledge the many institutions and individuals who have helped in discovering or providing sources for this study. Manvers Street Baptist Church and Oldfield Park Baptist Church in Bath, whose early histories this book explores, were most generous in opening their archives to me as a friend and fellow Baptist. Other archives and libraries were equally helpful in my quest for even the smallest of amount of information, including: Bristol Baptist College Library, the Angus Library at Regent's Park College in Oxford, Bath Record Office, Bath Central Library, Bath Industrial Heritage Centre, Somerset Record Office, Somerset Local History Library, Dr Williams's Library in London, the British Library and the Public Record Office or The National Archives as it is now known.

Most of the illustrations in this book have come from my own camera or are in my own collection, however I am grateful to Colin Johnston at Bath Record Office for permission to reproduce the images in his care, and to Eric Chandler of Manvers Street Baptist Church for being able to photograph a number of records and images from their archive.

There have been many individuals, some representing the institutions I have already acknowledged, some no longer with us, who have taken a particular interest and helped in many different ways during the course of my lengthy investigations: Stephen Bunker, Stuart Burroughs, Eric Chandler, Graeme and Heather Chatfield, John Davis, Mary Ede, John Evans, Trevor Fawcett, Steve Finamore, Roger Hayden, Meryl Hirons, Elizabeth Holland, Fred Hughes, Colin Johnston, Ian Kember, Godfrey Laurence, Russell Leitch, Michael Messer, Robert Oliver, John Rackley, Stella Read, Nigel Scotland, Shirley Shire, Gillian Sladen, Susan Sloman, Connie Smith, Hugh Torrens, John Wroughton, and others. If I have forgotten to name you, I am really sorry – and thank you. As this study was nearing completion, Susan Sloman's essay on Thomas Parsons appeared in *The British Art Journal*. Based on the previously unattributed diary of Parsons between January and August 1769, in the possession of the Huntington Library, California, Susan Sloman gives a fascinating account that fills in further background to events and personalities in this present study. I have not made reference to her essay in this text, but have added it to the bibliography and gladly refer you there. Thank you Susan.

Finally, there is a small group of people I want to acknowledge because they have, in addition to some already mentioned above, been the friends who have kept me grounded and sane in recent years. To Jonathan Philpott, Carl Smith, Brian and Mary Hooper, Seb Bees and Pete Everitt I offer my sincere thanks. And to you, Dad, for your ongoing love and encouragement in all I do, I shall forever be in your debt.

Kerry J Birch

Worcester, December 2009

We are a garden wall'd around,
Chosen and made peculiar ground;
A little spot enclosed by grace
Out of the world's wide wilderness.

    Isaac Watts, *Hymns*

Proud City of Bath with your crescents and squares,
Your hoary old Abbey and playbills and chairs,
Your plentiful chapels where preachers would preach
(And a different doctrine expounded in each)…

    John Betjeman, *The Newest Bath Guide*

Chapter 1: Introduction

Matthew Arnold on Nonconformity

> "May not every man in England say what he likes?"—Mr. Roebuck perpetually asks; and that, he thinks, is quite sufficient, and when every man may say what he likes, our aspirations ought to be satisfied. But the aspirations of culture, which is the study of perfection, are not satisfied, unless what men say, when they may say what they like, is worth saying,—has good in it, and more good than bad.[1]

Matthew Arnold's mid-nineteenth-century view of Nonconformity, expressed in *Culture and Anarchy*, was unequivocal. 'Certainly we are no enemies of the Nonconformists', he wrote, 'for, on the contrary, what we aim at is their perfection.'[2] Yet such 'perfection', to which 'culture' aspires, 'is made the harder for others to find, general perfection is put further off out of our reach, and the confusion and perplexity in which our society now labours is increased by the Nonconformists rather than diminished by them.'[3] John Arthur Roebuck, subject of Arnold's criticism, and by whose 'stock argument' for freedom of speech Arnold was particularly provoked,[4] had been dramatically elected Member of Parliament for Bath in 1832 on a clear reforming agenda.[5] The 1832 election hustings in Bath were accompanied by posters declaring 'Equal Rights' and 'All we ask is equal rights', along with a rousing chorus of 'Roebuck shall get in, whether or no.'[6] Among Roebuck's supporters were a number of Bath's newly politicised Baptists.[7] Baptists were among the many Dissenters or Nonconformists that Arnold manifestly despised as non-conducive to the cultural welfare of nineteenth-century British society, yet who by their political involvement were demonstrating that they were both culturally and socially engaged. However the culture that Arnold had in mind concerned the higher intellectual pursuits of the arts, sciences and politics about which, he believed, the Nonconformists of his day were either ignorant or cared little.

---

[1] Arnold, 1869, 17.
[2] Ibid, xvi.
[3] Ibid, xvii.
[4] Ibid, 17.
[5] Defeating Lord John Thynne, Roebuck won the 1832 seat as an Independent candidate, alongside Major-General Charles Palmer, to the first Parliament after the Great Reform Act had increased the electorate. Roebuck held the seat until 1837 when he lost to the Conservative candidate, William Bruges. Roebuck again held the Bath seat from 1841 to 1847. For Bath's eighteenth-century MPs see Fawcett, 2001, 80-2.
[6] Wroughton, 1972, 28-32, 108-9.
[7] Neale, 1981, 347.

Arnold's 'scathing denunciation' of a cultureless Nonconformity, which helped to 'establish the legend of evangelical philistinism', was the starting point for Doreen Rosman's study of Evangelicals and Culture between 1790 and 1833.[8] Her sweeping survey of Evangelicals both within Nonconformity and the established church convincingly demonstrated that they did engage in cultural, artistic and intellectual pursuits, but that their evangelical worldview often prevented their full participation and instead supported a separation of spiritual and worldly endeavours:

> Their subordination of passion, sense and imagination to spirit and intellect was in part a reflection of the thought of the day. But it was reinforced by what K. S. Inglis has called 'the evangelical schism between soul and body, between spirit and the world', a schism which evangelicals believed should characterise Christ's followers as well as Christ himself.[9]

In context within a discussion of the churches and social reform, Inglis had written 'The evangelical schism between soul and body, between the spirit and the world, appeared in the Church of England as well as in Nonconformity', adding that 'In the Church of England, however, evangelicalism was less mighty than in Nonconformity':[10]

> The crucial distinction within English Christianity on social questions was not denominational but doctrinal: it was evangelicalism, not Nonconformity, that offered a peculiar resistance to social radicalism. The sternest Christian opponents of reform were those who believed most completely that body and soul were antithetical, and that the duty of a Christian was to reject the world, not to sanctify it.[11]

Arnold was convinced, however, that it was Nonconformists who separated the spiritual and the physical most detrimentally to culture, citing Baptist minister Charles Haddon Spurgeon as a representative opponent:

> Mr Spurgeon and the Nonconformists seem to have misapprehended the true meaning of Christ's words, *My kingdom is not of this world*; because, by these words, Christ meant that his religion was to work on the soul; and of the two parts of the soul on which religion works,—the thinking and speculative part, and the feeling and imaginative part,—Nonconformity satisfies the first no better than the Established Churches, which Christ by these words is supposed to have condemned, satisfy it; and the

---

[8] Rosman, 1984, 1.
[9] Ibid, 246.
[10] Inglis, 1963, 305.
[11] Ibid, 304.

second part it satisfies much worse than the Established Churches. And thus the balance of advantage seems to rest with the Established Churches; and they seem to have apprehended and applied Christ's words, if not with perfect adequacy, at least less inadequately than the Nonconformists.[12]

From this an important question emerges concerning whether Nonconformists were socially and culturally engaged, and the nature of that engagement. Although the focus of this work is one specific local Nonconformist church community in Bath, this question nevertheless remains close to the surface.

In his study of *Churches and the Working Classes in Victorian England*, K S Inglis has identified a significant danger that,

> Some ecclesiastical historians, believing all too literally that the kingdom of God is not of this world, or that 'the history of the Church is neither more nor less than the history of its theology,' give little attention to the relationship between the act of worship and its social environment.[13]

Karen Smith, in her study of Baptist life in Hampshire and the Wiltshire border, likewise identified the danger of studying a Baptist community 'by placing emphasis solely on doctrinal statements and treatises which dealt almost exclusively with soteriology or the doctrine of personal salvation', and opts for a regional study in which the community's life and spirituality are explored in context.[14] This study therefore focusses on a specific local Baptist church community that emerged in a particularly interesting cultural and social setting: Georgian Bath – within the wider context of a rapidly changing cultural and social world.

The Long Eighteenth Century

Waters of the Son explores the origin and development of the Particular Baptist[15] community in the city of Bath during 'the long eighteenth century'—the Georgian era, from the accession of George I in 1714 to the end of the reign of William IV in 1837. This was a period of great cultural, social and religious change, encompassing the industrial revolution and the evangelical revival, and culminating in a time of political reform and steadily increasing personal emancipation. It might not have been completely true in 1837 that every man in England could say what he liked, but it was certainly truer than in 1714 when

---

[12] Arnold, op. cit, 209-10.
[13] Inglis, op. cit, 324. quoting R Lloyd, 1946. *The Church of England in the Twentieth Century.* I, 3.
[14] Smith, 1986. 6-7.
[15] Particular Baptists were Calvinistic in theology whereas General Baptists were Arminian, taking their epithets from the doctrines of particular and general redemption respectively. Bath Baptists were a Particular Baptist community. For clear explanations of the different origins and development of each Baptist group, see Hayden, 2005, 17-54, 69-111, etc.

freedom of speech and individual liberty was more restricted. This era of revolution constitutes an important background to the development of the Particular Baptist community which sought to establish itself in Bath at the height of the city's 'Georgian Summer'[16] and which continued to evolve throughout the period.

Due in large part to the late-seventeenth-century Royal patronage of its heated mineral water, Bath's eighteenth-century transformation was dramatic. Bath had been an attraction for over two thousand years but now became established as Britain's leading pleasure and health spa resort for the wealthy and those who followed them.[17] As a resort Bath took its place on the social calendar and attracted all the virtues and vices that followed the visiting company. Even at the very beginning of the century one anonymous visitor commented on the contradictory nature of what was to become Bath's eighteenth-century character:

> Tis neither Town, nor City, yet goes by the Name of both: five Months in the Year 'tis as Populous as London, the other seven as desolate as a Wilderness…'tis a Valley of Pleasure, yet a sink of Iniquity; Nor is there any intrigues or Debauch Acted in London, but is Mimick'd here.[18]

R S Neale reminds us that very soon these five months were 'spread over two seasons in the spring and autumn' and that by 1714 even the otherwise sceptical Alexander Pope had become enamoured with Bath, as he explained to a friend:

> If Variety of Diversions and new Objects be capable of driving our Friends out of their minds, I have the best excuse imaginable for forgetting you. For I have Slid, I can't tell how, into all the Amusements of this Place: My whole Day is shar'd by the Pump-Assemblies, the Walkes, the Chocolate houses, Raffling Shops, Plays, Medleys, etc.[19]

The question of just how far Particular Baptists, indeed any Evangelical[20] Christians, would be comfortable engaging in the cultural and social life of such

---

[16] Gadd, 1971, 83. 'The heyday of Bath lasted rather more than a century, roughly from the arrival of Nash in 1705 to the end of the Regency in 1820. Over this long period the city and the life lived in it altered considerably, and it is convenient to make a rough dividing line at the decade which saw the deaths of the three creators of the city, John Wood in 1754, [Richard 'Beau'] Nash in 1761 and Ralph Allen in 1764.' Gadd writes about the 'social peak' during the first half of the period, with the climax of 'new building' well into the second.
[17] Hembry, 1990, 111-158.
[18] Anon, 1700. *A Step to the Bath with a Character of the Place*. Quoted in Neale, 1981, 12.
[19] Sherburn, George. (ed). 1956. *The Correspondence of Alexander Pope*. Oxford. Quoted in Ibid, 13.
[20] For an outline of the development of Evangelicalism in the eighteenth century see Bebbington, 1989, 1-19. David Bebbington's definition has become a standard framework for understanding what historical Evangelicalism is about: 'There are four qualities that have been the special marks of Evangelical religion: *conversionism*, the belief that lives need to be changed; *activism*, the

a place is an important one. The challenge faced by Christians living and worshipping in the city was certainly not lost on the pioneer Methodist, John Wesley, who visited Bath on numerous occasions, from 1738 onwards. Despite preaching to large crowds, Wesley soon formed an unfavourable impression of the city, being banned from preaching in the parish churches, including the Abbey, and having to find other places from which to address his audience. On one occasion in 1739 he preached at the Ham, on land belonging to the local Quaker, Richard Marchant. He recorded in his journal:

> I was wondering, the God of this world was so still; when, at my return from the place of preaching, poor R-----d M------t told me, "He could not let me preach any more in his ground." I asked him, why? He said, "The people hurt his trees, and stole things out of his ground. And besides, (added he,) I have already, by letting thee be there, merited the displeasure of my neighbours."[21]

Nevertheless, Wesley returned to Bath several times before thoughtfully reflecting in his journal, towards the end of 1741:

> I had often reasoned with myself concerning this place, "Hath God left Himself without witnesses?" Did he never raise up such as might be shining lights, even in the midst of this sinful generation? Doubtless he has, but they are either gone "to the desert," or hid under the bushel of prudence. Some of the most serious persons I have known at Bath are either solitary Christians, scarcely known to each other, unless by name; or prudent Christians, as careful not to give offence, as if that were the unpardonable sin; and as zealous to "keep their religion to themselves," as they should be to "let it shine before men."[22]

Given the way that Bath was described by some visitors it is easy to understand why serious or nervous Christians might be tempted to remain under cover. Yet there were those who did not, and it is the experience of one such Baptist community that we shall consider in due course.

Bath's rapid growth as a leisure resort during the eighteenth century led to what Phyllis Hembry described in her groundbreaking study of English spas as 'concealed tensions between visitors and residents, commercial competition and the increasing unrest of the poverty stricken', and an 'undercurrent of

---

expression of the gospel in effort; *biblicism*, a particular regard for the Bible; and what may be called *crucicentrism*, a stress on the sacrifice of Christ on the cross. Together they form a quadrilateral of priorities that is the basis of Evangelicalism.' 2-3.
[21] Wesley, *Journal*. i, 212. Tuesday 17 July, 1739.
[22] Ibid. i, 349. Friday 11 December, 1741.

discontent' which occasionally resulted in violence.[23] Bath cultivated an image of culture, yet this was built at the expense of a resident community that was often ill-catered for. Recent social histories of Bath, since R S Neale's seminal and comprehensive work in 1981,[24] have again focused on these contrasting social cultures within Bath, re-visioning many of the early studies which focused mainly on the city's social elite. The best examples of this are Graham Davis and Penny Bonsall's *Bath: A New History*,[25] followed recently by *A History of Bath: Image and Reality*,[26] which seek to bring back into some balance the experiences of all parts of Bath's population.

Peter Borsay's *The Image of Georgian Bath: 1700-2000* has explored the way that the propagation of a positive cultural and social image has been essential to the life and development of the city, and the power and significance of the image of Georgian Bath over three hundred years. He argues that 'From its inception, Bath's Georgian image was closely associated with selling the city.'[27] The Georgian image of Bath has had a powerful effect on perceptions of the city and also the practice of living in the city in the present, yet 'the sheer weight of history in Bath, occasioned by the ascendancy of its classical image…raised doubts throughout the twentieth century as to the dangers of the nostalgic turn of mind, and suggested a fundamental human need to establish an equilibrium between past and present.' Borsay also demonstrates clearly the frequent dissonance between image and reality, between perception and experience of life in Bath, and the way this has been manipulated. This was certainly true in the eighteenth century:

> Representations of Bath which conveyed the impression that it was a city of unbridled licence, where greed, gambling, and carnal pleasures flourished, severely compromised the spa's moral image. To check this flood of censure Bath badly needed to emphasise some of its morally commendable assets. Religion was a potentially strong card to play.[28]

Bath's population spurt and building frenzy was accompanied by a growing number of chapels and churches – many of them chapels of ease, or privately funded proprietary chapels.[29] Borsay argues that the popular guide books were useful in changing perceptions of the city:

---

[23] Hembry, op. cit, 270.
[24] Neale, 1981. For his *Bath: A Social History 1680-1850* Neale chose the anonymous 1700 comment about the City as his subtitle: *or a Valley of Pleasure, yet a Sink of Iniquity*, thus highlighting the contrast.
[25] Davis & Bonsall, 1996.
[26] Davis & Bonsall, 2006.
[27] Borsay, 2000, 348.
[28] Ibid, 38.
[29] Hembry, op. cit.

> Whereas *The Bath and Bristol Guide* of 1755 could muster no more than two pages (or 3 per cent of the total text) on three churches and seven chapels (some of which must have been very small), *The Improved Bath Guide* of 1812 lavished eighteen pages (or 13 per cent of the text) on six churches and fifteen chapels, many of them new or rebuilt structures. By the early nineteenth century a lengthy description of the Abbey was becoming *de rigueur* for the guides and histories...Such stress on the religious landscape and life of the spa no doubt enhanced its respectability, but for much of the Georgian period the spiritual front was not one on which Bath was winning the war.[30]

Even Evangelical headquarters in Bath such as William Jay's Argyle Independent Chapel or the Countess of Huntingdon's Chapel cast a veil of respectability over Bath's religious and social reality. In 1792 Hannah More, a regular member of Jay's congregation when she was in Bath, had exclaimed, 'Bath, happy Bath, is as gay as if there was no war, no sin, nor misery in the world.'[31] Indeed the testimony of the Rev. John Penrose, a loyal Church of England clergyman who visited Bath from 1766 to 1767, would suggest that Bath's religious scene was a thriving one that catered for his particular needs. Yet by and large the life experiences of ordinary residents were hidden from the visiting company. Penrose was particularly horrified by the emerging Methodist movement in the city, and the encouragement that Selina, Countess of Huntingdon, was giving the new Evangelical movement.[32]

In the early eighteenth century the Church of England was not adequately addressing the social and spiritual needs of the growing local population. Attending the parish church was part of the visiting company's social routine, and anything that upset that routine challenged the social authority of the city – governed by the Master of Ceremonies.[33] John Wesley's reputation among Bath society had been secured since his contretemps with Richard 'Beau' Nash on Tuesday 5 June 1739.[34] Nash failed to prevent Wesley, along with George

---

[30] Borsay, op. cit.
[31] Quoted in Hembry, op. cit.
[32] Mitchell & Penrose, 1983, 14-16.
[33] The authority of the Master of Ceremonies in Bath was related to the Assembled visiting company and the City's Assembly Rooms. cf. Fawcett, 1989, 4-10; Fawcett, 2001, 75. "Beau Nash was not dubbed 'King of Bath' for nothing, yet he had no official position vis-à-vis the Corporation and owed strict allegiance solely to the polite company at Bath whose spokesman he was. The part he played in civic affairs during his lengthy reign (1705-61) was altogether more complex than this suggests, as he bridged the yawning social gulf between the visiting gentry and the burghers who ran the town...By taking charge of the amusements, calming the wilder forms of visitor conduct, promoting sociability, and acting as supreme arbiter of spa protocol, he served a function that the Mayor and his colleagues were ill-equipped to undertake."
[34] Wesley, *Journal.* i, 198-9. "Tues. 5. There was such a great expectation at Bath of what a noted man was to do to me there; and I was much entreated "not to preach, because no one knew what might happen." By this report I also gained a much larger audience, among whom were many of

Whitefield and many other preachers, from making converts within the city – indeed it has been suggested that it was the Evangelical conversion of the Countess of Huntingdon under Methodism, and her determination 'to make Bath a place where she could spread the new religion to the upper classes', that thwarted Nash from any further attempts.[35] It is popularly believed that it was to the Methodists that the poorer population of Bath flocked, but in reality Methodism was slow to become established in the city. Well known leaders, and the provision of a room in the poor Avon Street district, led to a prominent reputation but to little success:

> Hopes raised by the erection of the Avon Street Room were doomed to disappointment. The 1760s were probably the darkest years for Methodism's earlier story in Bath. The number of members listed in 1757…as 35. Five years later this figure had fallen to 31. Wesley commented in the autumn of 1769 that numbers had fallen to 11 or 12.[36]

According to the study of Bath Methodism by Bruce Crofts and others, 'venomous' attacks in the *Bath Journal* and satirical works from authors such as Christopher Anstey[37] and Richard Graves[38] would probably have done little to

---

the rich and great. I told them plainly, "The Scripture had concluded them all under sin," high and low, rich and poor, one with another. Many of them seemed to be a little surprised, and were sinking apace into seriousness, when their champion appeared, and coming close to me, asked, "By what authority I did these things?" I replied, By the authority of Jesus Christ, conveyed to me by the (now) Archbishop of Canterbury, when he laid his hands upon me and said, "Take thou authority to preach the Gospel." He said, "This is contrary to Act of Parliament. This is a conventicle." I answered, "Sir, the conventicles mentioned in that Act (as the preamble shows) are seditious meetings; but this is not such; here is no shadow of sedition; therefore it is not contrary to that Act." He replied, "I say it is: and beside, your preaching frightens people out of their wits." "Sir, did you ever hear me preach?" No. "How then can you judge of what you have never heard?" "Sir, by common report." "Common report is not enough. Give me leave, Sir, to ask, is not your name Nash?" "My name is Nash." "Sir, I dare not judge of you by common report. I think it not enough to judge by." Here he paused awhile, and having recovered himself, said, "I desire to know what this people comes here for?" On which one replied, "Sir, leave him to me. Let an old woman answer him." "You, Mr. Nash, take care of your body. We take care of our souls; and for the food of our souls we come here." He replied not a word, but walked away. As I returned, the street was full of people, hurrying to and fro, and speaking great words; but when any of them asked, "Which is he?" and I replied, "I am he," they were immediately silent. Several ladies followed me into Mr. Merchant's house, the servant told me, "There were some wanted to speak to me." I went to them, and said, "I believe, ladies, the maid mistook; you only wanted to look at me." I added, "I do not expect that the rich and great should want either to speak with me, or to hear me; for I speak the plain truth: a thing you hear little of, and do not desire to hear." A few more words passed between us, and I retired."

[35] Mitchell & Penrose, 1983, 15.
[36] Crofts (ed), 1990, 29.
[37] Anstey, Christopher. 1766. *The New Bath Guide*. In Letter XIV the fictional 'Miss Prudence B-n-r-d informs Lady Betty that 'she has been elected to Methodism by a Vision':
> HEARKEN, Lady Betty, hearken
> To the dismal news I tell;

damage its development. Rather, Crofts explains Methodism's slow start as a failure to successfully establish local leadership, which would only be reversed when fully authorised Methodist preachers and an organised Circuit were put in place towards the end of the century.[39]

When general Bath histories discuss Nonconformity during the eighteenth century it is usual that Methodism be most prominent, followed as the century progressed by the Countess of Huntingdon's Chapel and William Jay's Argyle Independent Chapel. Often missing from accounts are the other Nonconformist groups who had been present in the city and often hidden within phrases such as 'six other chapels'.[40] The reality is that even as John Wesley bemoaned the dearth of serious Christians challenging Bath's social climate and responding to the inactivity of the Church of England, there were groups of Bath Dissenters doing just that. The 1755 *Bath and Bristol Guide* had clearly recorded:

> There are also three Meeting-Houses here, viz. the Quaker's-Meeting, which is situated at the Upper End of Marchant's

---

> How your friends are all embarking
>   For the fiery gulph of hell!...
> For I dreamed an apparition
>   Came, like Roger, from above;
> Saying by divine commission,
>   I must fill you full of love.

Roger was a Methodist preacher. In Letter XV Mr Simkin B-n-r-d reflects upon what has happened to his sister: O how shall we know the right way to pursue!
> Do the ills of mankind from religion accrue?
> Religion, designed to relieve all our care,
> Has brought my poor sister to grief and despair:
> Now she talks of damnation, and screws up her face,
> Then prates about Roger, and spiritual grace;
> Her senses, alas, seem at once gone astray—
> No pen can describe it, no letter convey.

[38] Graves, Richard. 1773. *The Spiritual Quixote*. In his parody of the experiences of John Wesley and George Whitefield in Bath, Graves' hero, Geoffry Wildgoose, had begun 'to relish the doctrines of the Methodists; which began, about this time, to spread in every corner of the kingdom.' 20. Wildgoose was to preach to a Methodist public meeting on the Parade, which was interrupted by, in Edith Sitwell's words, 'a silly and bad-mannered guerrilla warfare of annoyance and noise' by Beau Nash: 'But Mr Nash though he himself had greatly reformed and regulated the manners and behaviour of his subjects in the public room; yet, being orthodox in his tenets, and very well content with the present state of religion amongst them, he did not desire any reformation in that article. Having notice, therefore, of this intended preachment, he got ready his band of music, with the addition of two or three French-horns and kettle-drums: and as soon as the Orator had exhibited his person on the Parade, stretched forth his hand…and was in act to speak, Nash gave the signal for the grand chorus of 'God save the king.' The music struck up; and playing so loyal a piece of music, no one had the hardiness to interrupt them. Nay, a majority of the company were probably pleased with Nash's humour; and, it being now breakfast-time, the mob was easily dispersed.' 145. Sitwell, 1932. 136.

[39] Crofts, op. cit, 30-31.

[40] Hembry, op. cit, 271.

Court, in the Market-Place; the Presbyterian-Meeting, situated in Frog-Lane; and a Meeting for Anabaptists, in Horse-Street, built by Mr. Robert Parsons, Carver. There is another Meeting held at the Cross Bath, at a House known by the Name of the Bell-Tree, for those Persons who are Members of the Church of Rome.[41]

The Methodists did not have their own meeting space in Avon Street until at least 1759, the Countess of Huntingdon started building her chapel in 1765, and the Independents broke away from the Countess's congregation soon after 1781. There had been a Moravian congregation in Bath from 1752, but it met in a hired room.[42] The 1755 *Bath and Bristol Guide*'s account of the older Dissenters' meeting places is significant for other reasons too: firstly, the accepted place these groups had within the social structure of the city, and presented as options for visitors as legitimate places of worship at a time when Evangelical novelty was being resisted; secondly, the diversity of Dissent in mid-eighteenth-century Bath, from the Friends to Roman Catholicism; and, thirdly, the naming of the Baptist, Robert Parsons, Carver, the only personal name of any Bath citizen connected with any church, chapel or meeting house listed in the guide. It is significant that in the mid-eighteenth-century Bath the Baptists were not only a notable community but were also publicly associated with the name of a local stone carver of some repute – Robert Parsons.

That there was an active Nonconformist presence in Bath before Methodism seems as unrecognised by some Bath historians as it was by the Church of England at the time. William Tyte, an early twentieth-century historian of eighteenth-century Bath, is a notable early exception and expresses surprise that the established church had failed to wake up to the significance of the rise and success of what the Nonconformist churches were achieving:

> It is surprising that the Church was not aroused from its lethargy by the growth of Nonconformity and the chapels it was enabled to erect by relying mainly on the voluntary gifts of its members. To this object lesson Churchmen or their pastors closed their eyes. They went on levying Church rates for the maintenance of the fabrics and other objects, which all had to pay, but no disposition was shown, as we have seen, to extend and improve the Church's ministrations by the individual liberality of those who ranged themselves under its aegis, and who formed the most numerous and wealthy section of the community. When with this state of things is contrasted the zeal, earnestness, and self-denial of the Dissenters, what wonder that sects waxed and

---

[41] *Bath and Bristol Guide*, 1755, 16. The first edition of this guide appeared in 1742, although no copies are known to survive. The 1755 edition was the third to be published.
[42] Ede, 1989, 1-3

the influence of the Church waned? As late as 1760 there were only three meeting houses, namely, that of the Presbyterians in Frog Lane (now New Bond Street), the Baptists in Horse Street, and the Friends at the upper end of Marchant's Court, High Street.[43]

Tyte's serialised history of *Bath in the Eighteenth Century* was the first general history of the city of Bath to take the Dissenting churches seriously. Little research had been carried out on their history up to this point, and in 1903 most of their records were still confined to the back cupboards and storage spaces of the chapels and churches concerned.[44] In his section on 'Dissent' in eighteenth-century Bath Tyte contributed a significant paragraph addressing Baptist origins in Bath:

> The first Baptist congregation was started in 1726 by Henry Dolling at his house near Widcombe Old Church, he having obtained a licence from the Bishop's Court at Wells. It ran thus: — "The dwelling-house of Mr. H. Dolling, Widcombe, is by this court lycensed and allowed for an assembly or congregation for religious worship, as law directs." Three of the worshippers from this little community—Messrs. R. Parsons (a nephew of Dolling), Singer, and Hathaway—took a piece of land in the rear of Southgate Street (Corn Street side) in 1752, and built a small chapel, where Mr. Parsons officiated. It was opened in 1754, and the following year Whitefield preached in it several times "to a vast concourse of people." The denomination grew rapidly, and in 1768 a larger chapel was erected and opened for its accommodation in Garrard (now Somerset) Street. Mr. Parsons' pastorate extended over forty years, and during the whole of that

---

[43] Tyte, 1903, 111-112.
[44] At Manvers Street Baptist Church, the direct descendant of Robert Parsons' Baptist Meeting, many of the historic records were deposited in the great iron chest in the basement, only to rot and decay in the damp over the years. As late as February 1994 Eric Chandler, Church Archivist, wrote in the Manvers Street News: 'From time to time people turn out their lofts or cupboards and discover records of organisations and clubs which once flourished or to which they once belonged in Manvers Street. They sometimes ask if these are of use or interest. The answer nearly always is "Yes". The notion occurred to me that there must be many more old minute books and so on about if we could only find them. It is certainly true that there were many things going on in our church of which we know very little today. So if you think you might have anything, please look and let me know if you have. I am particularly interested in getting more information about the following stalwarts of the church and city: Sydney W Bush who died in 1937, Frederick W Spear who died in 1935, George J Long who died in 1943 and Charles H Long who died in 194[?]...' Much of what was subsequently discovered is written up in Chandler, 2003.

time he received no remuneration for his services, gaining his livelihood by working at his trade of stone-carving.[45]

Recent histories of the city have taken much less interest in the Baptist community, although historians such as R S Neale, Trevor Fawcett and Mike Chapman have written positively about individual Baptists.[46] Neale's *Bath: A Social History 1680-1850*, highlighted the contributions of various individual Baptists, such as George Cox the Baptist hatter, undertaker and noted Chartist, and members of the Evill family, who had wide business interests around Bath. Neale's Marxist slant is evident when, in discussing the lifestyle and conditions endured by Bath's labouring poor during the eighteenth century and the role of the local church communities, he writes:

> Even in Avon Street some men and women sought and won relief in Methodism rather than in drunkenness and violence, while later in the century the Baptists provided a community of peace for many others.[47]

Although Neale's chronology needs adjusting, for the Baptists were on the scene earlier than the Methodists and were active at the same time, it does highlight one reason for the marginalisation of Baptists in the written histories of Bath: the Baptist community being perceived as having little relationship with the community at large, or at least with the impression of the city some writers were keen to convey. Baptists were more prominent in eighteenth-century Bath than previous accounts have tended to suggest.

Whilst Neale focused on the people, John Haddon's *Portrait of Bath* looked at the significance of some of the buildings occupied by Bath's Baptist community.[48] Written in the style of an amplified commentary to a walk around the city, Haddon takes seriously the many Baptist sites and experiences along the way.

---

[45] Tyte, op. cit, 112; Cater, 1834, 62-68, 75-76. Tyte's abbreviated account is not original, relying on the introductory chapters of Philip Cater's biography of John Paul Porter published in 1834, even down to style and turns of phrase.

[46] Neale, op. cit, 342-5 for George Cox; Fawcett, 1990, 68-70 for the Evill family; Chapman, 1997, 26 for Opie Smith.

[47] Neale, op. cit, 93.

[48] Haddon, 1982, 13. Haddon poetically introduces the city of Bath in the early decades of the twentieth century through his own eyes as a small boy: 'Our point of view, in several senses of the phrase, determines what we see. When I was small my parents sometimes took me to Bath on a real puffing, clanking train and my first impression of the city was a message in huge white letters which said, "We Have Redemption Through His Blood" and changed, as we drew into the station, to "Christ Died For Our Sins". I was greatly impressed at being addressed in this way from what I now know to be the roof of an Ebenezer chapel and I would probably have been even more affected if I could have seen the roofs on the other side which change from information to admonition—"Ye Must Be Born Again" and "Prepare To Meet Thy God". I did not really understand the message but it gave me the impression that Bath was a pretty stern place which shouted at you from the roof-tops. The only other thing I remember is that the water in the Roman baths looked like thin soup.'

He recounts how the Friends' Meeting House in York Street was originally built in 1817-19 as the Freemason's Hall, designed by William Wilkins who had designed the National Gallery in London, and was for a short time occupied by a Baptist group who referred to their meeting place as Bethesda Chapel.[49] Likewise, Manvers Street Baptist Church is described as 'a pleasant little neo-Gothic Baptist chapel with a rather jolly turret.'[50]

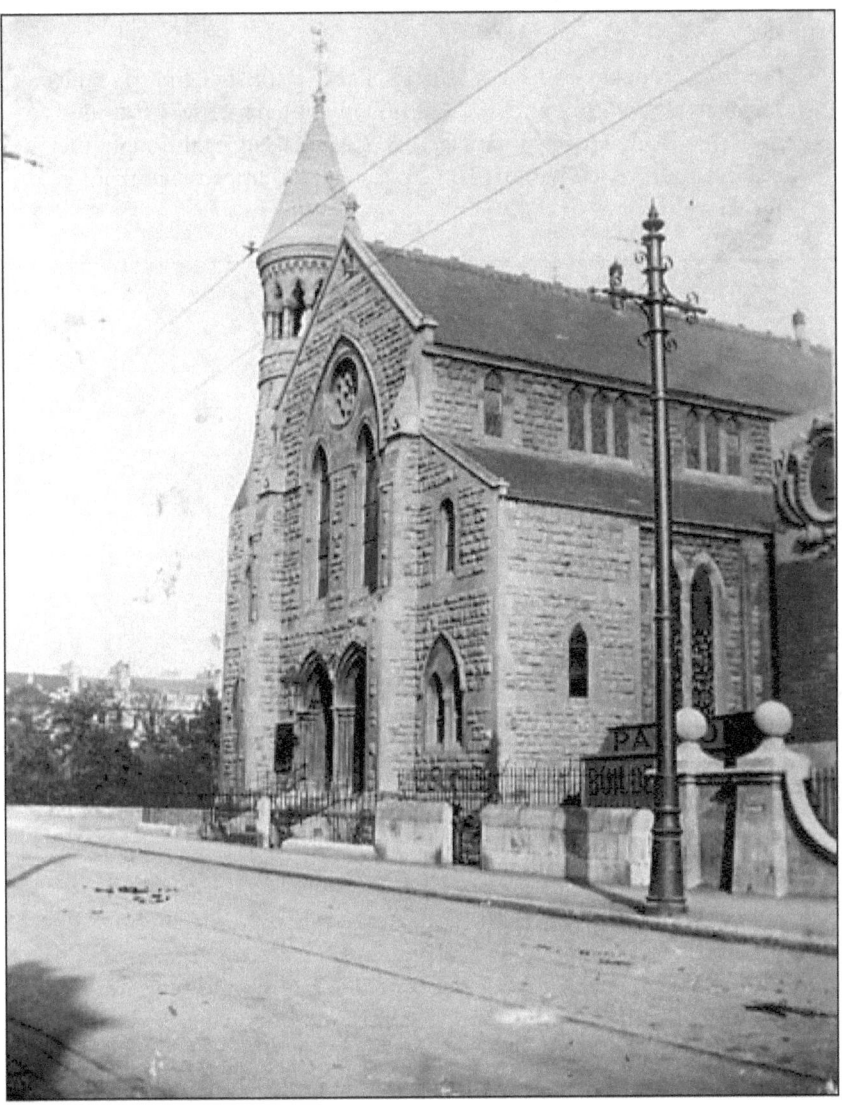

Figure 1. Manvers Street Baptist Church, 1902

---

[49] Ibid, 54.
[50] Ibid, 55.

We further learn that Widcombe Baptist Church, the Ebenezer Chapel he had encountered from the train as a child, had originally housed a set of bells which were subsequently relocated to St Thomas's Church, Widcombe, after St Thomas's bells had been moved to the new parish church of St Matthew in 1846-7. Ebenezer Chapel 'was at that time in Church hands, before being acquired as a Baptist chapel in 1849 by a splinter group from the Providence Chapel, Lower Bristol Road.'[51] In Oldfield Park, in Triangle North, Haddon points us to:

> the two blocks of the Oldfield Park Baptist Church built respectively in 1902 and 1929 although the chapel was founded in 1828. Both are in a satisfactory Classical style although the older, larger, block with its Ionic pilasters and impressive front is the more showy.[52]

Figure 2. Oldfield Park Baptist Church, 1928

Oldfield Park Baptists trace their continuity through the Baptist church in Twerton, mentioned briefly as 'in Mill Lane, the Twerton Baptist Church with an addition of 1928.'[53] Each of the Baptist buildings visited by Haddon in 1982 has significance for the Bath Baptist community which we shall go on to consider. Behind these glimpses of the past in the surviving architectural structures there are numerous stories of people and movements which constituted the living fabric of the Bath Baptist community.

---

[51] Ibid, 154.
[52] Ibid, 193-194.
[53] Ibid, 197-198.

Local Baptist Histories

Having surveyed how wider histories of Bath have tended to marginalise the Baptist community, we turn to examine the accounts of their history written by Baptists themselves. Bath Baptists have had no serious critical historian, and there is no substantial written history of the Bath Baptist churches—*Waters of the Son* is the first to bring together many diverse and previously unused sources and undiscovered details. There are a handful of short histories of individual Bath churches, and aspects of their history have appeared in a number of publications – suggesting that it is sufficiently important to be remembered and recalled – but these are of varied length, quality, detail, accuracy, and purpose.[54] An examination of the purpose of these previous accounts will show why many of them are partial or incomplete.

Baptist church or chapel histories form a genre in their own right, and often churches have produced these as small booklets or pamphlets for special occasions. Substantial church histories are rare.[55] Occasional papers on the history of particular churches have appeared in the *Baptist Quarterly* and its predecessor *Transactions of the Baptist Historical Society*.[56] An anonymous and misleading account of the Bath Baptists appeared in the *Baptist Quarterly* without comment or explanation in 1932:

> BATH. Josiah Thompson learned about 1770 that the Baptists began about 1744 in a private room, that Hugh Evans of Bristol opened at Kingsmead Square in 1747, moving soon to Collett's back yard on Horn street. A church of nine members was organised in 1752, with six more baptised at Paulton, and joined the Western Association at once. Bernard Foskett opened a meeting-house in 1755, and Robert Parsons was ordained. In 1760 the church was strong enough to entertain the Association, and two years later it enlarged the meeting-house, acquired a burial-ground, and started to register births in its families. In 1769 it shifted to a new home on Garrott street, having ninety members. So far the story is consistent, but there is a puzzling fact that from 1689 to 1697 John Gay represented "Bath Haycomb" at various assemblies. And in 1837, when the church was at Somerset street, and William Peachey was pastor, and the

---

[54] In mitigation it must be stated that this study would not easily have been possible without the serendipitous discovery of many isolated sources in unexpected places, not readily available to previous writers.

[55] Studies such as Clyde Binfield, 1984. *Pastors and People: The Biography of a Baptist Church, Queen's Road, Coventry* (348 pages) and Faith Bowers, 1999. *A Bold Experiment – The Story of Bloomsbury Chapel and Bloomsbury Central Baptist Church 1848-1999* (472 pages) are among the exception rather than the rule. Most church or chapel histories come in at well under 100 pages.

[56] *Transactions of the Baptist Historical Society* and *Baptist Quarterly* have appeared as a continual series since 1908.

church surrendered its registers to Somerset House, the claim was made that the church originated in 1720. The only justification seems to be that Henry Dolling, who was a trustee of the Presbyterian meeting in 1726, registered his house in Widcombe for public worship by Baptists; it is not certain that there is any continuity between that event and the organisation in 1752.[57]

However, the earliest and most substantial account of Bath Baptist history comes from Philip Cater, minister of York Street Baptist Chapel in Bath, and appears in his *Memoirs of the Life and Character of the Late Rev. John Paul Porter, More than Forty Years Pastor of the First Baptist Church in Bath*.[58] Published in 1834, just three years before the period covered by this study ends, he wrote about people and events that were within living memory. Based on the testimony of living witnesses and extant documents, Cater can be relied upon as a trustworthy historian – although there are many gaps, and at times his purpose is clearly to put his main subject in a positive light, serving as a biography and celebration of Porter's extraordinary long ministry in Bath.[59] Noteworthy from the title is that

---

[57] *Baptist Quarterly*. iv, 279. Although anonymous, the note was possibly the work of W. T. Whitley, pioneer early twentieth-century Baptist historian and editor of the journal. The sources of information are largely noted within the text, but it is strewn with unexplainable inaccuracies: e.g. Collett's back yard was on Horse Street not Horn Street; there is no reference in other sources to Paulton; Garrott Street should read Garrard Street; it was Richard Gay not John Gay who represented "Bath Haycomb"; etc.

[58] Cater, 1834.

[59] Cater's purpose is further stated in the dedication and preface: 'To Mrs Porter the widow, and to Miss Porter the daughter, and only child, of the late Rev John Paul Porter, and to the church formerly under his pastoral care, whom for the space of forty years he served in the gospel of Christ, as a testimony of regard to them, and as a token of veneration for the character of the deceased.' In other words, in addition to giving an account of John Paul Porter, it is Cater's purpose to give tribute to the service of pastor and church in the propagation of the gospel to which they had been united. It soon becomes clear from the preface, however, that the use of Cater's book as a source to reconstruct any historical narrative is problematic – not because there is any reason not to trust what he says, but because of the material available to him. Cater wrote the account at the request of Porter's widow, using verbatim extracts from Porter's personal diary from 1792 to his death in 1832. The diary does not survive, so we cannot be sure how representative the extracts are. Cater admits that at times he finds it difficult to 'maintain an unbroken succession of yearly occurrences', although he attempts to do so from 1800 onwards. Yet on the other hand Cater is aware of his own potential bias, so himself seeks to guard against it. He writes, 'Some disappointment may be felt that so little notice is taken of certain painful proceedings, a particular recurrence to which could scarcely fail to excite feelings of the most afflicted kind. No judgement is here pronounced on those proceedings, or on any individuals connected with them.—I praise none,— I censure none, —I conciliate none. Any opinion concerning them is neither settled, nor depreciated, nor disturbed, by any remark of mine. Here I maintain the strictest neutrality: I take neither one side nor the other, nor steer a middle course between both; but I stand in a situation that is aloof from the subject altogether, whence I am guilty of throwing out no innuendos, or of making any covert attack upon different persons for the views they may entertain or the part they may have taken in a transaction, than which there was the occurrence of nothing more painful or more important in the whole history of Mr.

Somerset Street is referred to as the first Baptist church in Bath, for by 1834 there were a number of Baptist congregations in the city. The origins of some of these congregations are mentioned in Cater's text. Although he was minister of the first Baptist church, Porter was not the first minister, nor the only minister to have had a long pastorate. Robert Parsons, the founding pastor of the church, himself served for over forty years. Two real values of Cater's work need to be emphasised. Firstly, in Section IV Cater devoted twenty pages to information about the Baptist community in Bath in the years before Porter's arrival, along with accounts of other Dissenting and Nonconformist churches in Bath. Cater is thus the first to give some coherent narrative from the very beginning, also highlighting the significance of the Haycombe and Presbyterian congregations to the early part of the story. Secondly, Cater's account is valuable for containing many unedited verbatim excerpts from Porter's diary, without which the story would contain nothing of his own perspective.[60] Cater's main value is that within his text he preserved extracts of valuable sources no longer available to the researcher.

The next known account was part of an anonymous report in the *Bath Herald* on Wednesday 21 February 1885, titled '*Manvers Street Baptist Chapel. Thanksgiving Services upon the Extinction of the Debt upon the Building.*'[61] A paragraph in the report summarised the historical overview as told by R H Moore at a social meeting on the previous day:

> This church has had a memorable history in this Fair City of the West. Nonconformity in Bath started with the Act of Uniformity in 1662, when the Rev. George Long, and his assistant, the Rev. W. Green, were ejected from the State Church for conscientious opinions. In 1752 this Baptist Church was formed, preceded in 1692 by the Presbyterians, and in 1693 by the Quakers. In 1768 Somerset street Chapel was built, and enlarged in 1807. On the 1st October, 1872, the church was transferred to the present site. It has been privileged with long pastorates. In 1790 Mr. Parsons, its first minister, entered into rest after 37 years of honorary labour. Mr. Porter succeeded him in 1791, and died in 1832 after a pastorate of 42 years, having received 562 baptized persons into Church fellowship. The

---

Porter's public life.' In the later decades of Porter's ministry there were indeed difficult times, culminating in a particular time of stress just three or four years before his death. Philip Cater, having only recently moved to Bath and with his experience as a writer, would no doubt have given Mrs Porter confidence that he would remain neutral and allow her husband's words to speak on their own terms without having been part of the local conflict.

[60] This material contains descriptions of Porter's life as a minister, a life of preaching, prayer, and pastoral care, as well as numerous accounts of the people he visited, the missionary causes he supported, and the difficulties he frequently encountered.

[61] *Bath Herald*. 21 February 1885. The report was subsequently reprinted for sale.

Revs. J. Jackson and William Peachey, who resigned on account of illness, filled the interval until 1839, when Mr. Wassell, who threw all his energies into the erection of this chapel, but was not spared to enter it, became the pastor. Many of us now present look back with pleasure upon his memory, his earnest ministry, large abilities, and genial Christian life, but after a pastorate of 34 years, in the May following the opening of this building, he was summoned to his rest with God.[62]

R H Moore was the acknowledged historian of the then recently opened Manvers Street congregation. When in 1908 the new minister of Manvers Street compiled a booklet about the work of the church and its new Institute building it was to R H Moore's manuscripts that Rev. Louis Parkinson turned. Moore was no longer around to work on *Praise and Progress, being a Brief History and Account of the Present Work at Manvers Street Baptist Church, Bath*, but his work was included in the booklet, as Parkinson explained in the foreword:

> The opening historical survey, by Mr. R. H. Moore, will prove especially valuable, giving a brief, permanent record of the rise and progress of the Church. We have felt it incumbent upon us, and due to him to insert his name, as one who bravely shared the burden of the erection of the present Chapel.[63]

The account was attributed to Moore out of respect and honour, although it would seem that the historical section, covering the years from the founding of the church up to 1905, may not have been entirely his own work. The account is much longer, taking seven pages to cover the same part of the narrative covered in the 1885 address, which itself may have been a journalist's condensed version of what actually transpired. Yet there are notable additions in the 1908 version, most obviously the inclusion of a brief account of the seventeenth-century Baptist congregation at Haycombe[64] and the connection between the Bath Presbyterian community and the subsequent foundation of the Baptist church at Somerset Street.[65] Minor differences and errors aside, Parkinson's aim had been to present a brief historical background to the present work of the church, demonstrating that the fervent life of the church in 1908

---

[62] Ibid, 4-5. As Parsons was founding minister and was responsible for the church well before its official constitution in 1752 his ministry was well in excess of the thirty seven years given here.
[63] Parkinson, 1908, 2.
[64] Ibid, 4.
[65] Ibid, 5. As well as these additions, the story being told in a fuller fashion, there are also other differences or errors between the two accounts. David Wassell's ministry numbers 33 years in 1908 compared with 34 in the 1885 account. This could of course be an amendment or otherwise a lack of care in transcribing from Moore's original manuscripts. The latter would more likely explain the most glaring error in quoting 'Irving's' *History of the Baptists*, when no such publication exists, rather than referring more correctly to Ivimey's *History of the Baptists*.

was a direct consequence of all that had gone before in a Baptist community committed to the culture and society of which it was a part.

Two accounts exist only in unpublished manuscript form. The first certainly had an audience, for around 1950 two members were set to present 'The History of Manvers Street' at a meeting of the Manvers Street Guild.[66] The Guild existed to fulfil a social and educational function in the church, particularly amongst younger people, and the event was to coincide with the upcoming bicentenary celebrations of the first independent Baptist church in Bath in 1952. It seems from a letter by Irene Willway included with the manuscript that the presentation was to have been made before 1947 but delayed whilst the research was continuing – providentially, according to the letter, which included reminiscences of people she had known during her 45½ years as a church member.[67] Another letter preserved with the manuscript was from Ellie Wilson, a direct descendant of Robert Parsons, who in 1948 was living in Australia. She was able to give valuable details from the Parsons family Bible.[68] F W R Deverell and S L Bush eventually gave their presentation in the form of a dialogue, interspersed with longer sections of description, in which each of them would take the lead in turn. The evidence suggests that Deverell had taken the lead in the research and writing of the project, which was evidently designed to be as entertaining as educational.[69] The manuscript takes the account well

---

[66] Bush & Deverell, 1950.
[67] Correspondence - Irene Willway to F W R Deverell, 31 December 1947.
[68] Correspondence - Ellie Wilson to F W R Deverell, 9 January 1948.
[69] Although detailed in many sections, the selection of material was patchy and obviously chosen to be entertaining, as this extract from the beginning demonstrates:
> B. Hullo. Hope I'm not late. You do look busy. You want me to help you compose a history of England, do you?
> D. Good gracious, no. We have to put our heads together to give an outline of the history of Manvers Street.
> B. Do you mean the building here or the church itself?
> D. Actually the church, but we can make reference to the building I suppose.
> B. Well don't you think (voice from the rear "Speak up please") I say, they want to listen. Well, as I was going to suggest, don't you think we had better get down to some general headings, and work to them. When did the church actually commence?
> D. According to the best information I can gather it was in 1752, although the suggestion for the formation was probably in 1750, but the church was actually formed in 1752 and that is why I asked you to bring some account of Bath halfway through the 18th century as a background.
> B. O I see the idea. Local background. Beginning of church.
> D. Then I suggest some account of the buildings.
> B. Yes, and something about the ministers and their little funny ways.
> D. And we might re-call some of the stalwarts.
> B. I should like to make some reference to the line of missionaries if there is time.
> D. Don't you think we had better leave the history of the various organisations such as choir, and Sunday school?
> B. Perhaps we could deal with them another time. I've some priceless pictures of the choir, with ladies hats about 3 feet across.

beyond the period of this study, but what is most significant is the way that the history is seen to be important, not just for the presenters, but for the audience too, as part of their reason for being, their identity. Thus it was presented imaginatively, and with reference to personal testimonies and reminiscences.[70] It is also significant that Irene Willway considered it providential that Deverell and Bush's Guild presentation had been delayed,[71] for she was busy writing her own history of the Bath Baptists, the second unpublished manuscript.[72] Willway's *History of Manvers Street Baptist Church* was completed around 1967, although were it not for the correspondence archived along with her notes the date would be unknown. For the period of this study her version adds nothing to the detail of what happened between 1714 and 1837.[73] Having written forty pages Miss Willway sent them to her friend F W R Deverell for comment, which he did in some detail:

> Now about your ms. I am sure you will realise that it is far from any final form yet. You have brought together a number of interesting items, but there are many gaps to be filled in before it could be of interest to any people beyond a small circle in the church itself.
>
> I wonder what became of Paul Porter's diary which I left in the vestry some time ago for Mr Darvill to take care of. That told of the development of the church from earliest beginnings. It recorded the words of the three founders. "Seeing the low state of religion in Bath we deem it expedient to commence a cause/work in the Baptist interest."
>
> I always remember those words & actually saw them in their own faded hand-writing, when it was on show in the Guildhall. They were included with other exhibits telling of the uprising of nonconformity in Bath. It must have been some sort of exhibition, but when & why it was I cannot remember.
>
> In Porter's diary there is an account of a great flood when a baby was carried down the Avon in a wooden cradle. Also of Andrew Fuller's visit to Bath & district when he was going around the country seeking support for the newly born B.M.S., of which he

---

[70] Preserved with the presentation notes is a further script for a drama based on a church members' meeting, or series of meetings, when the move from Somerset Street to Manvers Street was discussed. Given the length of the documents preserved it is doubtful whether this was part of the same Guild programme, but rather presented on another occasion.
[71] Her letter conveys that she had been unwell and not yet sufficiently recovered to be present. Whether she was there on the day is not known.
[72] Willway, 1967.
[73] What is important is that she wrote it at all, one generation passing on the story to the next. Here was an elderly member of the church, keen to keep its history alive and to add to it things that were within her living memory.

was the first secy. & much beside. I wish now I had kept that book. Bessie White gave it me, after Mr Archard's death.

There are several things to note about Deverell's response. Firstly the diary he referred to is Philip Cater's *Memoirs* of John Paul Porter; secondly, the annotated copy that Deverell referred to survives in the Manvers Street archive; and thirdly, the survival of the book confirms that Deverell's memory was good in remembering the wording on the paper he had seen at the Guildhall. Finally, it ought to be added, if Deverell had not left the copy of Cater's book in the Manvers Street vestry, the annotations might not have survived.

In 1972 Manvers Street celebrated the centenary of moving into their new building and published an historical booklet, *Two Hundred Years of Ministry and Witness, 1752-1972*.[74] The book was researched by Charles Attryde, one of the deacons, and written up by Leslie H Moore, a senior member of the church. The two pages covering the period of this study are based on details from Cater's book, particularly the references to Haycombe, which they inaccurately say is 'presumably the village we now know as "Combe Hay"',[75] and the Presbyterian connection. The account presents a fairly successful summary of the early history for the limited purpose of celebrating an anniversary. One of the dangers in writing local church history is to tell the story of a building rather than of the people that make up the community. This tension is picked up on the first page of the booklet where it is subtitled, 'The story of a Baptist Fellowship meeting in the city of Bath, first in Somerset Street and then in Manvers Street from 1752 to 1972.' The foreword was written by the minister, Rev. John H Matson, which declares:

> The Centenary of the present church building has been the occasion for thanksgiving for the past and dedication to the future in the name of God. This has been expressed in worship and in the complete renovation of the church building. It has also provided the incentive to record the story of the Church, not only during the past 100 years but since its beginnings in 1752.

Matson then goes on to define where the church's history fits into its present life and purpose as an agent of God's mission at the heart of the present and future community:

> This is a story that was lived. It is a story of men and women and boys and girls who found their spiritual home and came into

---

[74] Attryde & Moore, 1972.
[75] Ibid, 2. The mistake in the first sentence, referring again to Irving's *History of the Baptists* instead of Ivimey's, makes it clear that for the early period Louis Parkinson's 1908 compilation is also a major source.

> communion with God in Jesus Christ in this fellowship. It is a story of caring and service, devotion and faith.
>
> It is in this tradition that we stand. As the story continues to unfold it is our prayer that we may catch the vision and understand more deeply our place and mission in the centre of Bath now and in the years to come.

These accounts of Bath Baptists, compiled and written by members of the Bath Baptist community, have had the clear objective of preserving and communicating their own story. Two other Baptist historians have recorded Baptist events in Bath from a significantly different perspective.

In the decades before the 1960s Ralph F Chambers was researching the history of the Strict Baptist chapels of England for a series of books which were to be published by the Strict Baptist Historical Society. Chambers never completed the volume on Wiltshire and the West, which included Bath, but his manuscript account exists and is titled *Where Heated Waters Spring. The Story of the Strict Baptist Chapels of Bath*.[76] For the period covered by this study the main source used by Chambers was Philip Cater's *Memoirs* of John Paul Porter, although he makes the same error that was later repeated by Attryde and Moore, by assuming that Haycombe is the same as Combe Hay. Writing from a Strict Baptist perspective Chambers was looking at the Particular Baptists as the direct ancestors of the Strict Baptist congregations in Bath. Chambers' tone was strictly confessional, longing for the return of what was 'a once purer doctrine':

> In this city the glorious doctrines of sovereign grace have rung forth from many a pulpit; sounded out by Anglican and Nonconformist, Methodist and Independent, Presbyterian and Baptist. Men of renown have lifted up their voices and the spiritual giants of the past have drawn their thousands to hear the gospel's joyful sound.
>
> Our story of the Strict Baptist Chapels of Bath will occasionally give glimpses of these mighty men of God, but the general course of our history will be less spectacular, dealing with quiet but none the less effectual ministries of the Word of God.[77]

It is anachronistic to talk about Strict Baptist churches during the period 1714 to 1837, for the description only came into use from around the 1830s to describe those Calvinistic or Particular churches whose strict or limited communion differentiated them from other Particular Baptist churches who were linked around the evangelical sentiments of the Baptist Union and

---

[76] Chambers, nd. Faded copy in Bath Reference Library.
[77] Ibid, 2.

therefore in fellowship with General Baptists.[78] The Baptist churches in Bath at that time were Particular Baptist in doctrine and principle. But that was Chambers' argument. He continues,

> At the time of the outbreak of the second great war (1939) there were two Strict Baptist Chapels in the city, one called "Providence" and situated in the Lower Bristol Road; the other named "Bethel", and built at the rear of some shops in Walcot Street.

Chambers argues that the successors of these two Strict Baptist churches were the only true and doctrinally pure descendants from the original Particular Baptist churches in Bath. However Chambers also argues that the other Baptist churches in Bath had become General Baptist over the course of time, something which is strictly untrue and totally misleading. Of the Manvers Street church Chambers asserts, 'This church is now associated with the General Baptist body, and all its ministers have been of that communion.'[79] The Baptist body referred to by Chambers was the Baptist Union, but a majority of its members were originally Particular Baptists. Further, Chambers continues,

> There is every evidence that the cause at Twerton was like the parent church at Somerset Street a regular Particular Baptist church in its early days, but it has long since become General Baptist, and the General Baptist church in Oldfield Park is its direct descendant.[80]

Just as it is anachronistic to talk of Strict Baptists during the period 1714 to 1837 it is also equally false to refer to Somerset Street, Twerton and Oldfield Park as General Baptists in the later period also, where foundation and title deeds and subsequent trusts firmly define these congregations as Particular Baptist, as indeed their history continued to so define. This was corrected, however, when the volume Chambers was researching was finally published albeit in a severely edited form.

---

[78] General Baptists and Particular Baptists have distinct origins, although sharing many similarities. The main although not only distinguishing doctrinal differences were around the atonement – General Baptists holding the Arminian view that the saving power of the cross effects all people, with Particular Baptists holding the Calvinist view that salvation is effective only for the elect. For detailed accounts of the emergence of the Strict and Particular Baptists see Dix, 2001 and Oliver, 2006. In the early decades of the nineteenth century strong differences surfaced among Particular Baptists over the issue of communion, and a number of churches strongly concluding that communion like church membership should be restricted to those who had been baptised as believers by immersion. These churches adopted the term Strict and Particular Baptist, in contrast to those who were less restrictive in this regard. Somerset Street and Twerton were Particular Baptist churches, generally limited membership and access to communion, but never identified themselves as Strict and Particular, and certainly not General Baptist. Dix, 2001, 3.
[79] Chambers, Ibid, 12.
[80] Ibid, 11.

Volume five of *The Strict Baptist Chapels of England: The Chapels of Wiltshire and the West* appeared under the authorship of Robert W Oliver in 1968. The title page records that the volume is 'Based on the Original Manuscript of R. F. Chambers'. The chapter on the Bath churches is based on Chambers' research, although Oliver rearranged the material to give a more structured account of the early days of each of the churches, including the period beyond 1837. Although many of the details were printed in the same form as in Chambers' manuscript, including the mistaken assumption that Richard Gay had preached at Combe Hay,[81] Oliver's judicious editorship also moderated the polemical language of the original, enhancing the general although not complete accuracy of the final volume. This can be demonstrated by comparing Chambers' paragraph referring to Twerton, Somerset Street and Oldfield Park alongside the version which appeared in the published volume:

> There is every evidence that the church at Twerton was like its parent at Somerset Street, a regular Particular Baptist church. Its descendant is the open communion church in Oldfield Park.[82]

Oliver had wisely removed the confusing references to General Baptists, or that the churches at Twerton and Somerset Street had changed their doctrinal position, and instead categorised Oldfield Park as an 'open communion' church, emphasising that the communion table was open to all in Christian fellowship with the church and not just baptised members, and more accurately reflecting the reality of the situation.

Each of these accounts of Bath Baptist history has originated in one way or another from within the Baptist community. Paul T Phillips has thus far been the only serious attempt to objectively place the Bath Baptist community within the wider framework of religious life in the city as a whole. Phillips' 1973 article on 'The Religious Side of Victorian Bath, 1830-1870' was published in the journal *Social History*, and 'partially influenced by the fact that surprisingly little interest has been shown by historians in the "Queen of the West" in the Victorian Age.'[83] Despite its Victorian focus, Phillips' study engages considerably with the pre-Victorian period, and significantly for our purpose made use of Philip Cater's earlier history of the Bath Baptist community and had brief access to the Somerset Street Baptist minute books and records kept at Manvers Street Baptist Church. Phillips argues that this was an important period in the life of the church, particularly significant for the difference that the growth of evangelicalism and revival in the church had made to the moral and spiritual character of Bath since the eighteenth century, and amongst which the Baptist community had made a significant contribution. Phillips states that it is not just the observation of later historians looking back, but the assessment of

---

[81] Oliver, 1968, 83.
[82] Ibid, 88.
[83] Phillips, 1973, 224-5.

those living at the time, that 'Methodist and Evangelical Revivals were believed to have transformed the moral life of the community converting Bath from a city of sin to one of piety.'[84] Phillips adds to his footnote at this point that 'This is particularly apparent in the Chapel pamphlets of the period, e.g. Philip CATER, *Memoirs of the Life and Character of Rev. John Paul Porter* (Bath, 1834).' Phillips argues that Baptists were part of the evangelicalisation of the whole of Bath, a transformation which brought with it other less desired changes, as major pillars of Bath's economy were undermined and visitors stayed away from Bath in great numbers, preferring other spas and resorts appearing in the early decades of the nineteenth century:

> One of the most serious of the alleged consequences was that the new religious activity destroyed the basis of the old city's economic prosperity—the public and private amusements of the wealthy. Banquets, the races, opera, theatre, mixed bathing were all clearly on the wane by 1815. Two decades later the city was one of the nation's evangelical showplaces.[85]

Yet Phillips acknowledges that this was not the only shift in the economy of the city during this period. Citing the research of David Jeremy and R S Neale,[86] among others, Phillips suggests that another transformation had taken place by the early decades of the nineteenth century, arguing that 'Bath evolved into a multi-class society' with a vibrant new economy that was no longer based primarily on the patronage and amusement of the few amidst the survival of the many. Phyllis Hembry confirmed the transformation of Bath by 1837:

> Formerly the health and holiday resort of eighteenth-century aristocrats, it now attracted the consumer society of retired people and the professional classes ministering to them. The *Bath Journal* could still in November 1837 call the opening performance of the 'celebrated' Pump Room band on the 6th of that month the 'signal for the return of the resident gentry from summer excursions and for the influx of summer visitors from all quarters', but again residents came first.[87]

It is in this context that the transformation of the Bath Baptist community can be understood as a transition from establishment and survival under the leadership of the dynamic and charismatic Robert Parsons to a more fragmented and diverse community under the leadership of John Paul Porter and other influential business men and traders such as members of the Evill family and Opie Smith.

---

[84] Ibid, 225.
[85] Ibid, 226.
[86] Neale, 1963; Neale, 1964; Jeremy, 1967.
[87] Hembry, 1997, 62.

Phillips' use of the Bath Baptist story is significant in that it is the only study to seriously attempt to place it within its wider social context, which he analyses in terms of a broad social stratification:

> Dissent lagged far behind the Church in gross numbers of adherents. There were few status inducements to join a Dissenting chapel. This was as true for the servant class as for those on top of the social ladder. Domestics were probably more inclined toward the Church both because of their loyalty to family and their search for respectability in the eyes of the predominantly Anglican upper classes. The origins of Dissent in Bath were also humble but found amongst other groups—predominantly independent artisans and craftsmen. Presbyterians first met in a small shearing shop in 1700 for their services. Quakers and Baptists were also associated with basically the same elements before 1800. In the nineteenth century very predictably the records of the various Nonconformist chapels indicate that the bulk of the membership in these congregations was drawn from the tradesmen and shopkeeping classes.[88]

Phillips' use of the Bath Baptist story had been to argue that it contributed to the unique religious fabric of Bath but that it contributed little to the economic or political profile of the city. Overall, he concludes, Nonconformist 'religiosity' was 'essentially in the area of internal denominational activity, new sectarian interests or possibly in personal religious experience.[89] Yet in the example he used for the Baptist case there is as much significance in what is not said as what is included in his summary:

> Lack of men of much substance was apparent among the Baptists. It was also reflected indirectly in the special preoccupation of that denomination in dealing with the problem of poverty within the membership. One of its most famous institutions of this chapel was the penny club for poor members instituted by John Paul Porter in 1825.[90]

That a concern for the poor among its members is an important indication of the care taken by members of that community to look after each other practically; that there were substantial figures as the Evill family, Opie Smith and George Cox the Chartist present among the Baptist community—these things were not noticed or were ignored by Phillips in his otherwise important article.

---

[88] Ibid, 229-30.
[89] Ibid, 240.
[90] Ibid, 230.

Each of these accounts of Bath Baptist history has also been focused in one way or another on the original heart of the Baptist community in the centre of the city at Somerset Street. As the Baptist community expanded, further congregations emerged in other parts of Bath, and in nearby villages. The longest surviving and best documented of these other congregations was at Twerton, a neighbouring village which by 1837 had been practically subsumed within the boundaries of the expanding city although not formally part of it until the twentieth century. There are further publications that record the history from the perspective of the church at Twerton and which need to be included at this point.

In November 1928 the Baptist church at Oldfield Park celebrated its Centenary and published a booklet entitled *One Hundred Years: The Centenary Story of the Oldfield Park Baptist Church, Bath, 1828-1928*. Two important things need to be stated about this. Firstly, the Oldfield Park building was built during 1902 and opened in 1903, so it is the Baptist community and not the building that the centenary celebration commemorated – a community which originated in Twerton over a hundred years earlier. Secondly, the church community that had been started in Twerton under the auspices of Somerset Street now had its home at Oldfield Park, in East Twerton. The church community that met in the old chapel at Twerton and closed on Easter Sunday 2004 was one which had been re-established only a hundred years earlier.[91] Although the relationship

---

[91] *One Hundred Years*, 1828, 12-13. Whereas the congregation at Twerton had understood the church at Oldfield Park as their descendant or sister church, Oldfield Park themselves had a different perspective. Throughout the 1890s under the leadership of Rev Benjamin Oriel the community at Twerton had been planning to move out of their original buildings into the heart of the more densely populated newly developed Oldfield Park, east towards Bath but still within the parish of Twerton. The foundations were finally laid in 1902 and the buildings opened on 26 May 1903. What actually transpired is fortunately recorded in the 1928 account: 'When the Building Scheme was first formulated, it was the intention of the Church to remove *en masse* into new premises, but when a site on the Lower Bristol Road which had been offered to the Church was thought to be unsuitable, a few of the members who lived near the old chapel expressed the desire that services might be continued there as formerly. They urged with reason, that West Twerton was a large district, and that few would go from it to Oldfield Park, so that Baptist interests as well as their personal convenience would suffer. To this request the Church acceded readily. Mr. Henry Mallard, a valued deacon of the Hay Hill Church kindly undertook the oversight of the work at the West, and for years laboured with great love and faithfulness as lay-pastor. Mr. Henry Mallard is held in high honour for his noble character and his love for the Church. The Chapel at West Twerton was closed for five weeks whilst the Opening services of the new Chapel were held. Some few members returned to the old place of worship still so dear to them, and in the course of time were transferred to make a new church in the old home. The Rev. Alex. Findlay began his ministry at Twerton in 1927. His genial personality is welcomed everywhere. Since his coming, beautiful new schoolrooms have been built at Twerton and the Chapel altered and renovated. The work of the Church in all its branches is progressive; and the happiest spirit of co-operation between the two Churches, separated a mile from each other exists, and is perpetuated.' The text further records that 'The above notes are almost entirely the work of the late Mr. Frances J. Robinson, father of our present and honoured deacon, H. H. Robinson. Mr. Frances Robinson, a remarkable man, was baptised at the age of 74.'

between the Oldfield Park and the new congregation at Twerton was cordial, there was disappointment that the foundation date 1828 was taken to Oldfield Park when Twerton understood that the membership had purposefully divided and that they could have shared the same date.[92]

What is clear is that the history of its formation in the 1820s was important for the new Baptist church at Oldfield Park to record. *One Hundred Years* opens with a brief account of the Baptist community in Twerton. Commenting on the life and witness of Nonconformists in general during the early days the writer concluded, 'Their vitality was at once demonstrated by the fervour with which evangelical work was undertaken at home and abroad.'[93] The narrative refers to the twenty year period before 1828, when the Twerton community was being established and connected to the mother church at Somerset Street. Debt was acknowledged to Alderman Moore, 'the Senior Deacon of Manvers Street, and ever loyal friend of our church',[94] for the detail of the account. Moore had spoken about the early history whilst laying one of the foundation stones in 1902:

> He (Alderman Moore) was looking at the old books, written with trembling hands in the Rev. J. P. Porter's own writing, and found it recorded that on July 15, 1808, it was rumoured in Somerset Street that there was some building going on in Twerton, and a deputation was sent to find out what it meant. The Twerton people were extremely kind and very loyal to 'mother,' and the result of the meeting was that it was prescribed by Somerset Street that no individual should have ruling power as to filling the pulpit or otherwise, except as approved and appointed by the Church at Somerset Street. Thus she showed her disbelief in foster mothers; she intended to take care of her child. But Twerton was strong then and seemed to be a little precocious for eight years after she sent a letter to the old pastor at Somerset Street to ask that she might either be a separate church or that the church ordinances might be administered on the spot. That caused a flutter in the Somerset Street dovecotes, and the result was a very severe resolution stating that the request could not be granted, because as to the first suggestion the title deeds forbade, while the second was 'repugnant to the ministry.' He need not say Twerton behaved very loyally and loved the old mother still. It appeared almost as though she

---

[92] *Baptist Union Directory*, 2000-2002, 61. 'Oldfield Park (The Triangle) 1828; Twerton (Mill Lane) 1905.' This continued to be Twerton's position throughout the twentieth century until its closure in 2004 that from one church community two had been formed, thus maintaining continuity with what had gone before.
[93] *One Hundred Years*, op. cit, 9.
[94] Ibid, 9.

came back on her knees, for she prevailed on the old pastor to go down to Twerton now and then and administer the Lord's supper. Before the church was 21 she did get her separation.[95]

Moore may have overstated the humility and precociousness of Twerton and the overbearing control of Somerset Street and its minister, but as community historian and diplomat he did his job well in remembering the details, linking the continuity of past, present and future, particularly as his version is being recalled by Frances Robinson nearly twenty-five years later. The editor of *One Hundred Years* noted:

> Every care has been taken to present in the following pages an accurate history of the Church and some of its existing institutions. It is not intended to be a complete and detailed history but rather a sketch in broad outline of a developing Church…The book is issued in the hope that it will cement still more firmly the solid grounds of our fellowship.[96]

It is clear how importantly the editor considered past history as contributing to the present life of the church, in cementing relationships and moving the church forward. The cordiality of the Oldfield Park and Twerton relationship is further demonstrated in the front pages of their centenary booklet, which was 'dedicated in gratitude to Almighty God for His ceaseless love and guidance through one hundred years and to the revered memory of the founders, past-ministers, officers and members of the Twerton Baptist Church and of the Oldfield Park Baptist Church, whom the present members follow in the faith and hope of the Gospel.'[97]

In 1934 the Twerton historian, R G Naish, published a series of articles about Twerton Baptist Church in the *Bath and Wilts Chronicle and Herald*. An article of 6 July about the Twerton Baptist Sunday School, 'Pioneers of Sunday Teaching' in Twerton, was based on 'a finely printed old document of some 650 words preserved between sheets of glass. Mr. H. W. Bence, the present secretary, has allowed me possession of it for a few days.'[98] This was followed up by a series of eight short articles between 24 August and 5 September, which begin:

> Mr. H W. Bence…brought me, after I last wrote, a wooden trunk of about two cubic feet capacity. "I don't know what is in it; books and papers connected with our church," he remarked, after he had dumped it down.
>
> I put the box and its contents out in the sun and air, for everything was damp and smelly. I found account books bound

---

[95] Ibid, 9-10.
[96] Ibid, 8.
[97] Ibid, Dedication.
[98] Naish, 1934, 6 July.

in parchment over 120 years old; ancient letters and documents, deeds and valuable printed papers, all bearing on the early years of West Twerton Chapel. I arranged, and codified somewhat, and now construct my story.

Let me say at the outset that I welcome criticism and other points of view than my own, and I desire to disturb no bond of essential peace. But I cannot accept the main thesis of the pamphlet issued by the Oldfield Park Baptist Church, Bath, in 1928.

My quarrel is with the opening sentence: "In 1828 the Baptist Church was founded in Twerton." It was not founded, only formalised in that year.[99]

Naish then goes on to argue that the church had been in existence for twenty years by 1828, and that it had been founded by James Cadby and others in around 1808. Naish's willingness to accept criticism was fortunate, for the 1808 date was given in *One Hundred Years*. The debate that ensued concerned the practice of Baptists dating the foundation of a church from the time of formally setting up a separate independent membership roll, and celebrating communion independently, rather than the time of first meeting together – a highly significant point, as highlighted by one of the three correspondents to the *Chronicle and Herald* on 7 September.[100] However, it is clear that Naish was not willing to accept other points of view than his own, nor able ideologically to accept the denominational practice of "founding". If this was Naish's weakness, his strength as an early twentieth-century socialist was highlighting in the Twerton Baptist relationship with Somerset Street the struggle of the working classes of the villages, and their liberation from the tyranny of the city oppressors. Figures such as Opie Smith and James Evill, and the reforming woollen mill owner Charles Wilkins, stand out as supporters of this struggle in Naish's account, and a workers' hero is found in the twenty-three year old

---

[99] Ibid, 24 August.
[100] *Bath & Wilts Chronicle & Herald*, 7 September 1934. Correspondence from Henry Smetham, Harry H Robinson and E Barnes. Despite the particular dispute, all three correspondents are grateful to Naish for an interesting and important series of articles. Naish, a socialist teacher with an interest in boys' education and the social history of Twerton, of course had his own perspective on the story he was uncovering: 'Sir,—I thank Mr. Harry H. Robinson for his criticism, and extracts from the Baptist minutes of 1828. But we can never agree on the point at issue between us. He speaks more denominationally than historically. I expected this; that was why I said in my preface: "I decline to be trammeled by delicate points of Baptist formality." John Paul Porter's pastor-craft and astonishing presumptions abound in every syllable of those minutes. A church runs on in Twerton for 20 years; then this "old and obdurate" minister comes down to "found" it. The idea is ludicrous. My kind acknowledgements to Mr. Henry Smetham and Mr. E. Barnes. ROBERT GEORGE NAISH. Campgarden, Southdown.

James Cadby, who in 1808 was the 'founder' of the Twerton Baptists – and who Naish proclaims 'A Clothworker Saint'.[101]

Figure 3. Cadby House, Twerton

The argument of an appropriate 'founding' date for the Twerton congregation is given another twist in an article by Deryck Lovegrove on 'Particular Baptist Itinerant Preachers during the late 18th and early 19th Centuries':

> In the village of Twerton members of the church at Bath commenced regular preaching in 1804 using a house that had been rented and fitted up by an unnamed resident. As the numbers attending increased the original premises became too

---

[101] Naish, 1934, 28 August; Bath City Council Housing Committee, *Minutes*, 6 April 1965. This status was recognised in 1965 when his name was given to a new block of flats erected in Twerton, 'Cadby House', although even here the Baptist origin of the name is likely in time to be lost. That James Cadby was the source of the name given to the flats was affirmed by Cynthia Turner and Michael Messer, working on the history of Twerton at this time. More recently Peter Little erroneously states, 'Ebenezer Cadby who died in 1855 gave his name to Cadby House. His grave can still be seen in the churchyard today.' Little, 1995, 36. Naish returned to Cadby five years later in an article on education in Twerton: 'Mrs A. Brown, of "Westwood," Lower Oldfield Park, Bath, a great grand-daughter of James Cadby, has very kindly communicated some reminiscences to me which I hope to publish in due sequence. Naish, 1939, 24 November. But there is no further reference to these reminiscences, so this part of the information available to Naish in his assessment of Cadby and the Baptist community in Twerton is lost to us in understanding the history today.

small and in September 1808 a new meeting-house was opened with accommodation for some three hundred persons.[102]

Subsequent research has shown that there were Baptists in Twerton from at least 1754. Where Naish's perspective has contributed most is in demonstrating the social and cultural engagement of Baptists in Twerton at the start of nineteenth century, just as Baptists were engaged socially and culturally in the heart of mid-eighteenth-century Bath.

The final account of the history of Baptists in Twerton appeared in 1978 when Twerton and Oldfield Park jointly celebrated their Ter-Jubilee. The booklet, *How Firm a Foundation*, told the combined story.[103] This year marked a high point in the relationship, before the last quarter of the twentieth century saw a dramatic decline in the Twerton membership and its eventual closure. It is significant that in retelling the history of the early years there is, although the account is brief, a sense of unanimity and joint ownership of the events as recorded. The account culminates with a reappraisal of the events surrounding the move to Oldfield Park in 1903, and recognises the bond between the two congregations.[104]

Unlike the Church of England which was firmly established by law, the Particular Baptist community in Bath consisted of a voluntary association of people bounded by a covenant relationship in and through a specific

---

[102] Lovegrove, 1980, 137 referring to *Baptist Magazine*, i, 38.

[103] Joan Rusbridge researched and wrote the Twerton chapters covering the formation in 1808 up to 1928. In addition the story was produced as a series of historical dramas for a joint Ter-Jubilee Pageant by Joan Rusbridge and Faith A E Brettell.

[104] *How Firm a Foundation*, 1978, 20. 'Before the move to Oldfield Park a conference was held to consider the future of Twerton and Mr H Mallard a deacon of Hay Hill Baptist accepted the post as lay pastor stipulating that Twerton's finances must be separate and run by the friends there. It was also agreed to leave the organ at Twerton. The church at Twerton was closed for five weeks for cleaning and all the members joined in the celebrations at Oldfield Park, then a number of them returned to carry on what was now an uphill task at Twerton. They held their own officers and members meetings (the first one records two deacons and twenty members present). All previous activities of the church were continued and various repair and painting jobs were carried out by the members themselves to save money. By December 1903 they were electing deacons and receiving members (including one unable to be baptized for health reasons) and also raised money for the Triangle Church (£4..11s..6d). Reports of baptisms in 1904 indicate that the small church was growing again. It became increasingly obvious that there were in fact two separate churches, so in 1905 negotiations were entered into with Oldfield Park Baptist and Twerton agreed to pay £250 as their part of the debt on the new buildings and then on October 31st 1905, 75 members restarted the Roll at Twerton... In 1906 the church officially affiliated with the B.U and the B.B.A as a separate entity...' It is this final comment that brings the argument to its conclusion. The official dates were merely those of the new registration with the Baptist Union and the Bristol Baptist Association. This revised account marks an important point of reconciliation in the period leading up to the final closing of the Baptist church in Twerton, although the two separate Baptist communities could not see their way to again becoming fully united whilst there were still mutual benefits to be gained. Significantly the original Twerton Baptist witness continues at Oldfield Park.

understanding and experience of the Christian faith. This 'gathered church of covenanted believers'[105] stood in the tradition of separatist Protestants who had set themselves apart from the established church, and although they shared a degree of relationship in association with other Baptist churches they formed an independent community which faced its challenges substantially alone. The notion of a separated gathered community, expressed in one form or another, has always been an essential part of Baptist ecclesiology.[106]

Despite the number of introductory surveys of Bath's Baptist past, an extended reflection on the early history of the Bath Baptist community is long overdue. This present study seeks to somewhat fill in that gap. In exploring the origins and development of the Bath Baptist community, with an eye to its social and cultural engagement, the life of Robert Parsons will be examined, both as a member of the Bath Baptist community and also as a contributor to the wider social and cultural world. Then the experience of the same community will be examined in the period after Robert Parsons' death, exploring the engagement of some of its members in the wider social and cultural life of Bath and further afield. Finally the period of change after 1800 will be explored, when there was a rapid increase in the Bath Baptist community, and a growing number of other Baptist congregations established in the city. In terms of Arnold's definition of 'culture' as that which aims towards 'perfection' it is reasonable to at least enquire whether Baptist Nonconformist engagement in Bath in the century before Arnold tended towards perfection or imperfection, whether through the Baptist contribution people's lives were improved or otherwise.

It can be shown that during a period of just over a century there were substantial changes in the nature of the Bath Baptist community, just as found also in the cultural, social, political and missiological context of the Georgian period as a whole. A very different structure was necessary in the early days of establishing a Baptist church community in Bath from that needed at the end of the eighteenth and into the nineteenth century, when the Baptist community was no longer one united church but more scattered or fragmented with a number of different Baptist church communities.

Eighteenth Century Baptist Growth

A superficial glance at the statistics shows that during the eighteenth century Baptist churches were growing, both in numbers of members and numbers of churches. This trend is true nationally, as well as locally. Studies have shown that there was steady growth until the 1790s, when things then expanded more rapidly.[107] Within Bath, specifically, this growth was extraordinary – promoted by the strength of Evangelicalism in the city – although this growth was by no

---

[105] Durnbaugh, 1985, 95.
[106] Walton, 1946, 55-105.
[107] Gilbert, 1976, 32-42.

means confined to the Baptist community. Paul Phillips's study of religion in Victorian Bath points to the evidence of the 1851 religious census to show the significance of this growth, and the important part religion played in the developing city:

> Although the role of religion in the emergence of a new Bath economy in the early nineteenth century is an area of debate, there can be little doubt about the place of religion in this new society. Just as the economy and class structure of this urban area was quite different from most large towns so was its religious behaviour. The religious census of 1851…reveals that Bath had one of the highest attendance figures for a large town in the country…These figures together with the sheer fact that so many people thought that Evangelical religion had such a profound role in the shaping of this new society points to the fundamental importance of religion in the lives of Victorian Bathonians.[108]

The community of Baptists in Bath were thoroughly caught up in what was happening in the country generally.

The end of the eighteenth century was certainly not the same as the beginning, in terms of Baptist experience. By origin the Baptist community in Bath were Particular Baptists, firmly established in the stream and traditions of Calvinist doctrines of faith. By the end of the Georgian period a thorough change or transition had taken place as they moved from a fairly strict, albeit moderate, Calvinism at the beginning and middle of the eighteenth century towards a more open evangelical Calvinism at the end. This is what was happening elsewhere too, such as in Bristol and Northampton.[109] This may be the general trend, yet the experience at Bath needs a more nuanced or critical explanation, largely because the development of the eighteenth-century Bath Baptist community would seem to be as much associated with the personalities of certain characters, such as Robert Parsons, John Paul Porter and Opie Smith, as with the theological timeframe in which they lived. It would be difficult to argue that Bath is a unique or peculiar case, although its character as a premier spa city, with its constantly fluctuating combinations of resident and transient population, would suggest that it might well be.[110] Certainly Phillips' observation from the 1851 census leads us in that direction, and in the eighteenth century there were certainly very few places with which Bath could be compared.

---

[108] Phillips, op. cit, 227.
[109] Naylor, 1992; Haykin, 1994.
[110] Borsay, 1999, 8-9. If that were the focus of this study it would not be the first study of a Bath institution to argue a unique context influencing a unique form of institution. What made Bath unique was its naturally heated spring water.

That there is something of considerable significance about the Bath Baptist community has been apparent in the official records since the 1830s, when sufficient tables of statistics relating to Baptist churches had been compiled to highlight an unusual and fascinating trend. Indeed the story of how such statistics came to be compiled is interesting in its own right, as John Briggs has shown. In *The English Baptists of the Nineteenth Century* Briggs discussed the gathering and interpretation of Baptist statistics, a daunting task in the early nineteenth century as today, because of 'first a failure of churches to associate, and secondly the failure of associated churches to make regular statistical returns.'[111] Baptist churches were not acknowledging each other and meeting together as they were being encouraged to do by the Associations, nor were they always attending to the accompanying paperwork. Statistical tables showing the numbers of Baptist congregations in each place were published in John Rippon's *Baptist Annual Register* and *The Baptist Magazine* covering the period 1790 to 1835. The tables for Bath are given in **Figure 4**.

Publication	Year	Church	Minister	Settled
BAR vol. i, 11	1790	Bath		
BAR vol. ii, 11	1794	Bath	John Paul Porter	
BAR vol. iii, 11	1798	Bath	John Paul Porter	
BM 1811, 461	1811	Bath	John Paul Porter	
BM 1823, 28	1823	Bath	John Paul Porter	
BM 1827, 136	1827	Bath	John Paul Porter	1791
BM 1831, 204 (also 591)	1831	Bath 1...1752 2 3 4...1828 5 6 Twerton	John Paul Porter P Cater W Clarke O Clarke J Chalker S Saniger	1791 1830 1826 1828 1830
BM 1835, 562	1835	Bath 1 2 3...1828 4 5 6	J Jackson P Cater O Clarke J Chalker W Clarke	1833 1830 1828 1826
BAR = *Baptist Annual Register*, BM = *Baptist Magazine*. In the 1831 & 1835 volumes the churches are not named but numbered, apparently in order of foundation.				

Figure 4. Bath Baptists in Published Lists, 1790-1835

Although the names of the congregations are not given in the tables, they can be identified from the given names of the ministers. John Paul Porter was at Somerset Street, followed after his death by John Jackson; Philip Cater was at

---

[111] Briggs, 1994, 255-7.

York Street; William Clarke was minister of the Scotch Baptist congregation that met at Chandos Buildings; Owen Clarke was at Corn Street; John Chalker was at Thomas Street; and S Saniger is named as minister of another small congregation that is now difficult to identify. The Baptist church at Twerton was without a minister at the dates given.

John Rippon had compiled his lists from regional Association returns, as far as they existed, and from his network of local contacts and correspondents. The later tables published in *The Baptist Magazine* were compiled by Joseph Belcher, a long time advocate of the value of statistical analysis in the cause of spreading the gospel. Belcher demonstrated a threefold increase nationally in the number of Baptist churches between 1811 and 1831. John Briggs noted that the 1831 table is particularly significant. 'Clearly there were considerable areas of Baptist strength', he writes and points out that along with only one other place Bath 'had significantly more Particular Baptist churches than any other urban centre in this early period'. Indeed, the published tables show that Bath had one Baptist church until 1831, when the number jumps to six (or seven when Twerton is properly included). It is unlikely that this number would increase so suddenly between 1827 and 1831 without something significant having happened by way of explanation. What was throughout the eighteenth century a single Baptist community in Bath can no longer be described in quite the same way when manifest as six or seven distinct churches at the beginning of the nineteenth, although the varying relationships between the churches demonstrates a 'community' of Baptist churches in a different sense of the word. Unfortunately the records for most of these congregations no longer exist, but the records of the church at Twerton are important for giving some insight into the relationship between them, and showing the developing relationship between the new Twerton congregation and its mother church in the city from whom it gradually won independence.

In order to explore the history of the Bath Baptist community it is necessary to reconstruct a narrative from the primary and secondary sources that are available. Minutes books, accounts books, and a wealth of other papers and documents exist for both of the main churches examined. However, the purpose of this study is not just to reconstruct or retell a narrative, but rather to reconstruct a narrative in order to show its value and significance, illustrating the cultural and social engagement of its subjects. The Bath Baptist community certainly has an interesting story, introducing a number of fascinating characters and intriguing twists and turns, explaining how the community became established in the way that it did, and why it behaved in certain ways. It might be described as a colourful and passionate story, but that is for the reader to judge at its conclusion. If this were to be the judgement then this would be reason enough to retell the story on its own terms. *Waters of the Son*, however, is also about the significance of the story as lying in what it says about the relationship between the Baptist community and the Georgian city of Bath.

Chapter 2: Origins and Overview

Western Baptist Association

Having considered eighteenth-century Bath as the main theatre for the events of our study, it would be wrong to move on without further considering the wider Baptist context in the West of England into which the Bath congregation emerged. The numbers and locations of Baptist churches in the West Country during the late-seventeenth and early-eighteenth centuries fluctuated, and it would be the middle of the eighteenth century before things would settle. Something of the background, however, can be gained from exploring the development of the Western Baptist Association, with which most Particular Baptist churches were associated. The Association's roots were in the seventeenth century where the turmoil of the Civil War, Commonwealth and Protectorate years had stirred up the religious climate nationally and locally. The defeat of the Royalists by early 1646 gave the Presbyterian supported victors a short period of confidence under a more settled regime. Thomas Edwards, the diligent Presbyterian cataloguer of the many new religious 'errors' that were emerging at this time, recorded one of his correspondents writing that,

> There are two new Opinions risen about Bath and Bristol among the Anabaptists, and followed with much heat, as a glorious Discovery of a new Light (for so they call it) it hath been disputed pro and con, in severall Conventions, and increaseth much, &c.
> 1. That Christ's humane nature is defiled with Originall sin, as well as ours.
> 2. That there is but one person in the Divine nature.[1]

Baptists were eager to distance themselves from these erroneous doctrines, because sectaries were lumped together as 'Anabaptists'. Nevertheless here are embryonic signs of the later Quaker movement[2] and Unitarianism that would later come to challenge Baptist thinking. One of the early opponents of the Quakers was Thomas Collier, former chaplain in Cromwell's army and an effective Baptist evangelist. Thomas Edwards wrote about Collier in the second part of *Gangraena*, published in 1646:

> There is one Collier, a great Sectary in the West of England, a mechanicall fellow, and a great Emissary, a Dipper, who goes about Surry, Hampshire, and those counties thereabouts, preaching and dipping; About a fortnight agoe on the Lords day he preached at Guilford in the meeting-place, and to the

---

[1] Edwards, 1646, i, 49-50
[2] George Fox didn't discover his 'Inner Light' until 1647.

> company of one old M. Close, an Independent Minister, who hath set up at Guilford, and done a great deal of mischiefe, having drawn away many of the well-meaning people from the ministry of those godly Ministers, whom before they much prized; there this Collier exercised, and it was given about in the County he was a rare man, and the people came from the Towns about to hear him…[3]

Much of Collier's known influence lay in the South and West of England. In the third part of *Gangraena* Edwards refers to '*Thomas Collier* a great Sectary in the West of *England*', whose vision of a new social order governed directly by the Lord Jesus, and given over by the Presbyterian supported Parliament for that very purpose, made him a heretic in Edwards' eyes.[4] In a letter from Guildford dated 20 April 1646 'To the Saints in the Order and fellowship of the Gospel in *Taunton*', Collier exhorted the small Baptist community there

> … to wait upon the Lord in his own way, and not to look forth into the world; there is bread enough in your Father's house; There he hath promised his presence; though you seem to want gifts, yet you shall not want the presence of your Father, your Jesus, if you wait upon him…[5]

and then encouraged them to welcome 'brothers Sims and Row', who are not identified further but had been denied the 'unlimited power of the Presbyterians'. In another letter from London dated 2 May 1646, this time addressed to William Heynton the butler at Taunton Castle, Collier expressed his love towards the Taunton fellowship and urged them to live in the 'unity and fellowship of the Son of God' and not to live upon 'lower things', which are for him

> …but instruments to conveigh light and love unto us, I meane even Ordinances or the like, which indeed are but as a shell without the kernel, further then wee enjoy Christ in it.[6]

Emphasising the locally gathered and Spirit filled community over against the institutional church – the 'kernel' as opposed to the 'shell' – Collier and others like him posed a threat to the Presbyterian establishment, even in the relatively tolerant days of the late 1640s. The seven Baptist churches in London, 'those

---

[3] Edwards, 1646, ii, 148. The term 'Dipper' refers to someone who practices baptism by immersion.
[4] Edwards, 1646, iii, 27-30. Edwards relied upon the testimony of local witnesses, or from correspondence that had fallen into his hands. A Presbyterian himself, and now a member of the ruling party, Edwards considered other groups and sects to be in 'error' or 'heretics', but he is not always clear in what sense.
[5] Ibid, 51.
[6] Ibid, 52.

churches which are commonly (though falsly) called Anabaptists', had only recently found the courage to publish their *Confession of Faith* in 1644.[7]

In the West Collier was busy preaching and establishing new Baptist congregations, such as at Taunton, and by 1653 'churches from Gloucestershire to Cornwall [were] linked together under the general leadership of Thomas Collier.'[8] At some point during his travels Collier became associated with the London church pastored by William Kiffin, something that would have later consequences.[9] Collier held the view that all who have the gift of preaching should also have the freedom to preach, as recorded in *The Pulpit-Guard Routed* in 1652:

> those varieties of stations amongst men, must have varieties of distinct Callings to it; but this of Preaching and Prophesying is that which all the brethren that have the gifts are called to, as I have often proved; that in the Church all may prophesy, that have the gift, and yet no confusion, but peace and order: and indeed its nothing else but ignorance, and your pride, in being afraid of such an equality with your Brethren, as the Scripture presents you with.[10]

Under Collier's enabling leadership ministers and 'messengers' from the locally networked Baptist congregations gathered at least annually in 'Association', the first recorded being of eighteen churches[11] at Wells, on 'the 8th and 9th daies of the 9th moneth 1653.'[12] The proceedings of these meetings, usually taking the form of queries with their corresponding answers, and the occasional letter, were meticulously recorded until 1659. By then things had become dangerous again for Dissenters: the records of the Association at Dorchester only survived in detail because Mayor Stansby had refused the Baptists access to any of the churches and they were forced to retreat to the George Inn where proceedings were reported back to Cromwell by his government spies.[13]

---

[7] Lumpkin, 1959, 144-171. This confession was reprinted in 1646, and further editions appeared in subsequent years during the early Commonwealth.
[8] White, 1971-1974, ii. 53.
[9] See below, p.37. William Kiffin (1616-1701) was an influential London merchant and one of a small group of influential Particular Baptist ministers in the mid-late seventeenth century.
[10] Collier, 1652, 35. This was part of Collier's well-documented disputation with Thomas Hall (1610-1665), puritan clergyman of King's Norton, Worcestershire. Copson, 1997, 107-121.
[11] Jackman, 1953, 1. 'The eighteen churches represented at the 1653 meeting were as follows:- Bridgwater, Stoke, Taunton, Wells, Wedmore, Hatch, Ryden, Chard, Dulwood (Loughwood), Bristol (Pithay), Somerton, Abingdon, Sodbury, Lyme, Dartmouth, Totness, Upottery and Bradley.' Jackman continues, 'In addition we know that Dorchester had a meeting house by that date, Weymouth and Poole had been in existence at least seven years, Plymouth was flourishing, whilst there were churches in Exeter, Barnstaple, Honiton and the neighbourhood.'
[12] Ibid, 54.
[13] Underdown, 1992, 219.

The *Confession of Faith* around which the London churches associated in 1644 had been published 'to manifest their substantial agreement with the prevailing forms of Calvinistic orthodoxy.'[14] Articles twenty-four to twenty-six make it clear that the 'elect' would normally come to faith through the preaching of the Gospel and the grace of God working in the sinner's soul. In this they were staunchly Calvinist, renouncing any hint of Arminianism, denying that it is within human capability to respond freely to the offer of the Gospel:

> XXIV. That faith is ordinarily begot by the preaching of the Gospel, or word of Christ, without respect to any power or capacitie in the creature, but it is wholly passive, being dead in sinnes and trespasses, doth believe, and is converted by no lesse power, then that which raised Christ from the dead.[15]

In the West Country at first both General and Particular Baptists associated, although this would change in a very short time. With Collier's lead there was an emphasis upon evangelistic activity and Gospel preaching despite other doctrinal concerns, as is amply illustrated in the Association records. In 1654 at Taunton it was queried

> Whether any are to be received into the church of Christ only upon a bare confession of Christ being come in the flesh and assenting to the doctrine and order laid down by him?

The answer was direct, reflecting the inner spiritual emphasis already seen in Thomas Collier's understanding of the matter:

> ...they may not be admitted on such terms without a declaration of an experimental work of the Spirit upon the heart, through the word of the Gospel and sutable to it, being attended with evident tokens of conversion, to the satisfaction of the administrator and brethren or church concerned in it...[16]

At Chard in 1655 the question was asked,

> Whether Christ Jesus our Lord dyed for all and every man or for the elect only, and if for all, then how far?
> Answer: our Lord Christ dyed for all and every man...first, to reconcile all to God so as to have their being continued by him...Secondly, and that repentance and remission of sins might be preacht in his name to all men...Thirdly, that so he might be Lord of all...Fourthly, that he might raise all from the dead in

---

[14] White, 1968, 570. Lumpkin refers to the *Confession* as moderately Calvinistic: 'The Calvinism of the Confession is of a moderate type. The doctrine of election is balanced by the statement that the Gospel is to be preached to all men, and there is no teaching of reprobation.' Lumpkin, 1959, 146.
[15] Lumpkin, op. cit, 163.
[16] White, 1971-1974, ii, 56.

> the order and times appointed by the Father...Yet he died not intentionally alike for all...[17]

The following year at Bridgwater the subject of Gospel preaching was discussed in some detail. In fact Gospel preaching had been the usual practice of the associated churches, and had been acknowledged to have been blessed with some success. The issue was,

> Whether it be an absolute duty now lying on several churches speedily to send forth persons fitted for the great and good work of preaching the Gospel to the world?
> Answer: we judge it to be a duty and at this time much to be laid to heart and performed to send forth such brethren as are fitted to the work of preaching the Gospel to poor sinners that they might be saved.
> 1. That it's a duty appears by the commission of Christ...and by the churches that first trusted in Christ according thereunto...
> 2. That it's now to be performed appears by the open door that God hath set before us...the fields being white to harvest...and the abounding also of the mystery of iniquity.[18]

It was at this same meeting in 1656 that a new *Somerset Confession*, largely the work of Thomas Collier, was approved. The confession's aims were to set forth clearly the doctrines of West Country Baptists in Association; to counter the accusations and confusion that the emerging Quaker movement, particularly active in the Bristol and Bath area, was causing; and to restate the unity in doctrine and order of Somerset and Western Baptists with the Particular Baptist movement in London.[19] The *Somerset Confession* was distinctly and explicitly evangelistic in tone:

> XXXIV.
> THAT as it is an ordinance of Christ, so it is the duty of his church in his authority, to send forth such brethren as are fitly gifted and qualified through the Spirit of Christ to preach the gospel to the world...
>
> XXXV.
> THAT it is the duty of us believing Gentiles, not to be ignorant of that blindness that yet lieth on Israel, that none of us may boast...but to have bowels of love and compassion to them, praying for them...expecting their calling, and so much the

---

[17] Ibid, 61.
[18] Ibid, 64.
[19] Lumpkin, 1959, 200.

> rather, because their conversion will be to us life from the dead...[20]

Their understanding was that the church clearly has a duty to send out gifted preachers, expecting that people would respond to the call of the gospel. Such preachers were to be those who where 'gifted and qualified' by the Spirit, so that the Spirit might bring about the hearer's 'conversion' from death to life. Yet there was clearly some hesitancy in some churches in sending out preachers. At the meeting of the Association at Wells in 1659 it was again queried,

> Whether the answere of the brethren at the fifth generall meeting concerning the sending forth of the Gospell ministry to the world were a hasty conclusion or whether it bee the churches' neglect in not sending?
> Answer: it was then the sense of the assembly and still is that according to the capacity that the churches are in they ought to send there ministers to preach the Gospell to the world.[21]

It is unclear whether churches were unsure of their duty to send out evangelistic preachers, or whether churches were just not able or willing to do so for other reasons. Some churches, however, were sending out preachers. In Bristol, Andrew Gifford senior was baptised as a believer in 1659 and was actively preaching in the area between Bristol and Bath, at Hanham and Keynsham, both evangelistically in the open air and to newly founded Baptist churches. The duration of Gifford's ministry overlaps the end of Thomas Collier's, and Leonard Champion in his biography of Gifford's grandson (Andrew Gifford junior) finds every reason to agree with Joseph Ivimey's assessment that

> ...he might be considered as the Apostle of the West, as he was the founder of most of the churches in Somerset and Gloucestershire and used to visit them frequently until he became the settled pastor.[22]

What evidence survives seems to suggest a healthy growth in the number of new Baptist churches and the size of their congregations during the mid-seventeenth-century period.

1660, however, saw the Restoration of the Monarchy and subsequent years of persecution when few records of Baptist Association meetings were kept, although occasional Assemblies were held. Douglas Jackman concluded about this period that 'If it had not been for the Restoration and what followed, the West might have anticipated Carey and the cause of modern missions by nearly

---

[20] Ibid, 213.
[21] White, 1971-1974, 102. A 'long silence' overtakes the record from this point, and it would be many years before being safe for Baptists to keep such detailed records again.
[22] Champion, 1961, 2.

150 years,'[23] such was the productivity of the preachers and church planters of the period. The work of Thomas Collier, and later Andrew Gifford, was crucial to this drive. Yet despite Thomas Collier's pioneering work he later separated from the Calvinism of other contemporary Particular Baptists, arguing amongst other things that Christ's death was effective for all, not just the elect. In fact Collier had developed a double view of election in which he reiterated his belief in God choosing some for salvation, but also a 'second special election' for those who by God's grace would respond to the gospel and thus be saved – but from which they could fall away.[24] Collier's orthodoxy was now in doubt, so in 1677 two Western Association Messengers, Richard Gay, minister at Haycombe, Bath, and Walter Penn, minister at Porton, were sent to see Collier at Southwick, Wiltshire, where he had been minister for some years. A Baptist delegation headed by William Kiffin and Nehemiah Coxe had travelled from London to dispute with Collier over further deviations in his doctrine. In 1676 he had written *An Additional Word to the Body of Divinity*[25] in which he had repeated his view that limited atonement alone was contrary to the sense of the gospel, and this had incensed the London church pastored by Kiffin, who still considered Collier to be one of their members. For the London church this was a disciplinary matter, but Collier claimed not to have been communicant with the London church for more than twenty years, and therefore not a member with them for some time. Events reached a climax by 1677 as Nehemiah Coxe explained:

> …it hath either been answered many times already by those that have written against the Pelagians, Jesuites, and Socinians, in whose steps Mr. Collier very frequently treads; or else (where he doth transcend the Heresies of those mentioned) its weakness and impiety is more manifest than to need any refutation by another; yet on many accounts, some Answer to him was judged necessary, not only by my self, but by divers others…[26]

In his case against Collier, Coxe included the testimony of six London ministers who Collier later claimed had no knowledge of either him or his beliefs. Yet the charge of heresy was made and finally ruled, despite the support Collier had from his own church at Southwick who themselves saw the case from London against their minister as a direct challenge and threat to their own authority as an autonomous church. The Southwick church was urged by Walter Penn to submit to the Messengers of the London and Western churches but they refused, as Collier later recorded:

---

[23] Jackman, 1953, 6.
[24] Hayden, 2006, 5-8. Hayden argues that Collier didn't become Arminian as such, but stretched and used Calvinist terms in such a way that caused serious doubts as to his Calvinistic orthodoxy.
[25] Collier, 1676; Land, 1979, 341.
[26] Coxe, 1677, Forward.

> ...yet still he persisted to get the power of determining into their own hands, and Richard Gay, one of them, to declare that they were of one mind in the matter, spake to the same effect; but when they could no further prevail, but for advice only, they yielded then to proceed, using their own power of determining, though denied then by the church...[27]

The decision was made that Collier should no longer be in association with them, and a letter was accordingly sent to Collier. This had been signed on 2 August 1677 by fifteen Messengers, including Nehemiah Coxe and Daniel Dyke from London, who had gathered in the region for the ordination of Andrew Gifford on 3 August 1677.[28]

Evidence of the continued meeting of the Western Association during the 1670s and 1680s exists amongst the surviving papers of Andrew Gifford.[29] One such meeting was called by the churches 'to take Account of their present state, that our breaches may be repaired, our disorders rectified, our wants supplied'.[30] Andrew Gifford was a survivor, preaching when it was dangerous to do so. Although he had been licensed under legislation passed in the reign of Charles II, in 1672, Gifford experienced numerous spells in prison for his troubles: three times in Bristol's Newgate Prison, just a stone's throw from where the Baptist meeting house in The Pithay would stand, and once in Gloucester Castle.[31] In 1689 the Act of Toleration brought to an end this period of persecution. It also brought a new era of confidence for Baptists in London and in the western provinces. Seven of the London Particular Baptist ministers invited churches throughout England and Wales to a General Assembly to be held in London, from 3 to 12 September 1689. J G Fuller, in his history of the Western Baptist Association, commented on the atmosphere of 'love and sweet concord' at the Assembly.[32]

The Assembly finally approved a new *Confession of Faith* that had been produced for limited circulation in 1677. The 1677 or *Second London Confession* had the grand title 'Confession of Faith Put forth by the Elders and Brethren Of many Congregations of Christians (baptized upon Profession of Faith) in *London* and the Country.'[33] Its approval by the 1689 Assembly gave the Confession a greater audience, and the *1689 Baptist Confession*, as it was thereafter known, became a standard authoritative text amongst Particular Baptists throughout its numerous editions.

---

[27] Collier, 1677, 9.
[28] Land, 1979, 279-80; Hayden, 2006, 7; Collier, 1677, 15-16.
[29] The collection known as *Gifford's Remains* is kept at Bristol Baptist College.
[30] *Gifford's Remains*. Letter from the Church of Christ at Haycomb to the Assembly signed by Richard Gay and William Lyppeat.
[31] Champion, 1961, 2-3.
[32] Fuller, 1823, 17.
[33] Lumpkin, 1959, 241.

From 1689 to 1691 the General Assembly of Baptist Churches met in London.[34] From 1692 it was agreed that the General Assembly should meet in Bristol and London, which was the arrangement until the end of the century, each sending messengers to the other.[35] Clearly, however, Western Baptists met together as an Association independently of the General Assembly, as they did at Taunton during 1688 and 1689. Similarly, a circular letter dated 29 March 1692 from Frome called for an Association meeting 'at Westbury, at brother Cator's house, in the year 1693.'[36] Despite years of persecution, by 1689 the initial eighteen churches had grown to twenty-four, and very soon thirty-five.[37] For forty years from 1693 there is very little record of Association life, but clearly the preference was local Associations rather than General Assembly in London, which was in any case difficult to get to. The General Assembly in London soon lapsed despite some effort to resurrect it.

Reflecting the influence of Thomas Collier, Andrew Gifford and other evangelists, West Country Baptists practised a Calvinism that was open to preaching the gospel evangelistically.[38] As the eighteenth century progressed, so did the reputation of the London ministers for their hyper-Calvinism which 'robbed many Particular Baptists of evangelical preaching',[39] and so increased the divide between London and the West. J G Fuller argued that in general West Country Baptists resisted hyper-Calvinism:

> With all their Hyper-Calvinism, the churches belonging to this Association never avowedly sanctioned the pernicious principles of 'Antinomianism;' nor did they maintain the doctrine of 'Reprobation,' in the sense alleged against them by their opponents. Individuals apart, while they strenuously repudiated the former (as their Annual Letters amply demonstrate,) they considered the latter, not as a negative of Election, but as the opposite of Approbation; or Divine Disapprobation on account of sin.[40]

---

[34] *A Narrative of the Proceedings of the General Assembly, 1889-82.*
[35] Ivimey, 1811-30, i, 519.
[36] Ibid, 524.
[37] Jackman, 1953, 7. 'The 24 in the first list being:- Taunton, Bridgwater, Croscomb, Hallatrow, Haycomb (Bath), Hatch, Kilmington, Dunster, Perriton-evil, Frome, Sarum, Warminster, Sedghill, Westbury, Devizes, Calne, Melksham, Bradford, Southwick, Malmesbury, Ninfield, Sodbury, Broadmead and the Fryers, Bristol. To these were shortly added Plymouth, Looe, Southams, Bovey, South Molton, Tiverton, Exon, Luppit, Dalwood, Lyme and Chard. In addition to these churches, not all of whom attended the London meetings, are churches within our area at Dorchester, Yeoville and Pearot (Perrott) Wedmore and Knoyle who were all represented at the London meetings in 1689 and 1692.'
[38] Hayden, 1990, 84-88.
[39] Ibid, 85.
[40] Fuller, 1823, 20.

In 1715 the Western churches in the annual circular letter written from Taunton were urged to encourage the gifts of pastoral leadership to be found in their midst. The urgency of finding new leaders for the churches is clear, as those who lived through the years of persecution were aging considerably and the tasks of evangelisation and pastoring the existing congregations in the new century were immense. The circular letter written from Bampton, Devon, in 1716, continues in its appeal:

> As it was recommended to you, from our last Association, to do what in you lieth, to encourage and improve those gifts for the ministry God may raise up among you, by affording them those helps of profitable books for their study, or helps in learning they may be capable of, herein you will not only give an evidence of the sincerity of your prayers to the Lord of the harvest to send forth more labourers into his harvest, but also, by his blessing on your pious endeavours, the breaches he hath made, and is like to make, on many of the churches, in taking home to himself their faithful pastors and ministers, may in some measure be repaired, and the generation to come may call you blessed.[41]

1719 was a significant year in the relationship between General and Particular Baptists in the West Country. Hitherto they had co-existed peacefully, but theological controversy in Exeter over the divinity of Christ, particularly among the Presbyterians, brought a growing Arianism among some General Baptists, which among the Particular Baptists was more to be feared than their Arminianism.[42] West Country Baptists were involved in the Salters' Hall debate amongst Dissenting churches, which concluded with a fully Trinitarian statement – to which most of the General Baptists refused to subscribe. This only heightened the tension between Generals and Particulars, which Roger Hayden has demonstrated was still alive amongst Western Association churches in the 1730s,[43] contrary to the testimony of John Sharp of Frome who reported back to the Western Baptist Association meeting at Trowbridge in 1719:

> We have great cause to rejoice (say the brethren) that though it is a perilous day, wherein many of other persuasions depart from 'the faith once delivered to the saints,' – particularly in that great article of the Christian religion – the Deity of our blessed Lord and Saviour Jesus Christ; denying, or calling into question, his

---

[41] Fuller, 1823, 28.
[42] Brown, 1986, 22 & 27. Brown gives this as the reason for General Baptists being isolated from the Particular Baptist Fund: 'They were more afraid of Arianism than Arminianism. After all, however orthodox some of their London ministers might be, some General Baptists made no secret of their doubts concerning the deity and humanity of Christ as well as the doctrine of the Trinity.'
[43] Hayden, 1999, 193.

> eternal Godhead; suggesting that he is not of the same nature with the Father, – that he is not supreme God, but a mighty glorious creature, in his Divine nature superangelical; – though it is thus with others, we rejoice that none of the churches, or ministers belonging to this Association, hold any such pernicious doctrine…[44]

Hayden shows how it was the Broadmead church, under Bernard Foskett's leadership, that attempted without much success in 1723 to tighten the doctrinal constitution of the Western Baptist Association by proposing to the Assembly that it fully adopt the *1689 Confession* (third edition 1699) as a condition of associating.[45] All that could be agreed by 1724 was a brief declaration of belief in a Trinitarian understanding of God. Foskett addressed the issue once more in an Association sermon preached at Exeter in 1725, Exeter of course being at the heart of the Arian controversy, and the spiritual and doctrinal 'coldness and declension' that was being experienced among Western Association churches as a result:

> The comfortable and glorious truths of free election, efficacious grace, imputed righteousness, and the certain perseverance of the saints, have not been treated by some as they ought. Surely, did we set them near our hearts, they would warm them, and inspire us with more zeal for God and for religion. – We would stir up one another, and all our brethren in the ministry, to take heed to themselves and their flocks; and with all plainness, seriousness, and courage, to preach, maintain, and defend the great doctrines of the gospel…[46]

The matter was kept to the fore by the Broadmead church for almost a decade until 1732 when, due to a fortunate hiatus in the Association's annual meetings caused by a fire at Tiverton in 1731, the Association finally met as guests of the Bristol church. A new set of 'preliminaries' (outline constitution) were drawn up for a newly constituted Association which excluded both the General Baptists ascribing to Arminian and Arian views on one hand, and extreme (hyper) Calvinists with Antinomian tendencies on the other. This new Western Association gathered around the doctrinal position of the *1689 Baptist Confession* at its core.

Gradually Association life was rekindled, as evidenced by the many references and encouragements in the Association letters and breviates to making the Gospel widely known if the church is to fulfil its mission, and the growth of evangelistic preaching throughout the West Country. Records of participation in

---

[44] *Association Letter*, 1723; Fuller, 1823, 29.
[45] Hayden, 1999, 194.
[46] Fuller, 1823, 31.

the Association clearly show consistent growth in the period 1750 to 1795 from some twenty to over forty churches,[47] a trend that would continue into the following century such that by 1823 there were seventy-eight churches in membership.

Figure 5 shows the growing number of member churches of the Association for the period 1733 to 1823, by which year the Western Association had grown sufficiently to divide into smaller geographical areas and Bath came to fall within the boundaries of the Bristol and District Baptist Association.

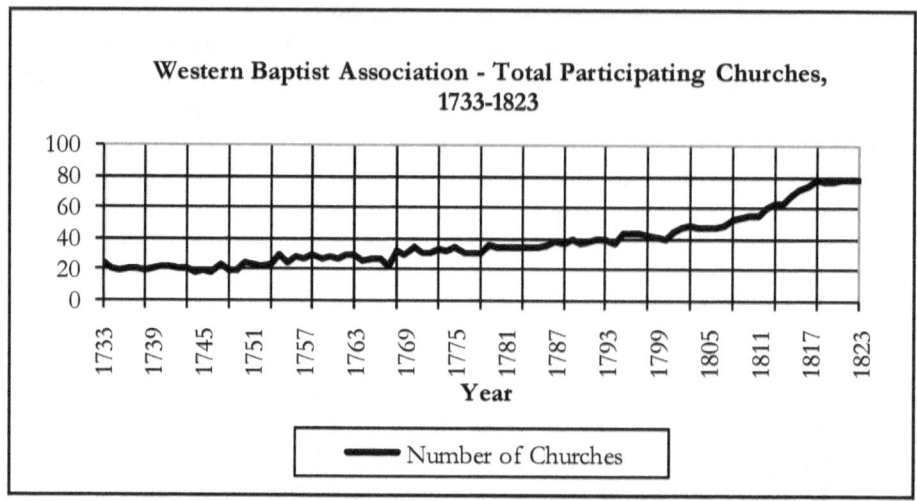

Figure 5. Western Baptist Association, 1733-1823.

Growth among the Western Baptist Association churches was not without its pains and struggles though. In 1760 the Association Circular Letter written from the Annual Assembly at Bath, during a brief spell when the Bath church was a member, exhorted the churches of the Association to re-read and study the *1689 Confession*. It was followed by the 1761 letter which complained of the 'Laodicean' state of the churches. Yet the Association and its churches were growing, despite the Association Letter of 1763 addressing 'the complaints which at your church-meetings you have solemnly subscribed' and a perceived stagnation from within:

> Give us leave to ask, whether they do not arise from your own indulged negligence? Whether you have felt the complaints you have subscribed? Whether you have made the same sincerely before God? Whether you have endeavoured and prayed to remedy and remove them?

The letter concludes:

---

[47] *Western Association Records*.

And now, brethren, as those who may possibly have but a little time to labour amongst you… warm yourselves at the fire of redeeming love; drink in vigour from the promises; submit to the attractions of eternal glory; – in a word, light afresh your torch at the Sun of Righteousness, and go on diffusing light and lustre all around you, till God shall bring you to that world where there is no light, and where the Lamb shall lead you to the living fountain in the realms of never-ending day.[48]

Despite the encouragement from the gathered Association that its member churches seek to rekindle their lives from within, there must be some considerable doubt as to the effectiveness of such a challenge due to poor levels of commitment to associating. For the period 1760 to 1796 the Association records not only list those churches who participated at the annual assembly, but also analyse the figures to show who actually attended and who only took part by sending an annual letter on the state of the church – which was one of the conditions of membership. **Figure 6** charts these figures and shows that during this period there was never a full attendance at the assembly and that on some occasions there were actually more letters received than church representatives present.

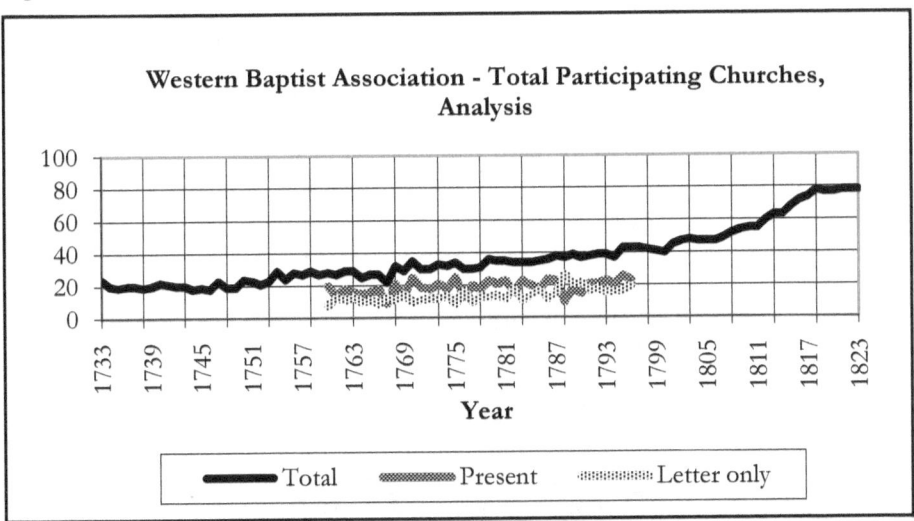

Figure 6. Western Baptist Association, 1733-1823 – Analysis.

Individual Baptist churches were at liberty to heed the Association as conscience dictated, and as we have seen it was difficult enough to get the churches to associate together in the early part of the century. This minor qualification aside, the data gathered by the Association indeed shows a pattern of growth as measured according to a number of different indicators. **Figure 7**

---

[48] *Association Letter* 1761; Fuller, 1823, 46.

charts the individual number of believers baptised in Association churches, and it shows a steady increase, in line with an increased number of member churches, with an accelerating growth from the 1790s into the following century – reaching a peak in 1816.

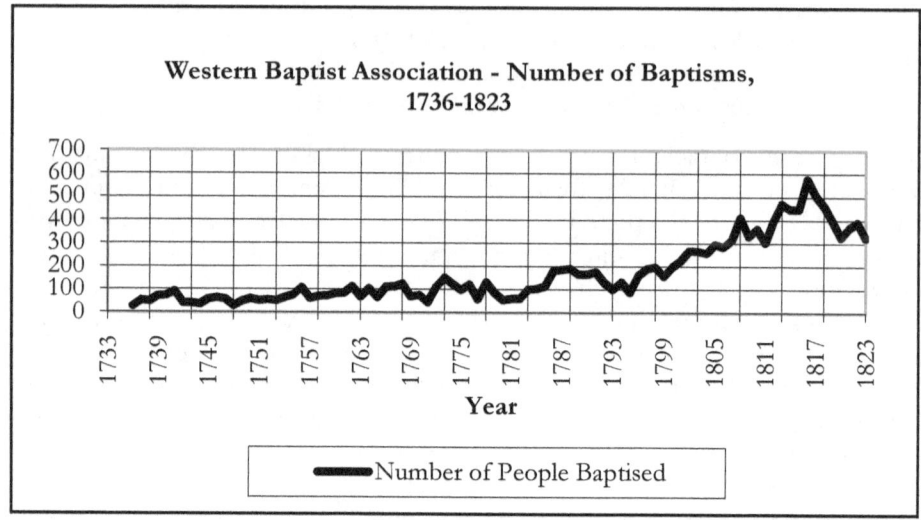

Figure 7. Western Baptist Association Total Baptisms.

Alone, however, this tells only part of the story. When an average number of baptisms in each church is calculated the resultant graph, **Figure 8**, continues to demonstrate this same progress, with churches baptising more people from the end of the eighteenth century into the nineteenth. Some churches were particularly successful, including at Bath.

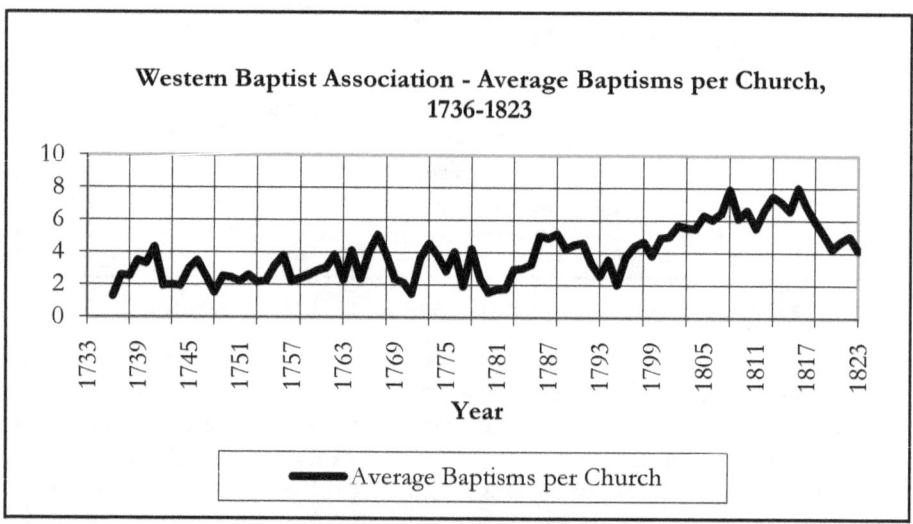

Figure 8. Western Baptist Association Average Baptisms.

A further growth indicator present in the Association records comes from the membership change data collected. Church membership grows or declines according to a number of different factors, including the baptism or transfer in of new members or the death, transfer out or dismissal for other reasons of existing members. A church's membership thus rises or falls year on year, and when the figures for the Association are totalled each year, starting with a base line of zero in 1733, the resulting graph – as shown in **Figure 9** – continues to demonstrate the same growth trend from the 1790s onwards, although there is only a small increase demonstrable in the earlier decades.

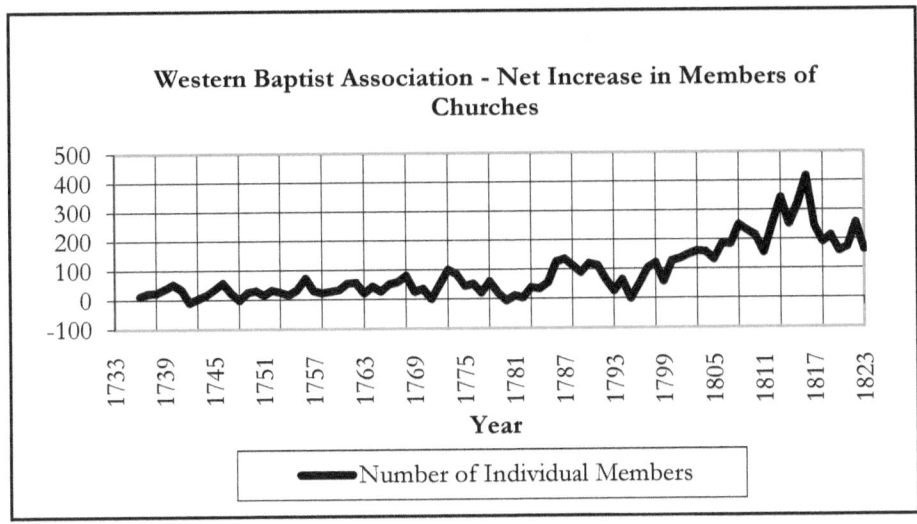

Figure 9. Western Baptist Association Membership Increase.

The Western Baptist Association grew steadily throughout the middle of the eighteenth century during the period of the Evangelical Awakening; that growth accelerated from the 1790s, a time usually identified as the era of missionary expansion. Locally, the drive for a thriving local Association united around the *1689 Baptist Confession of Faith* and dedicated to preaching the Gospel evangelistically, which the Broadmead church had envisioned within the constituency, was an important contributory factor for growth in the middle years of the eighteenth century and a catalyst for later years. The Broadmead church was at the centre of local Baptist life along with its Baptist Academy, which as Roger Hayden has shown, was a significant factor in the drive towards evangelical expansion. [49]

At the heart of Broadmead Baptist Church's desire to revitalise the Western Baptist Association in the 1730s was a passion, both in spirit and in practice, for the preaching of the gospel. It was at the Broadmead church in about 1740 that a young stone mason named Robert Parsons from Widcombe, Bath, who was

---

[49] Hayden, 2006.

engaged in decorative carving for John Wood's new Bristol Exchange, came under the influence of the minister Bernard Foskett. Foskett's colleague Hugh Evans baptised Parsons in 1742 and later in 1751 Parsons was charged with the responsibility of pastoring the new Baptist church in Bath, which Parsons had co-founded with John Clark of Frome in the intervening years.

Baptists at Haycombe

Having surveyed the Western Baptist Association history, attention now turns back to the Baptists in Bath. For those recounting the history of the Bath Baptist community at the beginning of the nineteenth century it was important that it began with the Baptist family that met at Haycombe in the seventeenth century.[50] Philip Cater included Richard Gay of Haycombe in his account of the Bath Baptists published in 1834,[51] and in the previous year William Jay preached a funeral sermon for Mariana Head of Bradford-on-Avon in which he stated,

> She could trace back decided piety in her family through at least three generations. One of her ancestors was the friend of the celebrated John Bunyan. This was Mr. Richard Gay, who lived at Hay Combe, a small village near Bath, where he preached the Gospel before any Baptist Church was formed in that famous city.[52]

Rather than being a village, Haycombe was little more than a farm settlement on the border of Englishcombe and Twerton —within the parish of Englishcombe and the Manor of Twerton. Evidence suggests that the Gay family were arable farmers, with land bordering the Langdon estate at Newton St Loe.[53] The earliest verifiable account of the Baptist community at Haycombe was in 1802 appended to some of Richard Gay's sermon notes by his great granddaughter Jane Blatch:

> The above writing was Mr Richard Gays of Haycombe in Sommerset — my great Grandfather. He was imprisoned In Ilchester Castle the same time as Mr Bunyan was
>
> Mr Bunyan greatly respected him & dedicated a Book of his to Mr Gay —
>
> My Great Grandfather was a Baptist minister preach'd at Haycombe in a house of his own set apart for the publick

---

[50] Birch, 1997b; Birch, 1998. The dissertation *Richard Gay of Haycombe: an exploration of a story and its influence in local Baptist family and church history* goes to great lengths to authenticate the various sources and family traditions surrounding the story of Richard Gay of Haycombe from contemporary records, including ecclesiastical and legal documents.
[51] Cater, 1834, 59.
[52] Jay, 1833, 24.
[53] Birch, 1998, 379.

worship of God built on his own Estate he lived in ye troublesome times I think by what I can gather from History & family circumstances in or before ye time of Charles ye 2nd —

He & his hearers were much persecuted for Religion He paid ye fine for Himself & hearers as long as they would take any money they then refused to take money any longer said they would have his person accordingly & they had him to Ilchester Castle where they confined Him for three years. His wife a pious woman was left with several young children under her care but she also trusted in God & was preserved. After ye Expiration of three years he was set at liberty & returned to his family He lived to be one hundred years old & used to recount the great goodness of God to him during his imprisonment with tears of Gratitude running down his cheeks

one text I remember hearing my dear & fond mother mention was In Isaiah 43: 1 & 2 But now thus saith ye Lord that created thee, O Israel, Fear not for I have redeemed thee, I have called thee by thy name: thou art mine. 2 when thou passeth thro' ye Waters I will be with thee & when through the Rivers they shall not overflow thee when thou walkest through the fire thou shalt not be burned neither shall the flame kindle upon thee, For I am ye Lord &c.

When my good venerable ancestor wrote this sermon he little thought a descendent of his family shd write in ye same book so long after as ye year 1802　　　　　　　　　　Jane Blatch[54]

The last documented reference to Richard Gay of Haycombe is a lease of 1704 in which he and his son John exchanged land with the Langdon estate, and it is probable that Richard died soon after. John Gay died in 1729 leaving his widow Jane and family at Haycombe Farm, and it is to this family that the Steele sisters and other family members made regular visits.[55] The Steeles were related to the Gays by marriage. John Froud's 'Verses written at ye Bath. Decb 1704' found their way into William Steele's commonplace book, and their inclusion clearly inspired by a visit to the city:

> Till now th' inclement seasons cold we mourn'd,
> And beauty left us, as ye frost return'd,
> But now more kind ye lovely Charmers stay
> Like winter flow'rs, all blooming, fresh & gay,
> Add brightness to ye walks, & summer to ye day.
> Lustre & heat are darted from their eyes,

---

[54] Gay, nd, 1-3. AL.
[55] Reeves, 1997, 3-11.

And Love affords us, what ye Sun denies[56]

Anne Steele, the Baptist poet and hymn writer known by the pseudonym Theodosia, and her sister-in-law Mary, whom she refers to as 'Sister' or 'Mrs Steele' interchangeably in her diaries and letters, had been to Bath on numerous previous occasions. They travelled again from Broughton to Bath in the spring of 1751 for the sake of their health. Unlike previous occasions, although the Steele diaries and letters are full of detail about their stay in Bath, curiously there is no record this time of these Baptist visitors having any contact with family at Haycombe or with the emerging Baptist congregation in the city. The Baptist congregation at Haycombe had certainly ceased to exist much earlier and after Jane Gay's death at some time in the early 1750s, and with the marriage of her remaining daughters, there were no men to carry on the family name. Gay Thomas Attwater, who as young Tom spent so much of his childhood at Haycombe and had a great fondness for the house and farm, looked back and remembered

> the [large] pile of Building composed out of houses and where ye meeting was kept wch had a [large] Chimney & fire place where stood up a high settle where our family used to sit. It must be the good Minister Richard Gay that built the House for that was built in 1665 who was so cruelly persecuted.[57]

After all, who other than Tom would have remembered and recalled after several years the comedy of the certain clock which 'as my Granmama Mrs Jane Gay was drawing up ye clock it fell down on her head'? Within just a few short years all traces of the Gay family at Haycombe had vanished. The present house on the site known as Haycombe Farm has the date 1766 high up on an outside wall,[58] which most probably marks the date of rebuilding after a serious fire had destroyed the original house.[59]

Although the mid-eighteenth-century Baptist community in Bath was fairly small, it is possible that the Steeles would have looked for other Baptists with which to share fellowship now that there was no family at Haycombe – indeed just three years later in 1754 Anne herself welcomed a visit from Bath Baptists Robert and Mary Parsons to her own home.[60] Of course there were other things on the Steele's minds, in particular Mary's health which was a constant cause of

---

[56] *Steele Papers.* Commonplace Book of William Steele IV, STE 4/2. Here the poem ends abruptly, and there is space left in the book as if to continue.
[57] *Reeves Private Collection.* Late eighteenth century account of the Gay family of Bath, most likely from the pen of Gay Thomas Attwater rather than one of the daughters of 'either Anna Attwater or Jane Gibbs', referred to in Reeves, 1997, 8 & 211-213 as paper *a*.
[58] Manco, 1995, 7-8.
[59] *Reeves Private Collection.* Account of the Gay family of Bath contained in a Notebook of Wassell-Smith ancestry, referred to in Reeves, 1997, 8 & 211-213 as paper *b*.
[60] See p.61.

anxiety. In a letter dated 11 May 1751—a progress report to her mother—Anne wrote:

> My Sister drinks the Waters and thinks they agree with her & intends to begin Bathing next week. She has been out of order but is now pretty well. I have left off drinking the Water for I have a cold and hoarsness attended with a little cough...I have been very uneasy about Sisters Toe which has been bad ever since she has been here...Her foot is very much swell'd and very painful I doubt the walk yesterday hurt I don't know what to do I want her to have advice and yet when I remember Sister Molly's foot am afraid of the Bath Surgeons...[61]

On another occasion, possibly later in the same year, Mary returned to Bath without Anne. In a letter to her sister-in-law, Anne longed for Mary to return home to her family at Broughton and it is clear that Bath wasn't her favourite place:

> Dear Sister...Your garden is my scene of amusement but it has of late been a perfect solitude, My Brothers return enlivens it, but still you are absent, What a pitty 'tis you shou'd lose this delightful Season when everything round us is so pleasant— How much more agreeable would these Fields and Gardens be with my Brother and you here than the crouded walks at Bath — Here the flowers are drest as fine as Belles and Beaus, but without their noise and flutter, How formal is the studdy'd negligence of dress, How mean its brightest ornaments compar'd with the unaffected ease and sweetly varied colours of these little amiable visitors Here I can admire the charms of Nature and listen to the artless music of warbling Birds nor envy the politer pleasures of the gay world.—Sometimes I enjoy a calm evening on the Terrass walk and wish though in vain for numbers sweet as the lovely prospect and gentle as the vernal breeze to describe the beauties of the charming spring, but the reflection how soon these blooming pleasures will vanish spreads a melancholly gloom till the mind rises by a delightful transition to the Celestial Eden, the scenes of undecaying pleasure and immutable perfection—This thought I have pursu'd in a few lines which I send you as the produce of your garden...[62]

Anne Steele had already expressed her opinion of Bath in a poem composed at the time of an earlier visit to the city:

---

[61] *Steele Papers.* Letter from Anne Steele to Anne Cater Steele at Broughton, 11May 1751. STE 3/7.
[62] *Steele Papers.* Letter from Anne Steele to Mary Steele, c1751. STE 3/9.

'On the Walks at Bath May 1751'.
Ah how unlike the solitary Groves
Where the Muse haunts, and thought unfetter'd roves
Those kind Companions love the peaceful shade
And fly the laughing Croud and gay Parade
These Walks indeed an ample theme supply
Satiric theme if Pope or Young were by
The Censor Muse might here her power display
To scourge the follies of the Vain and Gay
But gentler themes the Sylvan Muse delight
And rural Scenes the artless Lay invite
Dear Native rural Scenes for you I sigh
Where Nature's charms alone enchant the eye
Where uncontroll'd sweet Meditation strays
And tunes the humble song to notes of praise.
But see a lovely verdant Walk beneath
There tall Shades rise and gentle Zephyrs breath
I bend my steps to this delightful Shade
And pensive here invoke the Muses' aid
Ah if the sweet inspiring Muse were here
How far the varied Landscape would appear
Raised on the distant Hill with proud disdain
Yon stately Dome* surveys the humble plain   * Mr Alleins House[63]
The humble plain in artless beauties drest
Where the pleas'd thought with calm delight can rest
Here Meads with lively Verdure cheer the eyes
There Trees irregularly beauteous rise
Soft as the cadence of an easy Song
The cool Stream rolls its gentle Waves along
On its green banks delighted while I stray
The smiling Scene invites the Sylvan Lay
But hark yon waterfall with solemn roar
Whose white wave foams and murmurs to the shore
Reflection deep and serious thought inspires
Almost some awful theme my fancy fires
But serious thoughts just rising fleet away
And Belles and Beaus forbid the coming Lay
For Vanity has found this soft Retreat
And here for idle chat the busie Triflers meet.[64]

---

[63] Anne's note points to the home of Ralph Allen at Prior Park which spectacularly overlooks Bath.
[64] *Steele Papers*. Hugh Steele-Smith's research notes on Anne Steele's unpublished hymns and poems. STE, 11/2.

In these reflections there is a conflicting sense of ease and disease with Bath, yet overall a longing to flee from the vanity of the city back to the rural idyll of home. Steele's poem here is full of classical illusion, with which she is comfortable, yet she is equally at home expressing the same sentiments in her spiritual hymns:

> Hence, vain, intruding world depart,
> No more allure or vex my heart;
> Let every vanity be gone,
> I would be peaceful and alone.[65]

The Baptist community represented by Anne Steele was uneasy with Bath in particular as a place of vanity and excess, but very much at home in the artistic and cultural expression that the city represented. Anne was concerned to look beyond the present, temporal, fleeting experiences of this life, which lead to immorality and death, towards higher eternal values. Eighteenth-century culture, its arts and literature, provided the language to express the eternal yet in Bath, as elsewhere, there were many competing diversions and pleasures seeking attention. Bath had its own peculiar pleasures: its hot water springs around which were attracted all the attendant human vices.

The Presbyterian Connection

Whilst the earliest Baptists around Bath gathered at Haycombe, a movement that would lead to the founding of the Baptist congregation within the city was taking place within the Presbyterian congregation. In relative safety at the end of the seventeenth century the Presbyterians began meeting within the city walls, first in a shear-shop in Frog Lane (Old Bond Street), then as the congregation grew at the beginning of the eighteenth century they moved into their own purpose built meeting house. However, Bath was even then becoming an ever more popular resort for visitors who came for the waters, and according to Jerom Murch the nature of the Presbyterian congregation began to change – causing local families to feel increasingly alienated. Murch, in his *History of the Presbyterian and General Baptist Churches*, makes much of the connection between the Presbyterian congregation and the early Baptists in the city. He points out that the eighteenth century witnessed a transformation in the nature of the Presbyterian church:

> a gradual change had been wrought in the character of the congregation, so that the majority became composed of the rich rather than the poor. This circumstance is to be regretted wherever it occurs…large additions were made every year to the educated and highly refined population of the city; the increased attendance of such persons at the Presbyterian chapel naturally

---

[65] Steele, 1967, 76. Hymn LXVIII, 'Retirement and Reflection.'

encouraged its minister to adopt a more intellectual style of preaching; such a style might perhaps have been skilfully accommodated to the understandings of the poor, but it was not; and that large and useful class were obliged to go where they could be both interested and improved.[66]

This congregation was eventually to move fully towards Unitarianism, and Murch later became its minister. Murch concedes that long before this shift there had been a history of secession as members of the Presbyterian congregation had gone elsewhere to worship and find a spiritual home:

> Several new religious societies were formed in Bath in the course of the last century. A secession from the Presbyterians seems to have taken place as early as 1726. In that year Mr. Henry Dolling, a Baptist, yet a Trustee of the meeting-house, united with a few other Baptists and licensed his house in Widcombe for public worship. But it was thirty years before the new church consisted of fifty members.[67]

There is no reference to the full reasons for this secession to form another community, although recent research has revealed that Henry Dolling had previously licensed his house in Widcombe for Dissenting worship in 1718.[68] This was just at the time when the Arian controversy that led to the Salters' Hall debate in 1719 was coming to a head, and bringing to the surface some of the underlying fault-lines within Old Dissent.[69] So it would seem that Henry Dolling, one of the Presbyterian trustees, licensed his home near the old church in Widcombe for religious meetings in 1718 and again in 1726.[70] In fact Jerom Murch's error can be easily explained as he seems to have relied totally on the work of Philip Cater, whose historical account had been published just a year earlier, and Cater had himself failed to find reference to the earlier license![71]

We cannot be certain whether the meetings at Dolling's house were truly Baptist, although the tradition according to Philip Cater and others is that Dolling was increasingly thinking along Baptist lines and meeting with others in the city who were like minded. The meetings were certainly for Dolling's Dissenter friends who found it more convenient to meet with him there, and their gathered community continued regularly for some years. Another unknown is whether there was any connection or even communication with the

---

[66] Murch, 1835, 141-142.
[67] Ibid, 142.
[68] SRO, Q/RRW 1. Lists of Diocesan Dissenters Certificates for Somerset reveal: '725. The house of Henry Dollings. Wittcombe. nr. Bath. Somerset. Easter Session 1718.'; '816. The house of Henry Dolling. Widcombe. Somerset. Ephiphany Session 10 January 1726.'
[69] Brown, 1986, 27.
[70] Recent research by Mrs Connie Smith for the present owners has revealed that Henry Dolling probably lived at what is now 11 and 12 Church Street, Widcombe.
[71] Cater, 1834, 62.

Baptist community meeting at Haycombe,[72] although a possible link lies in the connections between female Dissenter poets.[73] The Presbyterian minister at the time of Dolling's secession was Henry Chandler, whose daughter was the renowned Bath poet and shopkeeper, Mary Chandler.[74] Her most popular extended poem *The Description of Bath* was first printed in 1734 and went into several editions. The connections go further, for Mary Chandler was a good friend of the poet Elizabeth Rowe of Frome, whose father Walter Singer had been imprisoned in Ilchester as a staunch Dissenter at the same time as Richard Gay of Haycombe.[75]

Dolling's nephew, Robert Parsons, started to attend the meetings with his friends Richard Singer and William Hathaway, and others. It is this latter small group who were to form the nucleus of the first fully Baptist community in Bath. Richard Singers and William Hathaway were both builders whilst Parsons was a skilled carver-mason, and it was this skill with stone that brought him into closer contact with both learning and with further Baptist ideas. His was an important trade in Bath, expanding at the rate that it was in the eighteenth century. Competent craftsmen of all types were required in all sectors of the local industry which was making its mark across the country. As we shall see, Robert Parsons was active in the stone industry that was one of the important keys for the growth and development of the city at this time; just as with his friends he was active in growing and developing a Baptist community within Bath. For this reason it is as important to consider Parsons' career in working with stone as it is his life as a Baptist, a part of the story that has only recently been uncovered.

---

[72] Later correspondence hints at possible links. *Steele Papers*. Letter from Anne Steele at Broughton to her sister-in-law Mary Steele in Yeovil, 26 July 1754. STE 3/9. Anne Steele reports the visit of 'our Bath Friends Mr & Mrs Parsons' to Broughton.
[73] Reeves, 1997, 39.
[74] Murch, op. cit, 150-3.
[75] Reeves, op. cit, 19.

Chapter 3: Community and Minister

Robert Parsons of Widcombe

Robert Parsons was born in Widcombe near Bath in 1718, the son of Thomas Parsons. He entered into the family business as a mason-carver, but to whom he was apprenticed is uncertain. Stone that had been cut from Ralph Allen's quarries in the hills above Bath was taken down into Widcombe to the stone yards to be worked, before transportation by river or road. There is a reference to a young Parsons in the correspondence of Ralph Allen which may well refer to Robert or another member of the family. In 1734 Allen was under contract to supply stone from his quarries on Combe Down to John Sidney, Earl of Leicester, for a building project in London. There was a delay in shipping stone, and Allen was concerned that the mason he had sent to London to supervise should not be an additional expense to Sidney:

> I should be sorry that since Parsons & his partner have behav'd to your satisfaction that at this Juncture they shou'd either quit your work or create an unnecessary charge to you. Therefore I do beg that what Loss they may sustain on this head ('til the stone arrives, or that they have notice from hence that 'tis not in my power to send any) may entirely rest on me…[1]

At this time Robert Parsons would have been sixteen years old.

In just a few years Parsons was working on one of John Wood's prestigious local projects in Bristol. In 1740 Wood was instructed by the Corporation of that city to undertake the design and building of their new Exchange. This was completed and ready for opening by Wednesday 21 September, 1743. 'Mr. Robert Parsons, of Widcomb, near Bath, Free-Stone Mason' was 'one of the House Carvers of the Exchange'.[2] He was proud of this work, and over his door in Claverton Street was painted his advertisement, 'R. Parsons, Stone-Carver to the Exchange, Bristol'.[3]

While working on the Exchange, in January 1742, Robert Parsons married Mary Giles, daughter of John and Mary Giles of Caerleon in Wales, who is described by Joshua Thomas as the only Baptist living in Caerleon at the time.[4] They were to have several children, most of whom died in infancy. Their only surviving child was their son Thomas, born in April 1744.[5] It is from this Thomas that

---

[1] Boyce, 1967, 55.
[2] Wood, 1745, subscribers list.
[3] Cater, 1834, 76.
[4] Thomas, c.1795, unpaginated ms. 'Caerleon…About 1740, or before, Mis. Mary Giles lived in the Town and was the only Baptist in the Place, and it is like she was not long there. She was married to Mr. Robert Parsons, who for many years, was a worthy Baptist Minister at Bath.'
[5] Wilson, 1948.

much of the information about his father comes, although the whereabouts of the original source is unknown. In 1950 Thomas Parsons' *Commonplace Book* was 'offered for sale by Messrs Myers & Co Ltd' but the offer of £15 from Bath Library was 'not accepted'. However local librarian, Elsie Russ, did manage to extract some of the information and presented it in her valuable manuscript, *Biographical Reference Book for Bath Celebrities*.[6] Thomas himself had a son named Thomas, and Thomas junior's Bible contained the family information that Thomas senior had copied onto page 100 of his Commonplace Book:

> Copy of an entry in my son Thomas's Bible.
> Robert, the youngest son of Thomas and Hester Parsons was born in November 1718. In January 1742 he married Mary the daughter of John and Mary Giles of Caerleon. They settled in his native place the parish of Lyncomb and Widcomb and had several children, all of whom died in their infancy except their second son Thomas. The said Robert Parsons formed the Society of Baptists in the City of Bath and devoted to them his ministerial labours gratuitously near forty years. In the year 1765 died his first wife Mary aged 47 years, in the following year he married Sarah Stibbs of London, widow, who died in March 1778 aged 69 years. In the succeeding year he married Lucy Atkins of Bath, widow, who survived him. He died February 28, 1790 aged 71 years.[7]

Independently of the Library, in 1948, F W R Deverell of Manvers Street Baptist Church was writing to Ellie Wilson of Myrtle Bank, South Australia, in preparation for the address he was giving about the history of the church in which he wanted to include reference to her ancestor Robert Parsons. In her reply she stated, 'I can tell you only what is in the Family Bible', and provides the following information:

> Robert, the youngest son of Thomas & Hester Parsons, he was born Nov. 1718. In Jan. 1742 he married Mary daughter of John & Mary Giles of Caerleon. They settled in his native place the parish of Lyncomb & Widcomb & had several children all of whom died young except the second son Thomas [born April 1744]. The said Robert Parsons formed the Society of Baptists in the City of Bath, and devoted to them his ministerial labours gratuitously nearly 40 years — In the year 1765 died his first wife Mary, aged 47 years. In the following year he married Sarah Stibbs, widow, of London, who died in March 1778 aged 69 years. In the succeeding year he married Lucy Atkins, widow, of

---

[6] Russ, 1925-1959, Parsons.
[7] The Commonplace Book entry then continues with details of Thomas's marriage and family.

Bath who survived him. He died February 28 — 1790 — aged 71 years.

The fact that these two summary accounts are almost completely identical strongly suggests that this is the Bible from which Thomas Parsons copied information into his Commonplace Book, and which also survived at least until 1948 in the possession of descendants of his eldest son.[8]

Having previously introducing Anne Steele as an eighteenth-century poet and hymn-writer,[9] able to engage eloquently in both the artistic cultural world of her day and the Calvinistic Particular Baptist world which was clearly her preference, it is important to recognise that she was by no means unique amongst Particular Baptists.[10] So, in Robert Parsons' forty prolific years as a carver-mason we also see someone at ease with his cultural and artistic engagement with society at large, even involved in its improvement architecturally, yet who also withdrew from so much that eighteenth-century society stood for. The work of the carver-mason was a decorative trade, and in the eighteenth-century this meant images from classical mythology and symbolism as well as geometrical designs – and as we shall see below, Robert Parsons was prepared to accept such widespread commissions whilst also expressing the need to withdraw into a separate spiritual world.

The origin of the Bath Baptist community as a withdrawal from the Presbyterians demonstrated an increasing dissonance from an intellectualism in faith that tended towards Unitarianism. As Jerom Murch pointed out, this rationalist religion was associated with the educated and wealthy elite that were increasingly populating the city. The Baptist community was to become separated from Presbyterians on principles of doctrine, faith and morality, yet this was not accompanied by a total separation from all of society, and certainly not from the arts and sciences. Robert Parsons' biography as it unfolds demonstrates a full engagement in the business and artistic-cultural life of the city, whilst in the second generation Parsons' son Thomas was fully engaged with intellectuals including Unitarians in the early work of the Bath Philosophical Society and the Bath and West Society whilst maintaining religious separation.

Robert Parsons' commercial engagement can be seen, along with his speciality for carving stone vases and urns, in his numerous advertisements. An illustrated handbill or poster of 1745 declared:

---

[8] Efforts to trace the Commonplace Book and Family Bible in the UK, Australia, and the USA, have so far failed.
[9] Examples of her poetry, hymns and connection with Bath and Haycombe appear above, pp.47-50.
[10] For a further example, see the reference to Eleanor Coade on p.64, fn 15.

> URNS, VASSES, FLOWER-POTS, SUN-DIAL PEDISTALS, And all Other Sorts of Ornamental work Curiously wrought in Free-Stone. Variety of the above Executed with a Collection of Drawings by Robert Parsons, LATE CARVER AT THE EXCHANGE IN BRISTOL and to be Seen at his Yard Over the BRIDGE BATH. NB: Orders Directed as above will be Punctually Obey'd.[11]

Similarly the *Bath Journal* of 11 June 1753 carried the following advertisement:

> WHEREAS a Report has prevail'd, that R. PARSONS, MASON and CARVER, at the Bridge-Foot, BATH, has declined working in Marble; this will satisfy his Friends that such a Report is not true; that he continues to work Chimney Pieces, Monuments, &c. in various Sorts of Marble, as Italian, Irish and English: Together with his other Business of making Bath-Stone Ornaments, and fine Chimnies, in a beautiful Stone, he has for that Purpose, as usual; great Variety to be seen at his Yards, between the Bridge and Gibbs's Mill, leading to Claverton-Down. He executes Orders, by Letter, as punctual as Personal, both in Neatness of Work and Price.[12]

According to Philip Cater in 1834 the house that Parsons lived at in Claverton Street is the house that is occupied by Mr Lloyd and his stone yards were on the site occupied by the shops of Mr Cook.[13] The collection of drawings referred to in the 1745 advertisement is not known to have survived, although a sketch book from later in the eighteenth century, compiled by his son Thomas, includes original Robert Parsons designs as well as many others that he is known to have executed during his lifetime.[14] Many of the designs in the book come from well known artists and sculptors such as 'Gainsborough, Wedgwood and Bentley, Gibbs, Cipriani, William Kent, Chambers, G Romano, Mrs Coade, Ware, Wyatt, Adam, Thomas Baldwin and Lord Burlington.'[15]

---

[11] Parsons, 1745.
[12] *Bath Journal*, 11 June 1753.
[13] Cater, 1834, 75-76.
[14] Parsons, c.1770.
[15] Davis, 1991, 115-122. Some of the information in this section comes from John Davis in *Antique Garden Ornament* and correspondence and discussion with the author prior and subsequent to its publication. Although far from complete, it nonetheless acts as a necessary corrective to the inadequate entry for Robert Parsons in Gunnis, 1951, 292-293. In personal correspondence dated 11 February 1991 Davis concludes, 'From information in Parsons' book of designs—references to Lords etc, it now appears to have been executed between 1776 and 1784. Unfortunately several of the pages including designs by William Kent and Giulio Romano are missing!' Mrs Coade was also a Baptist engaged in the manufacture of high quality artificial stone, whose story is told in Kelly, 1990. See also the entry on Eleanor Coade in the *Dictionary of Evangelical Biography*.

Figure 10. The Parsons Vase at Stourhead

To say that Robert Parsons' career as carver-mason was prolific is in some ways an understatement. Country houses and estates around England contain evidence of his work which is only just being appreciated. For example, between 1745 and 1751 we know that Henry Hoare paid Robert Parsons £110 for vases at his splendid new gardens at Stourhead.[16] Henry Hoare was the influential banker, whose clients included many of Bath's elite – including Beau Nash, and another branch of whose family were influential artists in Bath.[17] John Davis concludes that

> in view of this it seems reasonable to assume that the Bath stone vase by the Temple of Flora at Stourhead was supplied by Parsons. Certainly the design features in Thomas's sketchbook in which it is described as 'Antique'. The source of this design comes from Bernard de Montfaucon's popular L'Antiquité Expliquée et Representée en Figures, published in 1719.'[18]

On the evidence of Thomas Parsons' sketches it would be reasonable to conclude that Robert Parsons also referred to the important classic source books for his designs:

> These include Vardy's "designs of Inigo Jones & Wm Kent", Montfaucon's "Antiquity Explained", Ware's "Inigo Jones", and Robert Adam's "Works".[19]

In 1747 Parsons executed some work for Lord Fitzwalter at Moulsham Hall, Essex,[20] the same year in which he apparently partnered John Ford of Bath in a monument to Winchcombe Packer at Bucklebury, Berkshire.[21] There was work in 1753 for Lord Burlington's house at Londesborough Hall, twelve vases and six plinths, for which he was paid on 29 June.[22] In 1759 and 1769 Parsons supplied vases to Lord Folkstone and according to Gunnis in 1951 'The two vases made in 1759 are still in the garden of Longford Castle…'.[23] The original account book

> records payment in January 1759 to 'Mr. Parsons for two vases from Bath packing cases &c. £6 18s 0d'. This probably refers to the vase… and its pair (whose design [is] in Thomas' sketchbook…), rather than another set of four Bath stone vases,

---

[16] Gunnis, 1951, 292.
[17] Hutchings, 2005, 62.
[18] Davis, 1991, 117. Source: Gunnis, 1951, 292. 'Information supplied by Leslie Harris.'
[19] Davis, *Correspondence*, 11 February 1991.
[20] Gunnis, 1951, 292.
[21] Ibid, 293.
[22] Lees-Milne, 1962, 143n.
[23] Gunnis, 1951, 292.

almost certainly also by Parsons, which adorn the same gardens.²⁴

Gunnis reported in 1951 that of the many vases known to be carved by Parsons,

> ... a dozen more, made for Castle Hill, Devon, are also in situ. These particular vases cost £2 15s. each, and in Lord Fortescue's archives is Parsons' original drawing for one of them.²⁵

Petworth was also a destination for Robert Parsons's vases, £58 paid in 1760 and £91 paid in 1762. 'Many of these remain in situ.'²⁶ Also for the Grotto at Oatlands Park Robert Parsons supplied 'fossils of different sorts' and 'rockified stone' in September 1762 for the sum of £6.²⁷ In 1766 Parsons made six vases for the front of Corsham Court;²⁸ and in the late 1760s or early 1770s provided a sundial pedestal for Bowood House, and another for Amesbury Abbey.²⁹ There were further vases in the 1770s for the Duke of Argyll for his estate at Combe Bank.³⁰ This is of course just a selection of the work undertaken by Robert Parsons for which evidence either remains or has been traced.

When Rupert Gunnis was compiling his *Dictionary of British Sculptors* he had sight of sources since lost. He noted that

> In Parsons' manuscript Commonplace Book (now in private possession) is an account of how he went in 1764 to see Ralph Allen on the day before the latter's death, in order to show him designs for tombstone and memorials. Parsons, therefore, is presumably responsible for the pyramid in Claverton churchyard under which Allen lies buried.³¹

This raises the question of whose Commonplace Book Gunnis refers to. He seems to imply that it belonged to Robert Parsons, but Gunnis was writing his book in the same year that Elsie Russ failed to secure Thomas Parsons' Commonplace Book for the Bath Library. Furthermore, the entry is curious for the plain design of the pyramid over Ralph Allen's tomb would not have required the skills that Parsons possessed. The known Parsons examples and

---

²⁴ Davis, 1991, 117. Source: Longford Castle Muniment Room.
²⁵ Gunnis, 1951, 292. Davis, *Correspondence*, 11 February 1991, adds that 'the documentation is now lost.'
²⁶ Davis, *Correspondence*, 11 February 1991.
²⁷ Correspondence from Hugh Torrens in *Geological Curator*, 1983, iii, no.7, 421. in response to erroneous endnote in *Geological Curator*, 1983, iii, no.6, 386. Source: Symes, M. 1981. "New Light on Oatlands Park in the Eighteenth Century", *Garden History*, vol 9, no 2, 136-156 (esp. 148).
²⁸ Gunnis, 1951, 292.
²⁹ Davis, *Correspondence*, 11 February 1991. Davis reports that the sundial pedestals at Bowood and Amesbury still survive.
³⁰ Davis, *Correspondence*, 11 February 1991. Also reported by Davis to still remain *in situ*.
³¹ Gunnis, 1951, 292.

designs are all far more complex, and more classical in form, and there is little or no ornament on the Allen monument. It seems likely therefore that Robert Parsons' designs were rejected. David McLaughlin rightly raises a doubt that he was actually responsible for the pyramid, for 'Richard Jones, Ralph Allen's Clerk of Works, claims to have designed the mausoleum himself.'[32]

The contacts between Robert Parsons and Ralph Allen are certainly interesting ones. Ralph Allen had laid out his gardens at Prior Park with ornamental lakes and grottoes, under the influence of Alexander Pope and others of his frequent artistic and literary company,[33] and it is difficult to imagine that Robert Parsons was not involved in the work in some way. John Davis discovered that

> Parsons seems to have supplied garden vases for Sir William Stanhope. This must refer to the Stanhope that acquired Alexander Pope's house and garden at Twickenham, and extended the gardens adding statues to the grotto and seemingly vases to the gardens. Incidentally Pope's vases as designed by William Kent were almost certainly made of Bath stone.[34]

Such was the significance and diversity of Parsons' sphere of influence as a stonemason. Yet alongside this influential career under serious patronage lies another more familiar to the Baptist community for whom Parsons was himself the patron pastor.

During the period 1741 to 1743 whilst working on the Exchange for the architect John Wood, Parsons was regularly in Bristol and he probably lodged there. Here his contact with Broadmead Baptist church became regular. It was here too that in January 1742 he had met and married Mary Giles, and was soon after baptised as a believer by Hugh Evans in the river Avon at Bedminster. Broadmead minutes record that

> On Lord's day, 27th June 1742, Robert Parsons was proposed to the church and approved. On the 6th of August, Robert Parsons was baptized by brother Evans at Bedminster, and on the 8th was received to full communion at the Lord's table.[35]

Robert and Mary were members of Broadmead, but lived in Bath, and they gathered around them a community of others of a similar mind. In 1744 John Clark, a member of the Baptist church in Frome, came to live in Bath. He and Parsons held similar views and formed 'a religious association which was held at their respective houses for nearly two years' as well as a close friendship.[36] They

---

[32] McLaughlin & Gray, 1989, 28.
[33] Clarke, 1987, 32-33, 37-39.
[34] Davis, *Correspondence*, 11 February 1991.
[35] Broadmead Baptist Church, *Minutes*; Cater, 1834, 76; Hall and Mowvley, 1991, 20. Hall and Mowvley erroneously state Parsons' baptism as 1724.
[36] Cater, 1834, 64.

described what happened in the following terms: 'Seeing the low state of religion in Bath we deem it expedient to commence a cause in the Baptist interest.'[37] Clark's *Memoir* in the *Evangelical Magazine* records:

> Soon after this (August 1742) Mr. Clark, finding a desire to unite himself with religious persons, became a member of the church at Frome, of which Mr. Thomas Hurne was then pastor. Providence, however, occasioned his removal to Bath, where he formed an intimate acquaintance with Mr. Robert Parsons; and there being, at that time, no society of their denomination in that city, a few friends used to meet at one of their dwelling-houses on the Lord's Day, spending their time together in reading, prayer and religious conversation. Thus the ministerial gifts of Mr. Clark began to be exercised with acceptance.[38]

Parsons and Clark led the Bath group of Baptists, and their meeting was now made more public. Because they were expanding they had to move into larger premises.

An important record of all this was made by Josiah Thompson, the Baptist minister from London who in the 1770s surveyed the state of English Nonconformist churches, and almost certainly visited Bath. Indeed during the period concerned he was co-pastor of the Pithay Baptist congregation, Bristol, alongside John Beddome and so would be writing from his own experience. He may even have visited Haycombe. He wrote:

> The Baptist Congregation at Bath was formed about 30 years ago. The latter End of the year 1744 a few of them met together in a private House on a Lords Day for the Purpose of religious Worship. In 1747 they took an upper Room in Kings mead Square which was opened by Mr Hugh Evans of Bristol & an Evening Lecture was supplied & kept up by ye Bristol Ministers of this Denomination, Here they continued for a year and half & then removed to a more convenient Room fitted up in Collets Back Yard Horse Street where they continued several Years, & were Supplied by a Variety of Ministers from Bristol, Bradford, & elsewhere.[39]

This is the earliest known eighteenth-century account, and although important has been totally ignored in previously written histories, probably because its existence in manuscript was largely unknown to later writers. Indeed the general

---

[37] Inscribed in the front cover of a copy of Cater, 1834, owned by Manvers Street Baptist Church, Bath. See F W R Deverell's account above, p.20. Investigations have failed to produce the original paper.
[38] *Evangelical Magazine*, November 1803, 462.
[39] Thompson, 1774, iv, 172.

accuracy of Thompson's account is confirmed by the Bath Quarter Sessions books which record licenses for both the places mentioned, although correcting the dates:

> January 13th 1746 The Dwelling house of Stephen Collins Mason Situate in Kingsmead Square in the Parish of Walcott within the Liberties and precincts of the said City is Lycensed and Allowed for an Assembly or Congregation of Protestant Dissenters called Baptists for Religious Worship as the Law directs.
>
> October 31st 1748 'An Outhouse belonging to Thomas Collett Distiller situate in Horse Street in the said City being put into proper Repair is Lycensed and allowed for an Assembly or Congregation called Anabaptists for religious Worship as Law directs.[40]

This later premise was situated off Marchant's Passage in Horse Street or Southgate Street, somewhere underneath the Southgate shopping area, where there was once a plaque on the wall marking its location.[41]

Figure 11. Possible site of Marchant's Passage Meeting House

---

[40] BRO, *Bath Quarter Sessions Books*.
[41] The plaque which was installed as part of their bi-centenary celebrations still exists in MSBC archive, along with an unidentified 1921 newpaper cutting, and reads: '1752-1952. The traces here preserved of this window are believed to mark the site of a meeting house where Baptists gathered to worship prior to establishing themselves in Somerset Street (now demolished) from whence they moved to Manvers Street.'

Figure 12. The plaque from Marchant's Passage

In 1750 John Clark left to become minister of the Baptist church at Crockerton, and Robert Parsons was left in sole charge of the Bath congregation. According to Philip Cater, these were difficult years of disillusionment and deliberate persecution, with meetings occasionally disturbed, and many people staying away. Baptists were encouraged when they were about to give up by a particularly poignant challenge from one of their members, Matthew Madden. It is recorded that he rose to his feet and proclaimed:

> For God's sake abandon not your object. You know not what good may yet be done. You behold the city devoted to amusement and every sinful pleasure. Relinquish this meeting and where then shall we find a people with whom we can consistently unite in the spiritual worship of God. Are you poor, and is the expense an object, then sooner than the meeting shall be abandoned on that account, I will bear it all myself. God hath so blessed the meeting to me, that I am prepared to make any sacrifice that circumstances may require, or necessity may demand.[42]

Soon afterwards Richard Singers and William Hathaway were baptised publicly in the river Avon near Gibbs's Mill in Widcombe.

The Community and its Pastor

Robert Parsons had been leading the Bath Baptist community for a year on his own, and a number of years with John Clark before that. Yet Bath Baptists were still members of the Baptist church at Broadmead, Bristol, meetings and services in Bath being mainly led by supply preachers from there, as well as

---

[42] Cater, 1834, 66.

informally by Robert Parsons and others locally. That was until 1751 when Parsons was finally called to preach by the Broadmead church:

> On Friday the 7th of June, 1751, being the first time of keeping our preparation on that day, beginning at two in the afternoon; having heard our brother Robt. Parsons exercise his gifts in preaching before, from "Eat O friends, drink, yea drink abundantly, O beloved;" and now from "Blessed are they that mourn," agreed to desire him to preach again.
>
> On Thursday the 10th of October the church agreed to call our brother Robt. Parsons to exercise his ministerial gifts where he may be desired.[43]

Now with fully recognised leadership the time was coming when the Bath church could be known as a Baptist church in its own right. It was only a year later that the Baptist church at Broadmead gathered and:

> On Monday 10th of August 1752, our brother Robert Parsons, and sisters Mary Parsons and Abigail Brewer, with six more were formed into a church to meet in Bath; in the presence and by the assistance of our Brethren Hugh Evans and Ebenezer Browne; Mr Richard Haynes, minister of Bradford, and Mr John Clark, minister of Crockerton.[44]

The new church was very small, with just nine members. However, the number of hearers, those worshipping either regularly, or when in the city, was substantially higher. Josiah Thompson wrote of 'Their numbers now beginning to increase both as to Members & Hearers & meeting with considerable Encouragement'. It was growth that led to a further move. So later in 1752 a piece of land was secured in Corn Street, behind Southgate Street, where Robert Parsons and Richard Singers built another meeting house.

It was while on a preaching tour to raise funds to build the meeting house that Robert Parsons had met Anne Steele. In the summer of 1754 Mary Steele was visiting her father, George Bullock, at his home in Yeovil and had written to invite her sister-in-law Anne to join them. In a letter dated 26 July Anne replied:

> My thanks are due to Mr. Bullock & your self for the invitation but I don't think I shall go so far from the house this Summer — Last week we had the pleasure of a visit from our Bath Friends Mr. & Mrs. Parsons, They are collecting assistance to build a Meeting house, He preach'd here and is thought likely to be a useful man My Brother was not at home but heard him at

---

[43] Ibid, 67.
[44] Broadmead Baptist Church, *Minutes*.

Portsmouth Their conversation was very agreeable, I wish'd their stay longer, it was but two nights...[45]

Robert and Mary Parsons were known to the Steeles, and warmly received as friends. What is significant is the warm approbation for Robert Parsons, pastor to the new order of Baptist life in Bath, from such a significant representative of the old order of the Baptist family that had been connected with Haycombe. And a 'useful' man Parsons was. He was a hard worker, working long hours, travelling many miles, and making many contacts in his business as a stone-carver. At the same time he worked indefatigably for the church, claiming no income from them, only expenses as they became necessary. What was needed was money for a new meeting house, and it was Parsons himself who travelled widely preaching appeal sermons for the cause.

Indeed it would seem that from time to time the church at Somerset Street was considerably indebted to Robert Parsons financially. For example, the account books such as they are refer in 1761 to 'The Standing Debt Due last year to Robt Parsons' of £24.18s.4d. On 1 January 1762 we read that 'The Debt now due to RP' is £13.6s.11¾d. During 1762 the church received £40 from Robert Parsons 'for a piece of Spare Ground at the Burying Yard', the location of which is unknown. Subsequent years saw similar sums due to Parsons.[46] We have suggested that Parsons travelled in the course of business, and the same was true in preaching the Gospel. There are thus also references in the account books to items such as 'Horse hire in supplying Melksham Church' £1.10s. in 1772 and 'Expenses in supplying Country Churches including Horse hire' £3.3s. in 1774. Parsons' itinerant ministry was clearly appreciated in the 1760s by the Baptist church at Westbury Leigh, according to the later reminiscences of Joshua Marshman writing from India in 1824:

> ...and Bath I assure you was ever endeared to our Christian friends at Westbury Leigh. Old Mr Parsons was every thing but adored there. He baptized (if I recall it rightly) my Father at Westbury Leigh in 1763, and the veneration my Father had for him I can scarcely describe. He and Mr Hains the Baptist Minister at Bradford in 1762 and two others, supplied the church at Westbury Leigh quarterly at that time...[47]

As a city dedicated to the comfort and convenience of its visitors more than its inhabitants it is not surprising that it is possible to track the progress of the Baptist meeting houses through the cheap tourist guide books and city plans. Readers of Cornelius Pope's New Bath Guide in 1761, would have read that as well as other Dissenting chapels 'There is likewise a Meeting for the Anabaptists

---

[45] *Steele Papers*. Letter from Anne Steele in Broughton to her sister-in-law Mary Steele at Yeovil, 26 July 1754. STE 3/9.
[46] SSBC, *Accounts*.
[47] Reeves Collection. R4/12.

in Horse-street, built by MR ROBERT PARSONS.' This meeting house in Horse Street, now Southgate Street, was enlarged in 1762. The number of church members was also growing steadily through the period: there were nine members in 1752, and by 1762 there were forty. Frustratingly the number of attendees at Sunday worship is unrecorded, although it can be determined that the total congregation was usually far higher than merely the number in membership. In the early days the number of members could be accommodated in a fairly large domestic house, whereas it appears they were frequently looking for a larger place to meet — suggesting not only room for expansion but that at any one time there were substantially more worshippers than the membership figures would suggest.

In 1765 tragedy hit the Parsons family and Mary Parsons died at the age of 47.[48] Although Mary had given birth to several children who had died in infancy, it is thanks to her surviving son Thomas that we have a brief description of his mother, which he penned in his Commonplace Book:

> My Mother was named Mary, a pretty florid little woman, in her person, more than commonly pious and devoted and very useful in assisting to form the infant Society which my Father was establishing in Bath. She was particularly zealous to suppress rising animosities and to reconcile differences before they became incurable. She was a true economist in her domestic concerns, active and smart in her little business, for she kept a shop, and remarkably open and undisguised in her address — She was very free in reprehension when occasion required and would sometimes be thought blunt. Somewhat quick in her temper and very plain in her dress. She was a very good Mother did everything for me that duty required, but kept me at a distance from her heart — She would often reply to an apprehension of my being spoiled, as I was an only child, that "Tom will never say that I have spoiled him."[49]

---

[48] Wilson, 1948.
[49] Russ, 1925-1959. Parsons. To the end of the brief memorial he wrote, 'In grateful remembrance of my Mother, her name devolved to my eldest daughter - my lovely Polly, as we ever called her. She was born January the eighth 1773 and lived to the age of six years four months and four days dying May 20, 1779.' Elsie Russ concluded by saying that 'The remainder was not of any great interest being an account of the last days of Mary Parsons. E.A.R.' The remainder would undoubtedly have been of great interest, and had Elsie Russ the use of a photocopier, instead of a typewriter as in 1950, we would have undoubtedly have known more. Wilson, 1948. Ellie Wilson wrote that the 'account of illness & death of first wife Mary' was also in the Family Bible. She continued, 'It's interspersed with various verses of hymns & scriptures - I read it to our family Dr. one day & he said undoubtedly it was appendicitis. It is very quaint, but I don't think your audience would be edified by it.' How wrong she was!

Figure 13. The 1759 Garrard Street Communion Cup

Within a year however Robert Parsons had found himself a new wife, and in 1766 married Sarah Stibbs, a widow from London.[50] Where or how he had met her we do not know, but they were together for twelve years. These were years of rapid growth and change in the life of the Baptist church in Bath. As we have already observed, members were by far outnumbered by hearers at Sunday services, especially during the season. Josiah Thompson's account of 1774 continues:

> ...they have been gradually increasing, so much as that their place of Worship being too small in the Year 1762 they enlarged it at near the Expense of 100l. having before this at a considerable Expense purchased & wall'd in a Piece of Ground to bury their Dead But still wanting Room & being so crouded particularly at ye Seasons for drinking the Waters, they at length came to a Resolution once for all, to have a Room sufficient to accomodate all that might attend with them. They began, finished & opened their present Meeting House in Garrott Street the latter end of the Year 1769 which will hold double the Number their last Place could contain & which is occasionally very well filled. There are 90 Members belonging to this Society at present. The Hearers are uncertain, that depending in a great Measure on ye Principles Taste & Inclination of those who resort hither for ye Benefit of the Waters which of late years has

---

[50] Wilson, 1948.

not been less than 9 Months out of 12 it being only the 2 or 3 hot Summer Months that empties Bath of its Inhabitants.

They actually opened their new self-built meeting house in Garrard Street on December 25th 1768. Richard Crutwell's *New Bath Guide* of 1771 directed visitors to 'the Baptist Meeting-house in Garrard-street'. Garrard Street was later re-named Somerset Street during the later half of the eighteenth century, so Somerset Street is the name by which the Baptist church became more familiarly known.[51] The church, now meeting in the home it would occupy for the next hundred years, found things difficult but organised itself as a Particular Baptist congregation along strictly disciplined community lines which it had some years earlier set out formally in the form of a covenant agreement.

Figure 14. The 1807 James Evill Communion Cup

The Community and its Covenant

From its formation members of the church agreed to accept a twelve part church covenant which laid down the boundaries of the church meeting together. The covenant was both experimental and experiential, in that it defined the theological position of the church and the nature of their

---

[51] Local tradition recalls that Garrard Street developed an unfortunate reputation for prostitution which led to the eventual change of name, although this cannot be authenticated. A pair of double handled silver communion cups (based on loving cups) from this period bear the words 'Baptist Meeting, Garrard Street, BATH. 1759.' The date on the cups predates the move to Garrard Street in 1768. 1759 is the date of the earliest surviving minute book, which is probably the first.

understanding of Christian community.⁵² Practically, there is also the sense in which the covenant helped to protect the new church emerging from a period of persecution, bolstering the sense of commitment of its members towards each other. The covenant began with a preamble containing classic Particular Baptist articles of faith, moderate but nonetheless Calvinistic in nature, defining the boundaries of the enclosed community. After the preamble there were twelve practical resolutions to safeguard the life of the community:

> We who desire to walk together in the fear of the Lord, under the gracious influence of the Holy Spirit, holding the Doctrines of the everlasting Love of God, manifested in Election, Redemption, and Salvation in and through his free Grace and by the Blessed Lord Jesus Christ, and by the effectual operation of his good Spirit, Regenerating, Converting, Sanctifying, and preserving of his people unto Eternal Glory, do hereby signify our desire, and determination to give up ourselves to God the Father, and his Dear Son Jesus Christ, to be our Lord and Lawgiver, and to the all wise unerring conduct of the Holy Spirit, and do in the Name and fear of the one Great and Holy God, unanimously agree to these following particulars.
>
> First. As we have given up ourselves to God, we do also to each other, and will to the utmost of our power walk together, as one Body; and as near as we can in one Mind, in meekness of spirit and Brotherly Love toward each other as becometh the disciples of Jesus Christ.
>
> Secondly. That we will jointly contend for the Faith, and purity of the Gospel, The truth of Jesus Christ, and the order, and ordinances, honour and privileges of his Church against all opposers.
>
> Thirdly. That we will with care, diligence, and conscience, Labour and Study to keep the unity of the Spirit in the bond of peace, in the Church in general, and with each other in particular.
>
> Fourthly. That we will carefully avoid all causes, and causers of divisions, as much as we are able, and shun all seducers and teachers of Error and Heresies.
>
> Fifthly. That we will sympathise and Labour to have a fellow feeling with each other, in every condition, and endeavour to

---

⁵² In her study of Baptist churches in Hampshire and the borders of Wiltshire, Karen Smith has helpfully provided examples of nine covenant documents. Each is different, highlighting its unique relationship with the church to which it relates. Smith, 1986, 289-305.

bear each others burdens, that we may be material helps to each other, and so answer one great end of our near Relation.

Sixthly. That we will exercise mutual forbearance, and bear with each others infirmities, in tenderness, meekness, and patience, not exposing them to the world, nor among ourselves, except it be according to the rule of the Gospel, endeavouring all we can for the Glory of God, and the credit of Religion, willing to cover the failings of each other, when they arise from the common Infirmities of our nature, and are not of a gross or profligate kind.

Seventhly. That if perilous times should come, we will as God may enable us, cleave fast to each other, to the utmost of our power, and we will endeavour to strengthen one another's hands, and encourage each other to persevere in the Lord, whatever may be the consequence.

Eighthly. We think it a duty incumbent upon us, to keep the secrets of the Church, not divulging them to any who are not of this community, though otherwise near and dear to us, for we believe that the Church ought to be "a Garden inclosed, a spring shut up, a fountain sealed."

Ninethly. That we will watch over each other for good, as to conversation, and conduct, so as not to suffer sin upon our Brethren, but use all kind and holy means to bring the offender to a sense of his Sin, and Repentance of it, with a reformation of life, and we will endeavour to provoke one another to love and good works.

Tenthly. That we will make conscience of praying for the peace and growth of the Church in general, the ministers of the Gospel, and especially for the prosperity of this Church. This we will do at all times, but especially in times of affliction.

Eleventhly. That we will never give up our duty and priviledge of singing the praises of God, to a set of Worldly men, nor resign that part of our worship to any man or men, who are not of this community.

Twelfthly. That we will always endeavour to the utmost of our power, to promote, encourage, maintain, and preserve a Holy, regular, and gifted minister, to take the charge of us, to go in and out before us, as the Shepherd before the Flock, together with all such Officers as are by Christ appointed, for the maintaining of Holy Order in the Church and regular discharge of all acts, and discipline, according to the appointment of Jesus Christ.

These and all other Gospel duties, we humbly submit unto, professing, and purposing to perform, not in our own strength, conscious of our weakness, but in the power and strength of our God, whose we are, and whom we desire to serve. All duties we desire to be found in the performance of, through the gracious assistance of the Holy Spirit, while we both admire and adore the grace, that has given us a name in his House better than that of Sons or Daughters. [53]

It is significant that this covenant was still in use by the church, and was signed by members of the church, as late as 1830, as the church identified with and used the covenant as the basis of its constitution. In addition to the biblical text and the doctrinal position according to the 1689 *Confession of Faith*, the church covenant forms both the formative and the normative narrative defining the community of Baptists in Bath meeting at Somerset Street. It defines how they understood themselves to be.

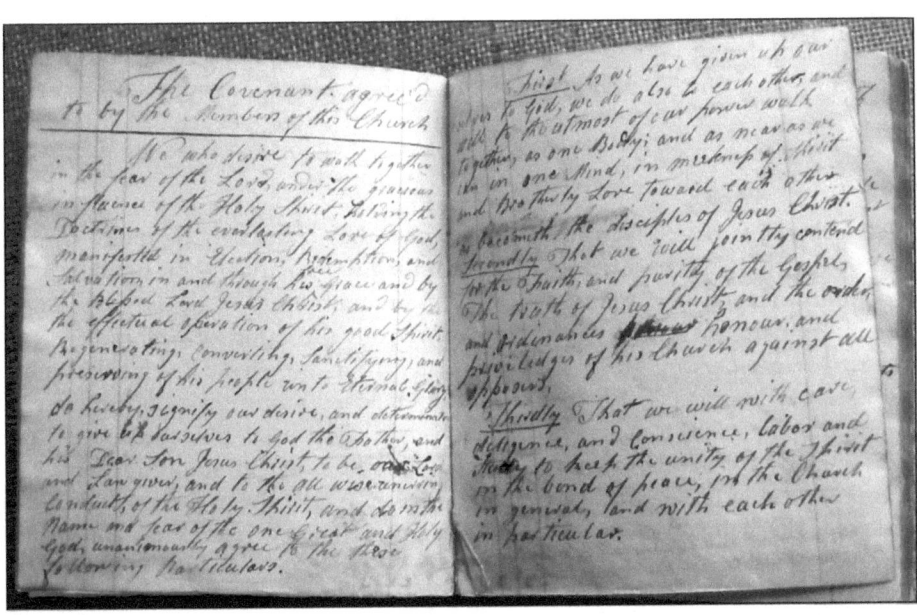

Figure 15. The Somerset Street Covenant

In the first resolution after the doctrinal statement the community highlighted their desire and willingness to be united in love as Christian disciples. This unity of body, mind and spirit, evidenced by total submission to God, formed the basis for the statements that follow. The nature of the unity of the community is

---

[53] SSBC, *Minutes*. There is no surviving early copy of the covenant, but a later copy described as 'the covenant which has been in the Church more than seventy years, from its first formation' was re-signed on 25July 1830.

worked out in practical steps. Resolution two concerns their unity as believers upholding the truth and purity of the Gospel of Jesus Christ against all opposition. This was significant in their early days when opposition was at its height, although in later days after the death of Beau Nash in 1761 opposition was less obvious. If maintaining unity against outside pressure was important, so in resolution three was the importance of maintaining good peaceful relationships within the community. Such pressure towards disunity from within or without makes the resolution especially significant for it deals with the need to avoid all causes or causers of division, whether that be in the realm of doctrine and belief or in moral and ethical behaviour. The resolutions had one purpose in mind, to protect the spiritual health of the community and its members. Yet the solidarity of the community is expressed in more practical ways too as the covenant progressed. Resolution five specifically addressed the issue of bearing each other's burdens, being as much practical help to each other as necessary. The strength of the community was based upon the strength of its members' relationship with each other and this, as resolution six reminded them, included bearing with each other's weaknesses and, unless grossly sinful, not exposing them to the outside world but keeping them within the confines of the community. In the early days of the Bath Baptist community persecution was apparently a frequent occurrence, and so as resolution seven sets out it was important that they 'cleave fast to each other', in other words, sticking together and encouraging each other to persevere in their faith.

The reality of their experience was that they understood their church community to be not just guarded and bounded in principle but in practice also. A common metaphor in referring to the church amongst Particular Baptists in the mid-eighteenth century was that taken from the Song of Solomon of an enclosed garden. Song of Solomon chapter four and verse twelve is where resolution eight finds its origin: 'A garden enclosed is my sister, my spouse; a spring shut up, a fountain sealed.'[54] Amongst Calvinistic Dissenters this had long since been a favourite image, and indeed the Song of Solomon had been commonly taken to be an allegory of the love of Christ towards his church, the bride and the beloved. This image was taken further by Isaac Watts in setting the Song of Solomon to verse as a hymn:

> We are a garden wall'd around,
> Chosen and made peculiar ground;
> A little spot enclosed by grace
> Out of the world's wide wilderness.[55]

Although allegorical this had come to be taken literally as the basis for a protective community, where boundaries were strictly maintained not just for the sake and safety of the community as a whole but for the protection of its

---

[54] Song of Solomon 4:12. King James Authorised Version.
[55] Watts, 1707, i, 74.

individual members. This meant that what went on within the church was to be kept within the church, and 'not divulging' any 'secrets' outside its walls. Further, as resolution nine testifies, it meant looking out for one another and being accountable to each other to protect each other from falling into sin – both in 'conversation and conduct'. The bounded community was intended to be both a pure and a holy community, set apart for the glory of God and to reflect the nature of the kingdom of God.

To this end the final three resolutions were important. Resolution ten committed the church to pray for three things: firstly the peace and growth of the church in general, then for the ministers of the Gospel, and finally that the church might prosper. It is acknowledged that this prayer is necessary at all times, but most particularly during times of trouble and conflict. Prayer was seen as important, just as the 'duty and privilege' of 'singing the praises of God' in resolution eleven. Having established the godly pattern of hymn singing within worship, through all the controversy that surrounded it in other places and at other times, the church was not about to give up the practice of appropriate singing under pressure from 'Worldly men' or those 'not of this community'. The final part of the covenant, resolution twelve, concerned the importance of appointing and supporting a godly minister to lead and guide the church and protect all that was important to it according to the principles of the Gospel. For the community of Bath Baptists this was also about preserving its identity as Particular Baptist.

There is little in the covenant to define the church's theological position accurately, other than moderately Calvinist – but that assessment is based on what the covenant omits rather than includes. There were in the eighteenth century a range of flavours of Calvinism, and a tendency in the first part of the century towards hyper-Calvinism.[56] Peter Toon has traced the stages in the theological journey from high (or strict) Calvinism to hyper-Calvinism. In practice the Bath Baptists were clearly Calvinist, adherents to the *1689 Confession*, and there is no reference in the covenant document to reprobation or similar doctrines which would suggest a very high or strict position. Furthermore the covenant talks of the 'free Grace' and 'Converting' nature of God. Indeed the terms of the covenant would seem to mitigate against the Antinomianism seen as often accompanying hyper-Calvinism.[57] Robert Parsons

---

[56] Toon, 1967, 91-103.
[57] According to Andrew Fuller, Antinomianism is '…that which is contrary to the law; because those who are denominated Antinomians profess to renounce the moral law as a rule of conduct, and maintain that as believers in Christ they are delivered from it.' Fuller, 'Antinomianism contrasted with the Religion taught and exemplified in the Holy Scriptures', *Works*, ii, 744. Fuller continues by outlining the dangers of Antinomianism: 'If there be no law, there be no transgression; and if no transgression, no need of forgiveness. Or if there be a law, yet if it be unjust or cruel, either with respect to its precepts or penalties, it is so far no sin to transgress it, and so far we stand in no need of mercy. Or if there be a just law, yet if on any consideration its authority over us be set aside, we are from that time incapable of sinning, and stand in no need of

came under the influence of Foskett and Evans in Bristol in his early ministry, and they were not high Calvinists, but tended towards an Evangelical Calvinism, as Roger Hayden has shown.[58] Parsons was certainly engaged in evangelistic preaching, but his reputation was for being strict in doctrine. It is not easy to label Parsons' position, to distinguish doctrine from personality.

An awareness of the dangers of hyper-Calvinism is possibly behind John Wesley's earlier criticism of 'serious Christians' in Bath being apparently unwilling to be as evident and proactive in preaching the Gospel as they might. Indeed, Wesley's Arminianism often brought him into disagreement with those of Calvinistic persuasion, both within the early Methodist movement and beyond. In 1737, a year before Wesley's first visit to Bath, West Country Baptists had, as we have seen above, met as an Association at the invitation of the Broadmead Baptist Church in Bristol under the doctrinal banner of the *1689 Baptist Confession of Faith*, which they had determined upon in 1733 and thus effectively disassociated the Arminian General Baptists who were largely becoming Unitarian.[59] This Arminian-Calvinist difference was one factor which eventually led to Wesley and Whitefield's divergent paths, and also the serious personal rift between Wesley and Selina, Countess of Huntingdon. The confrontation between Wesley and Caleb Evans, a leading Particular Baptist, pastor at Broadmead and Principal of the Baptist Academy in Bristol, is also well documented.[60]

One of the principles upon which the Evangelical Awakening of the eighteenth century depended was 'inviting the unconverted to trust Christ' – and this, Brown reminds us, was by 1737 becoming divisive amongst Particular Baptists as well as others. Further, the terms 'Arminian' and 'Antinomian' were respectively used detrimentally to dismiss, often inaccurately, those who took opposing views – either in freely offering the Gospel on the one hand or preserving the Gospel for a predetermined elect on the other.[61] It has been commonly held that before the Wesleyan revolution was underway, Baptist churches suffered badly. This has been the classic view, as stated by Underwood. He claimed that 'Instead of advancing' Baptists 'stagnated and even retreated.' He continues,

> A cold fog of indifference descended upon the nation which for a century had been preoccupied with religious questions. It now began to think of other things, such as commerce and science. Religion was displaced from the centre of interest. The eighteenth century was an age of reason...Lethargy had

---

mercy. The sum is, that whatever goes to disown or weaken the authority of the law, goes to overturn the gospel and all true religion.'
[58] Hayden, 2006, 62-70.
[59] Brown, 1986, 71; Hayden, 1991, 35; West, 1984, 158.
[60] West, 1984, 161.
[61] Brown, 1986, 73.

overcome them, as if their fight for existence had exhausted them.[62]

The main debilitating factor for Particular Baptists, according to Underwood, was the hyper-Calvinism espoused by many influential London preachers, such as Brine, Skepp and Gill:

> The notion that for multitudes of men no salvation was either intended or provided in Christ, devitalised evangelistic preaching and effort, depriving men of any feeling of responsibility for extending the Kingdom of God.[63]

Yet, as Underwood points out, 'The first Particular Baptists had never allowed their Calvinism to abate their evangelistic zeal.'[64] Roger Hayden, in his thesis, has challenged

> the commonly received view of eighteenth-century Particular Baptists as obscurantists, ill-educated hyper-Calvinists. From the very beginning Particular Baptists had been evangelical in their Calvinism. In the seventeenth century this was true of all Particular Baptists who shared the 1644 Confession of Faith and sought to promulgate it in various parts of the country.[65]

Of course John Gill could never seriously be charged with being obscurantist and ill-educated, being one of the most learned and widely published Baptists of any generation. But the charge of high, verging on hyper, Calvinism is more difficult to refute. There has been in recent years considerable effort to rehabilitate hyper-Calvinism from its charges.[66] Furthermore, Hayden seeks to argue that rather than a deadly hyper-Calvinism,

> Evangelical Calvinism was the decisive theological force in ministerial training, church life, and the wider life of the Particular Baptist Western Association. West-country Baptist ministers like Andrew Gifford, John Ash, John and Benjamin Beddome, Benjamin Francis, the younger Robert Hall, John Sutcliffe, Joshua Thomas and John Rippon are far more representative of Particular Baptists in the period than the three London Johns, Brine, Skepp and Gill.[67]

Nevertheless, Peter Morden more recently concludes that hyper-Calvinism was a powerful disincentive for mission,[68] and that it would take the influence of

---

[62] Underwood, 1947, 117.
[63] Ibid, 134.
[64] Ibid.
[65] Hayden, 1991, iv.
[66] For a survey of the recent debate see Morden, 2003, 10-17.
[67] Hayden, op.cit, iv-v.
[68] Morden, op. cit, 16.

Andrew Fuller to become effective towards the end of the century before things would substantially change.

Tracing the development of the Bath Baptist congregation during this period it is difficult to see where they fit into the theological debates and discussions. At various points the Bath church belongs to the local Association, whilst at other times operates outside of its fellowship. The Baptist church did gain a reputation for being strict in discipline under the authority of Robert Parsons, which would have stood in direct contrast to the moral and social behaviour of the growing city around them. Walter Wilson, church chronicler and commentator in the Congregational tradition, noted of the Bath Baptists of this period that 'This people have always been distinguished for their high Calvinistic notions.'[69] This as much reflects their strict sense of community as outlined in their church covenant as their theological position. Wilson's comment will stand further exploration in the light of his own conservative reactions to the evangelical energy of the beginning of the nineteenth century when he was writing alongside his own preference for an academically rigorous orthodoxy of a previous generation's Dissenting churches.[70] On this basis Wilson would have neither approved of the Bath Baptists under Robert Parsons, nor under his later successor John Paul Porter. On the one hand the church covenant, which gave the Bath Baptists their constitution, is weak in doctrinal content other than summarising a classic Particular Baptist doctrinal formula – yet it is one of very few records of what they themselves stated they believed and how they put those beliefs into practice. On the other hand, however, that kind of pragmatism is one of its greatest strengths, as it prepared the church for life and faith within the challenging context of eighteenth-century Bath.

Right through his ministry Robert Parsons is said to have maintained 'an honorable character for integrity, consistency, and disinterested benevolence.'[71] Philip Cater observed that days of prayer and fasting were kept regularly before the quarterly administration of the Lord's Supper, and continued:

> If any of his members had only once participated with paedobaptists in the Lord's Supper, they were on that account cut off from Christian fellowship. It was also a regulation of the church in his time that no person who had been sprinkled in their infancy should be interred in the Baptist cemetery without paying an additional fine![72]

Cater's assessment of Robert Parsons was that he was 'a Baptist of the old school; very strict in point of discipline, and very rigid in the maintenance of

---

[69] Wilson, nd, i, 98-101.
[70] Dale, 1906, 602-3; Gilbert, 1976, 40, 52, 58 & 156; Sellers, 1977, 3 & 57; Ward, 1972, 71-2.
[71] Cater, 1834, 75.
[72] Ibid, 77.

certain peculiarities generally attendant on a limited and defective education.'[73] Cater ungraciously concludes that Parsons' strictness was due to a degree of ignorance; and yet as we have seen in his business and cultural engagement, Parsons was far from uneducated. Indeed Cater, who wanted to maintain objectivity when commenting on John Paul Porter's ministry, clearly breaks his own rules when commenting on Parsons' ministry in the previous century. Cater admits this weakness, but barely redeems himself as he asserts the superiority of nineteenth-century knowledge:

> In many respects it was disadvantageous to have lived a hundred years ago, since the progress of time has conducted us into more enlarged and liberal views, and made us better acquainted with almost every subject that is profitable or interesting to man. An individual ought not therefore to be viewed apart from the age in which he lives, as there must always be taken into the account the mighty influence of existing circumstances in the formation of human character.[74]

Cater is correct in saying that you cannot project the understanding of a later period onto an earlier one, yet this is exactly what he did. Furthermore, the main factor guarding and protecting the life and character of the mid eighteenth-century Baptist community in Bath was not so much the character and personality of its pastor, significant though that was, but rather the covenant relationship established by the covenant document to which members assented and by which they sought to live. Indeed the boundaries set up by the covenant were strictly maintained.

The working of the community and its strict discipline can be seen throughout the pages of the church meeting minute books which date back to 1759, as deacons and messengers were sent out to counsel and admonish unruly members. A structured Christian discipline was adopted; moral and spiritual belief and behaviour were kept in close check, and 'dealt with' accordingly. On 1 January 1759, for example, the minute book opens by recording the number of members and their status: 'Thus the number is 24, of which 2 are under dealings Viz Wm Hathaway & Reba Cabble & one in Bedlam Jane Hurne and all the Rest in full Comunion'.[75] The story is continued in January 1760:

> Thus our Number is 29 having lost one by death Mary Hiller & Received 5 Women by Confession of Faith & Experience & Baptism and one Man upon his Experience having been Baptised 40 years ago. 2 are still under dealings Wm Hathaway &

---

[73] Ibid.
[74] Ibid.
[75] 'under dealings' means that the normal disciplinary process for whatever misdemeanour was being dealt with – anything from being visited by the Deacons to the expectation of improved or reformed behaviour.

Reba Cabble & we fear we must also soon Deal with John Maguire who inclines of late to the Quakers. Jane Hurn is still a Lunatick.[76]

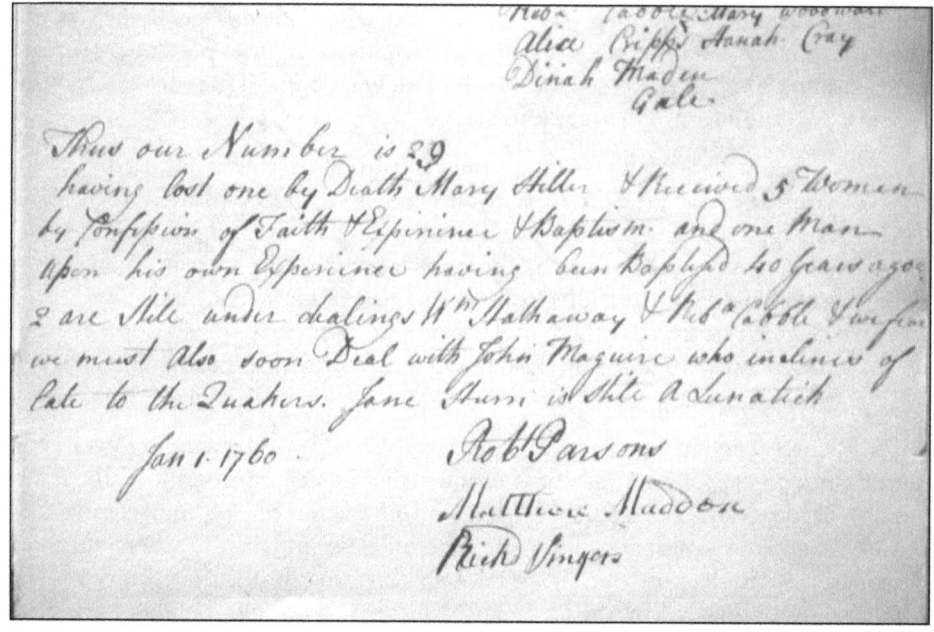

Figure 16. An Account of Bath Baptist Strength, 1760

William Hathaway was finally 'Cut off' from membership in 1772:[77]

> Jan 17 1772 at A Church Meeting held this Day and after Several Hours Solumn Prayer, it was Unanimously Agreed to Cut off and dismember William Hathaway & Benjamin Thresher from this Society for Negligence in Attending the Meetings & Other misdemeanours, after several years Dealings in Vain to recover & restore to their duty...

Matters like this were not taken lightly. It is apparent that the discipline of the church not only protected the standards of the gospel as they understood it but also reflected a response to the standards of the wider community around them in the growing city, and there was no doubt in their minds that they were right to act in this way. This was later expressed in these terms: 'although it is our

---

[76] SSBC, *Minutes*, January 1760.
[77] 'cut off' means being dismissed or removed from church membership, or otherwise 'dismembered'.

grief thus to act yet it is the Word of God must be our guide. 2 Thes. 3 & 6.[78] Above all, however, the church covenant encouraged a life of devotion and commitment to each other in brotherly love, when times were good as well as in adversity. It would seem that the church was moderate yet orthodox in its Calvinism, but strict in its observance and strict in its discipline.

Propagation and Growth

In addition to the cases of church discipline the minute books record the day to day activities of the growing community. For example, on 9 January 1764 was recorded an early declaration of the rights of church members to use the pews in the chapel for which they have paid a subscription or pew rent:

> It is agreed by Us the Pastor, Deacons & principle members of the Baptist Church in this City that any Person who hath or may pay an Acknowledgement for a Seat or Pew in this Meeting shall have the Libberty with his or her Family to fill & sitt in it from Time to Time during his Life, nor shall any Purchasser of a Seat have Libberty to sell it to any Other Person during his Life nor give it by Will Or otherwise at his or her death…[79]

Yet alongside the continual attention to guarding and protecting the community, there is also evidence in the minute books throughout the 1760s and 1770s of the church setting apart those men it believed were called to preach the gospel among them:

> May 18 1766
> This Day being the Lords Day After Several Months Tryal & Solumn Seeking Unto God in Publick & Private we Judge & accordingly have cald our Brother Sanny Parrott to the Work of the Ministry…

> May 9, 1771
> This being a Day of Solumn Prayer and after Seeking to God & Hearing of our Brother Richard Singer Exercise in Giving a Word of Exhortation for many Months we whose Names are Under Do Approve of him to Speak Occasionally Here or Else Where in the Ministry as God May Call Him and Employ Him…

---

[78] SSBC, *Minutes*, 25 September 1791. 2 Thessalonians 3:6 reads 'Now we command you, brethren, in the name of our Lord Jesus Christ, that ye withdraw yourselves from every brother that walketh disorderly, and not after the tradition which he received of us.' Authorised Version.
[79] On the one hand it might be argued that the charging of pew rents demonstrates a strictly disciplined church community lacking an eagerness to freely offer the gospel to all comers. However, there is no indication that all the pews were chargeable, or indeed what proportion would be free.

> May 9, 1771
> We the Church of Christ met this Day in Solumn Prayer do Unanimously agree that our Brother Thomas Parsons who hath for Several Months been Tryd in Speaking a Word of Exhortation to Us that he has Gifts for Usefulness & do Aprove & Call him to that Great Work where the Great Shepherd shall employ him...
>
> 5 May 1774
> At a Meeting of solumn prayer held by the members of this Church, it appears to be the sense of this Church that Brother Freeman, having occasionally spoken by way of exhortation for a considerable time is a proper Person, and is blest with Gifts to be employed in public, and the Members of the Church present unite in giving him a call to the work of preaching the Gospel when and where God shall direct him...

Deryck Lovegrove has demonstrated the significance of 'itinerant preachers' to the transformation of the Dissenting churches in England in terms of a 'growing enthusiasm' for such preaching from the 1780s onwards.[80] The impression given by Lovegrove's research is that across the country there was a rise in the number of largely uneducated itinerant preachers at the end of the eighteenth century, such that by the beginning of the nineteenth century they were having a significant impact in both a positive and negative way. Positively the number of congregations was increasing, whilst negatively there was criticism of the educational calibre of the preachers. Lovegrove cites William Wilberforce's disapproval of what was reportedly happening at Salisbury and Bath 'of a number of raw, ignorant lads going out on preaching parties every Sunday.'[81] Although it would seem this was atypical,[82] the question of education

---

[80] Lovegrove, 1988, 41-46.

[81] Ibid, 41 - citing R I & S Wilberforce, 1838. *The Life of William Wilberforce.* ii, 361.

[82] Ibid, 66 & 202. Lovegrove adds: 'With the ephemeral character of itinerant preaching and the passage of almost two centuries, it is difficult to know if the situation at Salisbury and Bath which attracted the condemnation of Wilberforce represented any more than local imprudence. The impression gained from church and association minutes is that the use of "raw, ignorant lads" by Calvinistic Dissenters was certainly exceptional. Since the matter was brought to the attention of Wilberforce by William Jay, the conviction that this was untypical is merely strengthened, for Jay, as a product of Cornelius Winter's academy at Marlborough, approved of a theological training whose academic ingredient was firmly related to practical evangelism.' Further in his endnotes Lovegrove adds: 'It is possible that a connection existed between the preaching parties mentioned by Wilberforce and the evangelistic activities of the Bath Sunday School Union.' For this last point Lovegrove cites Ward, 1978, 15-16. The link is indeed made by Ward who writes that 'Sunday schools were soon linked closely with itinerant evangelism, and the inter-denominational Bath Sunday School Union was itself itinerant, despatching corps of teachers into surrounding villages to revive flagging Sunday schools or organise new ones, and, having trained new teachers, to move on and repeat the performance.' However the presence of 'raw, ignorant lads' in the process is immediately negated, as is the connection with William Jay's remarks. Firstly, the Bath

and training for ministry was nonetheless a huge issue at this time of church transformation and expansion. The Bristol Education Society, which was formed in 1770 to provide a more stable foundation for the Baptist Academy at Bristol, sought to address the education of ministers and improve the standard of preaching. The examples that the minute books of the Bath Baptist community provide, however, suggest that the practice of appointing locally approved preachers was an established part of the Bath church's experience in the two decades before those cited by Lovegrove as significant, and there is no evidence of any education or training for the task. The minute books may be silent as to the education of the preachers, but a threefold process of discernment can be seen in the above examples: firstly that the preacher was called by God, then that call thoroughly tested by experience, and then finally approved by the members of the church. The question of qualification for ministry would by the mid-1770s become an issue in the Western Baptist Association that Robert Parsons would address in print.

In the second half of the eighteenth century Bath Baptists were thriving, just at the time other Calvinistic Dissenting congregations were becoming established in the city. Regular Bath visitor and occasional resident, Selina Countess of Huntingdon, who admitted that Robert Parsons preached the Gospel, but as he was a Baptist she was at variance with him,[83] built her meeting-house in the Vineyards on the fashionable slopes above the city in 1765 and attracted a different kind of congregation. The Independent secession from the Vineyards, later William Jay's Argyle Chapel, was established with the support of George Welsh, a London banker, who is reported to have said:

> When I come to Bath, I find that I have no home: I go to the Vineyards, and there I find a flock; but it has no fence: I go to hear Mr Parsons in Garrard Street, and there I find a flock surrounded with water, through which, I, at my time of life cannot pass.[84]

It can be seen, therefore, that the Baptist community was distinctive and well known to visitors and residents alike. It was strongly fenced with a doctrinal and disciplined rigour.

Sunday School Union was not founded until 1813 and then on a strictly educational mandate; and secondly, William Jay's congregation at Argyle Chapel were enthusiastically engaged in the enterprise. See *Bath Sunday School Union: A Glance Back Over One Hundred Years* reprinted from the *Bath Chronicle* 29 March 1913; and *The Sunday School Centenary in Bath* containing a full programme of the events and reprinted from *The Bath Herald*.
[83] Cater, 1834, 70.
[84] Cater, 1834, 74.

Figure 17. Former Somerset Street Chapel, 1912

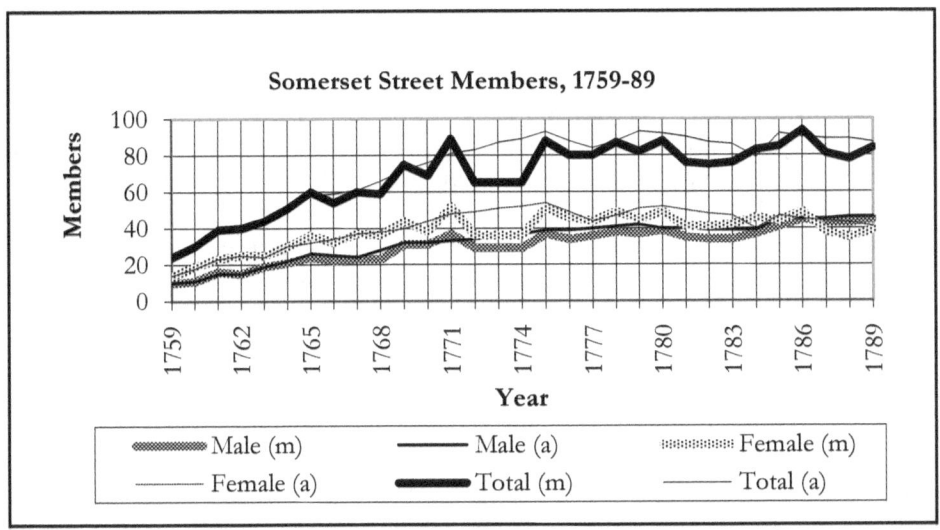

Figure 18. Somerset Street Members, 1759-89.

The minute books and membership rolls for the Somerset Street Baptist community between 1759 and the conclusion of Robert Parsons' pastorate in 1789 also allow the trends and growth in membership of the community to be traced with some accuracy. Although some of the Somerset Street records are missing, a further set of annual figures were kept by the Western Baptist Association – even during those years in the 1770s when Somerset Street was not in direct membership. **Figure 18** plots the growth in membership from the twenty-four in 1759 mentioned above to a peak of around ninety-four in the mid-1780s, although it must be remembered that membership only tells part of the story, for there were often many more in worship on a Sunday than were actually members of the church.

Further analysis of the records, including the association records, allows male and female members to be plotted independently. It can be seen that for most of the period there were about twenty-five per cent more female members than male members, although this trend begins to even out towards the end of the 1780s. Making a comparison between the church's own minuted records (m) and the association's records (a) helps to confirm the reliability of the surviving figures, and helps to verify the overall accuracy of the Association's statistical record. Where the church's figures are a little at variance with the Association's there are two factors at work: firstly Somerset Street's records are incomplete and some extrapolation has been necessary; secondly there is no indication as to the source of the Association record, for example whether the source was always the church itself.

The First Burial Ground

The story of the Baptist congregation at Bath is undoubtedly one of growth and success, however little this fact has been celebrated. This growth can be plotted in many ways, in the need to move to larger meeting accommodation and by measuring and comparing the membership figures. Yet growth in the Baptist community also meant practical considerations other than just meeting accommodation and annual statistics. There was the important consideration of a burial ground for the increasing number of dead, which as we have seen above was deemed significant enough to be mentioned in Josiah Thompson's brief account in the 1770s.[85]

The land had been purchased some time before 1762, but it was not until March 1764 that 'all that triangular plot, piece or parcel of ground, lying and being in the Parish of Walcot in the County of Somerset, next the turnpike gate there, and which was enclosed with a wall,' was entrusted into the hands of fifteen trustees. As the trust deeds for the Somerset Street property appear no longer to exist, the trustees of the burial ground are one of the few pictures we have of who were the responsible and influential members of the Bath Baptist community. The fifteen were Lazarus Brown, John Stock, Thomas Ludlow, William Ludlow, John Harris, Simon Nash, Peter Holland, Robert Cottel, Isaac Stephens, Joseph Mason, James Giles, John Evill, William Evill, John Latty and John Williams. These trustees represented local Association interests as well as the interests of the Bath church. Thomas Ludlow, William Ludlow and Peter Holland were deacons at the Pithay Baptist Church in Bristol, and Isaac Stephens was also a member there.[86] John Stock, John Harris, and possibly others, were members at Broadmead, Bristol.[87] The last five named were members of the Somerset Street church: James Giles, John Evill, William Evill and John Latty were all baptised by Robert Parsons in 1760, and John Williams joined them a year later. The trust deeds and indentures relating to the burial ground were reported as being destroyed by a flood, however details of their contents were given as evidence in a case brought before the Lord Chancellor in 1829. This case will itself be considered later in this study. The trustees held the ground in Walcot 'used and employed as and for a burial ground' for 'the congregation of protestants dissenting from the church of England, under the denomination of particular baptists, holding the doctrines of personal election, imputation of original sin, effectual calling, free justification, and final perseverance of the saints' worshipping at Somerset Street.[88]

The ground was small and an awkward triangular shape. It had been larger, but a church meeting in July 1762 had decided 'to sell a piece of Ground next the

---

[85] Birch, 1997a, 20-32.
[86] Merritt, nd, 68-70.
[87] Hall and Mowvley, 1991, 27.
[88] *The Case of the Baptist Church meeting in Somerset Street, Bath*, 1829, 1-5.

burying Ground for to Build two Houses upon to the best advantage'. This would in the long term appear to be a mistake as the ground was quickly filled. The details of what happened to the land and its management however tell a fascinating story of an area of church life and an important part of the story that is rarely heard. Firstly, as Dissenters the church wanted their own burial ground, although there is no record of Bath Baptists being denied burial elsewhere; secondly, this suggests that the concept of a bounded community and mutual responsibility extended beyond death; and thirdly, although burial grounds usually represent a memorial to a church's presence in the community, that part of the story has been lost since the clearing and redevelopment of the Walcot ground.

£40 was received from Robert Parsons for the land, which helped offset the £71.8s.8d. bill for the walling, gate, and finishing of the ground. There is no contemporary description of the ground, but some of its features can be gauged from the minute and account books. In 1768 13s. was paid for 'a Pump for the Burying ground'; in 1777 Thomas Bolwell was paid £2.9s.11d. 'for work at the Burying Ground'; and in 1781 'a Bar & Webing for ye Burying Ground' were secured for 6s.7½d. The pump needed repairing in 1795, costing 19s.6d. In 1793 £4.4s. was spent 'for Raysing the Wall', and 1s. 'for Letters in the Wall': the total £4.5s. being paid 'By Cash collected for the Burying Ground'. The letters referred to were to mark the position of individual graves according to their rows, the reference letter being recorded in the register purchased in 1785 for 13s. Typically locations were recorded as 'In the letter D 5 feet 6 inches from the lower Wall to the middle of the Grave', 'A new Grave in the Letter A 25 feet 4 inches from the lower Wall', or 'Grave seven feet deep 16 feet from the lower Wall in the Letter A Foot of the Coffin close to first line'. The ground was in the charge of Robert Harper until 1793 when Thomas Durnell, who had previously received a £4.4s salary for looking after the Somerset Street meeting house, took over. There is evidence that quick lime, used to aid speedy decomposition of remains, was perhaps produced on site. Accounts in 1795 record £2.9s.6d. 'pd Thos Durnell for Limestone & Labor', and £1.8s.9d. 'pd Thos Durnel for Limestone at ye Burial Ground'.

The written record mostly concerns the conditions which governed who could be buried in the ground. Members of the church and their children could be buried there without payment. Yet there were charges. At first these reflected the Bath Baptist community's theological views, more than the costs involved. As we have already seen above, discipline in the church was strict, infant baptism specifically attacked, and in the early days any member associating with paedobaptists could be cut off from fellowship. The church meeting in January 1785 agreed

> that all Children not Sprinkled may be Buried in our Burial Ground free of Fine – Such who are Sprinkled and under Ten

years of age to pay Five Shillings and for grown Persons who have been Sprinkled a Fine of Ten Shillings shall be paid.[89]

The only acceptable baptism was the total immersion of persons professing faith in Christ Jesus, according to New Testament teaching, which at Bath was usually in the River Avon or at Gibbs's Mill in Widcombe until a baptistery was installed in the chapel. A year later more detailed conditions were laid down. The February 1786 church meeting agreed

> 1st. That no Stranger shall be interred in the Burial Ground belonging to this Society, without the consent of the Minister and Deacons of this Society nor without paying a fine of twenty Shillings if above 12 years of age and ten Shillings if under that age. NB. By Strangers we mean Persons that are not Members of this Church and who have a claim to burial elsewhere.
>
> 2. Nor shall any Stranger be permitted to erect any Monument, Tomb, Gravestone or Headstone &c other than a flat stone or slab close to the Wall or inserted in the Wall.

Burial 'fines' were revised in 1791. The July church meeting set the charge as 8s. plus 2s.6d. for digging the grave of children under twelve years, and 16s. plus 5s. for digging the grave of adult persons over that age. It was further determined that

> the money to be paid before the corpse is interd & no persons to be excused the above fines except it be for members of this Church or their Children. We find ourselves necessitated to adopt this measure because our burying Ground is small & it is impractible to enlarge it.

Clearly the fines were not aimed at raising funds, for despite the number recorded burials usually only accounted for between 10s. and £3. annually, although a good year such as 1794 raised as much as £5.12s.8d. Later decisions were more practical; there was very little space.[90]

The transition from the 1780s to the 1790s saw the transition of the ministry from Robert Parsons to John Paul Porter. By 1795 ten of the original trustees of the burial ground had died, and so according to the terms of the deeds the church was consulted about replacements. The church meeting in October resolved to put 16 names forward in addition to the existing five, which were to

---

[89] SSBC, *Minutes*, January 1785. Subsequent Church Meeting decisions regarding the burial ground were also recorded in the minute book, along with accounts of expenditure.

[90] Minutes continually stress the lack of space as the reason for the baptismal qualification and the high cost of burial for those not members of the church, but the effect was to make burial a privilege of membership – unless you were wealthy enough to pay. There is no sense, either, that they were acting in a way contrary to the Gospel. If someone needed burial and could not pay, there would have been some way of either finding the money or waiving the fines.

comprise '2 from Broadmead Church Bristol, 1 from Pithay Bristol, 2 from Devizes and 11 from this congregation.' The resolution was signed by the minister and deacons on behalf of seventy-two church members, 'male & female'. John Smith—brewer, Opie Smith—brewer, James Evill—silversmith, William Evill, James Thomas—baker, Jasper Gay, Moses Gay, Edmund Davis—shoemaker, John Millard—carpenter, William Taylor and Henry Voisey represented Somerset Street's interests; Arthur Tozer, John Nash, William Stockham, John Sloper and William Brackstone were from the Bristol and Devizes churches; and John Harris, William Ludlow, Robert Cottel, John Williams and James Giles were original surviving trustees. John Williams and James Giles were still members at Somerset Street chapel. There is no record of whether James Giles was later buried in the Walcot burial ground; but John Williams, the Walcot Street silversmith and deacon of the Baptist church, buried his wife Ann in the ground in the following year, aged 64 years, and joined her in 1801 aged 71 years.

Throughout this period the church was looking for a second burial ground, but with little success. In the spring of 1798 they thought that they had found a suitable site, but in June the church meeting recorded their decision 'to let the intended Purchase of the burying ground rest where it now is having bid £120 for it & has been refused.' The following February Thomas Durnell relinquished his responsibilities for the ground, and the job was given to John Millard, the carpenter of Bradly's Buildings in the parish of St James, who had joined the church in 1784. On his death in 1809 Thomas Durnell was also buried in the Walcot ground, aged 76 years.

From the 1760s there is no record of who were buried in the Walcot burial ground. However the register purchased in 1785 to record births and burials still exists, and records 480 burials up to 1837, when the book was surrendered to the Registrar General.[91] Of this total 134 burials are known to be male and 182 female. 120 of the remaining 164 burials were infants, with no name and no age, illustrating the high mortality rate among the very young during this period. The occupation and address information recorded against many of the entries is sparse, but demonstrates the mainly artisan composition of the Baptist congregation, and shows residences mostly in the more modest poorer parts of the city. For most people very little information was recorded, except the brief mention of a name, age and date of burial. Only occasionally were members of the church given fuller entries.

For example, Charles Willis of the parish of St James, Deputy Surveyor of the city, was buried on 22 November 1785, aged 30 years. On the 26 of the following month John Timbrell, a baker of the parish of Lyncombe and Widcombe was buried 'with 2 Grand Children in his arms, Same Coffin & Grave' aged 68. And on 29 April 1787, Robert Strudock, 'Weaver of Twerton

---

[91] TNA. RG4/1790.

but lately of the Parish of Lyncomb & Widcomb', was buried aged 78 years. This is probably the 'Robt Strudick' whose house in Twerton was licenced for worship by 'Anabaptists' at the Epiphany Quarter Sessions on 15 January 1754.[92] On 1 February 1792, James Osborn, a 28 year old 'Servant to Opie & Wm Smith, Brewers of this City' was buried in the Walcot ground; followed on 25 April by an unnamed 29 year old servant, also of Opie and William Smith. An unnamed 18 year old servant of Moses Gay, of Stall Street, was buried on 16 March 1795. Opie Smith and Moses Gay were still trustees of the burial ground at this time.

There are entries in the burial registers that reflect the good relationship between the Baptist and Independent congregations in the late eighteenth century. Firstly there is William Jay's predecessor, Rev. Thomas Tuppen, the Independent minister instrumental in moving the Independent congregation into their new chapel in Argyle Street, but who was never to preach there. He was buried on 28 February 1790, aged 45, a year before the Independent congregation secured their own burial ground further up Snow Hill.[93] Secondly, however, is a more curious entry in the Baptist register which records the burial on 13 January 1795 of Stephen Gay, 'Clerk of the Markets in the City of Bath', aged 65 years, because 'He was inter'd in the Independent Burying ground, Walcot'! One suggestion is that his burial was conducted by John Paul Porter, the Baptist minister, in the Independent burial ground – and thus his entry appeared in the Baptist register.

In 1785 there was no consistent legal means of registering births, other than the records of infant baptisms in the established church. This to the Baptist congregation in Bath was anathema, and so they recorded their own births in the register. Together the births and burials record the development of family patterns within the church during this period, or those in close contact with it. By far the largest group identified is the Evill family, with thirty burials alone. The family was united around four brothers, who from the mid-eighteenth century appear as proprietors of a number of Bath retail and manufacturing businesses.[94] The eldest was George Evill, draper, of the Market Place, who was buried on 10 December 1785, aged 65 years. His widow, Ann, lived another 11 years before she joined him on 12 December 1806.

John, the second brother, resided at Southcot House before his death in December 1791. As senior deacon, John Evill's family had opened their home to the newly arrived John Paul Porter only a year earlier; and John's death was a great loss to the whole church. After his burial on 19 December Porter

---

[92] SRO. Q/RRW 1.
[93] Ede, 1989, 9. For the *Memoir* of Thomas Tuppen see *The Evangelical Magazine*, March 1805, 97.
[94] For further information on the rather complicated story of their retail and manufacturing businesses see Fawcett, 1990, 68-70.

preached the sermon from Zechariah 3:2, '...is not this a brand plucked out of the fire?', in which he gave details of the deceased's character:

> About thirty-six years ago, it was the pleasure of God to remove the veil of ignorance from his mind. He searched the Scriptures for himself, as the only rule of faith and practice with regard to the ordinance of baptism. In the year 1760, he, with two of his brethren, (both in the flesh and in the Lord), were baptized by Mr. Parsons....Twenty-five years our deceased friend was a deacon of this church: how he fulfilled the duties of his office, let those who were acquainted with him testify. His life was steady, circumspect, and exemplary; with manliness and fearlessness did he stand forth in defence of the gospel.... The last time I visited him, which was two days before his death, he said I know not what the Lord is about to do with me; but I know on whom I have believed. It was then the general opinion that he would recover; but sitting in his chair, he quietly and unexpectedly expired.[95]

He left £10 to the poor members of the church, £5 of which was 'put to the little fund for the poor'. The remaining £5 was divided among 13 poor members, including Thomas Durnell. John Evill's widow died the following year, and was buried on 28 September. She left £20 for the poor members, along with a further £10 'from Mr John Evill that was to be paid at Mrs Evills Death'. As a result the 'Little Fund for the Benefit of the Poor' was £10 better off; 21 poor members, including Thomas Durnell and Robert Harper, received 15s.6d; and 10s.6d. was given to 6 others. It appears that she and her husband died childless.

The third brother, William Evill, was a deacon of the Baptist church, as had his older brothers been. He was also a trustee alongside his brother John, and later James (either his son or nephew). After a successful career, he was buried on 25 April 1793; and also left money for the poor. £5 was divided amongst 21 of the poorest members. The youngest brother was Matthew Evill. Unlike his brothers, Matthew was not a member of the Baptist church, although his children and family burials are recorded in the Baptist books. He was widowed in 1790, and buried Elizabeth, his wife, at Walcot on 5 March, aged 50 years. Five years later and only five years older, on 23 April 1795, Matthew, 'Brother of George, John & William Evill of the City of Bath', was laid to rest amongst his family.

Comments in the register such as 'In the Letter E close to the Lower wall room in the Grave for one more', and 'In the Letter E close to the Wall Grave Full

---

[95] Cater, 1834, 81, 85.

Lower Wall', betray how full the ground was becoming; and the burial fines were adjusted accordingly. In June 1813 the church determined

> that the fines in the Walcot burying ground belonging to this Church shall be Twelve Shillings for persons buried under twelve years of age — and one pound one shilling for all above that age from this time.

The church's desperate need was met early in the nineteenth century, however, when a second burial ground was made available to them by their member and trustee, Opie Smith.

Chapter 4: Challenge and Change

Association and Gospel

From early on in its life the Baptist church in Bath was a member of the Western Baptist Association. As we have seen, during the early eighteenth century and championed by the church at Broadmead, the Association increasingly articulated the importance of propagating the gospel both for the survival of the church and more importantly in obedience to Christ. The early Bath Baptist community was planted and grew within this climate in the 1730s and 40s. In 1760 the Bath church had hosted the Association meetings, as ministers and messengers from Association churches gathered in Bath for their deliberations. Yet as the church grew in confidence and its own sense of identity, it would seem that certain differences arose between Bath and the Association. What the exact nature of those difficulties were is difficult to ascertain, although at the root would seem to be Robert Parsons himself and his own sense of call to ministry and understanding of the nature of the church. From the evidence it is impossible to judge to what extent Parsons was acting alone or with the support and encouragement of the church. As we have already seen, the closely bound nature of the church covenant and the strict position of the pastor were tightly interwoven. In 1763 Robert Parsons wrote the Bath church's annual letter to the Association meeting at Tiverton in which he is very critical of certain practices amongst the churches, in particular an elevated view of ministry and a worldly view of the church:

> The Baptist Church of X meeting in the City of Bath, Robert Parsons being Pastor, believing the Doctrine of Trinity, Eternal & Personal Election the Original guilt & depravity of Mankind, Free Justification by the imputed Righteousness of Jesus X, Efficacious Grace in Calling & final perseverance of the Saints to Glory.
>
> To the Elders & Messengers of the Several Baptist Churches of the Same Faith & Order met in Association the 25 & 26 Days of May 1763 at Tiverton Devon.
>
> Dearly Beloved in the Lord,
>
> Tho. We are Absent in Body yet would we be present in Spirit & ernestly pray that Grace from God the Father & our Lord Jesus X may plentifully descend Upon, Bless, Assist, & Direct, you all, this Yearly Meeting calls Upon Us, (more especially Us) who compose the Churches United together in it, to stand still, make a solumn pause, look back, consider, & gratefully Acknowledge what Jehovah hath done for Us; And as A People, while Neighbouring Nations struck with admiration, are saying the

Lord hath done Great things for them, shall we not as Brittons Say, with thankfullness say to the Lord hath done great things for Us where of we are Glad. How wonderful his Goodness during a Long, wasting & Bloody War, how remarkable in that all the Thunder & Confused Noise of War are Hush'd into silence & Peace, extends its self like a River far & wide. Our Eyes see our British Jerusalem a quiet habbitation & every man sitting under his Vine & Figg Tree enjoying Peace, Plenty & indearing Libberty, But what a Cloud gathers round what a Gloom spreads over this delightsom Scene when with the Candle of the Lord we are capable to enter in and take a Survey of our Hearts & ways Amidst all the Goodness of the Lord, who but finds Occasion to Say Wo. & Alass & Start back at the Shocking Contrast. Nor are we calld thus to Lament our own Account only but also National Ingratitude, General & Abounding Iniquity. In the Church too once the Ground and Pillar of Truth are these not the Chambers of Imagery & Striking instances of Pride & increasing conformity to this World. Partiality & Idolitry; Dear Brethren, Pompous Appearances, Grand Assemblies Idolized Litriture & Exalted Priestcraft may corispond with & be agreeable to the Spirit & Temper of this World but not so, to the Spiritual Mistical dispised & opposed Kingdom of Jesus Xrist O when shall Zion put on her Beautyfull Garments & Appear in Her Symple Primitive Glory & stand at a distance from thy Grace aid defiance to a Proud self seeking Ungodly Perishing World for this O help Us dear Brethren in your Solumn Approaches to the Divine Throne. As to our present circumstances As a Church Blessed be God we are at Peace Amongst our selves & enjoy plenty of the Means & humbly hope at Times God in them. Have had only one added & two are under Dealings. Our Meetings Well Attended and are in prospect of some lively stones preparing for God's Building & now dear Brethren we commend to God & to the Word of his Grace which is Able to Build you up & to give you an Inheritance among all them which are sanctified, Brethren Pray you for us your very Affectionate tho' unworthy Brethren in our Dear Lord.[1]

We have very few of Robert Parsons' own words, so this letter gives some insight into his thoughts at this time. Parsons demonstrates that he is strict Calvinist, but certainly not high or hyper. Following a general call to unity

---

[1] Parsons, 1763. Parsons' appeal to simplicity (according to the Oxford English Dictionary 'symple' is an early variant spelling of 'simple') is something he will come back to in 1774 – see pp. 105, 107.

among the churches, Parsons reflects upon the importance of the recent peace from a war that had affected many nations over recent years. The Seven Years' War had come to an end in 1763 with the Peace of Paris. Initially Britain had entered the war in support of Frederick II of Prussia, but the war was not confined to Europe and saw Britain at war with France in Canada, leaving Britain in control of much of Canada when Quebec fell as the French retreated. Notable British casualties at Quebec included Major-General James Wolfe, who himself had Bath connections.[2] From the war itself, Parsons moves on to condemn the nation's arrogance and ingratitude to God, and to contend that an increasing worldliness has become apparent within the church. There are things that may have a place in the world, he says, but have no place in the church, namely 'Pompous Appearances, Grand Assemblies Idolized Litriture & Exalted Priestcraft'. What the exact reference is within the life of the Association we cannot be sure. It could be that Parsons was answering criticism of the way that the Association had been hosted in 1760, if certain members of the Association had expected something grander than was actually experienced. It is more likely that Parsons was responding to a movement in the Association with which he was increasingly less comfortable. Parsons was concerned that developments amongst the Baptist churches of the Association were detracting from the Grace of God and the work of his Spirit. This positive aspect of the good things that God is doing indeed forms the bulk of the letter. He was also concerned that the church was reflecting the manners and modes of wider society, as demonstrated regularly and exuberantly at Bath, rather than being a Gospel critique of it. However it is also possible that the second half of the condemned 'Pompous Appearances, Grand Assemblies Idolized Litriture & Exalted Priestcraft' are references to a move towards a more educated and professional ministry. There were those seeking to extend and expand the training of ministers through the Baptist church at Broadmead, Bristol, since the death of its minister, Bernard Foskett, in 1758. Robert Parsons had been called to exercise his preaching gifts during the ministry of Foskett, but had not been formally trained as a 'student' of the Bristol Academy based at Broadmead. Now under Hugh and Caleb Evans at Broadmead there was a broader liberal education available for ministers, leading eventually to the founding of the Bristol Education Society in 1770, as we have seen above.[3]

Perhaps it was this other more worldly side to the forming of 'able, evangelical, lively, zealous ministers of the Gospel' that Parsons had in his mind, and to

---

[2] Lowndes, 1982, 112-3. 'He had often visited Bath, staying with his parents who had taken a house at No. 5 Trim Street. After returning to England following the siege of Louisbourg in 1758, he wrote to a friend from Salisbury: "My health is mightily impaired by the long confinement at sea. I am going to Bath to refit for another campaign". Shortly afterwards, he was given command of the Quebec expedition...And after his death, it was discovered that he was wearing a miniature portrait of a young woman next to his heart. She was a Miss Lowther of Bath, a close friend whom he had known and admired for some time.'
[3] Moon, 1979, 10-11.

which he objected – and perhaps clashing with Parsons' own tendency towards high Calvinism. Parsons' entire ministry had been supported by his continuing to trade in stone carving and other associated businesses. For Parsons there was something to be resisted in the increased professionalizing of the ministry implied by the movement by many churches to want the means to support a full-time minister. A growing number of churches were increasingly able and wanting to call a full-time trained minister, but there were insufficient funds to support their adequate training. A letter from four Bristol ministers inviting the formation of the Bristol Education Society on behalf of the Bristol Academy was addressed to 'the Friends of Religion and Learning among the Baptists':

> It has long been Matter of Complaint, that there is a very great scarcity of Ministers to supply the Congregations of the Baptist Denomination; and that many of those who have been called to the Ministry amongst them, have been unable, from want of more effectual provision for their support, to prosecute those preparatory studies which, under a divine blessing, would have enabled them to exercise their ministerial gifts with more general acceptance.
>
> To supply this defect, a small number of Pupils have been for many years past, instructed in various branches of useful knowledge in Bristol. But many of these students have been obliged to break off their studies very abruptly, to make room for others, owing to the scantiness of the present provision for the support of this seminary. Notwithstanding which disadvantage, it is presumed that the Baptist Churches in various parts of the kingdom have experienced the utility of this institution.
>
> Now it is hereby proposed to establish a Society, under the name of the Bristol Education Society, for the enlargement of the Number of students in this seminary, and their more effectual and permanent support: to the end that the respective Churches may be more disposed to encourage promising gifts, and that vacant Congregations, if it please God to succeed the design, may be more speedily and effectually supplied, with a succession of able and acceptable Ministers.[4]

This would increasingly become the pattern for the training of ministers during the succeeding decades, a pattern of which Parsons distinctly disapproved. In trying to understand Parsons' reasons for disapproving it may be significant that, as Roger Hayden has identified, Robert Parsons was among a small number who although recognised as a minister by the Baptist church at

---

[4] Swaine, 1884, 70-71.

Broadmead were not included among those listed by Bernard Foskett as students of the Academy.⁵ It is a matter of speculation whether he was denied the opportunity, and thus subsequently reacted against the education of ministers, or whether these views were longstanding and had influenced the path he had earlier taken.

Other clues to Parsons' thinking come from his published writing. Rupert Gunnis tells us that 'He published in 1772 Letters to the Rev. Mr. Fletcher of Madely on the differences subsisting between him and the Hon. and Rev. Mr. Shirley.'⁶ This 'Letter to the Rev. Mr. Fletcher' is indeed attributed to Robert Parsons in the bound volume in Bath Central Library, presumably consulted by Gunnis in 1950 in the course of his research. There are a number of reasons for doubting its correct attribution: the subject matter is a particular dispute within Methodism; Philip Cater refers to another work of 1774 as 'The only instance in which Mr. Parsons committed any of his productions to the press';⁷ and furthermore it is anonymous. One might from experience, as we have seen, reasonably expect Parsons to stand up for his own views and sign the letter. Yet there are also reasons for accepting the attribution. Firstly the letter is in a collection of works by Robert and Thomas Parsons bound together and annotated early on in the nineteenth century, and presented to Bath City Reference Library from the distinguished personal library of A W Page, a noted Bath Baptist, in 1923. Whilst maintaining anonymity the author of the letter makes his views known as follows:

> Sir, As I am an entire Stranger to your Person, and so little acquainted with Mr. Shirley as never to have exchanged one Word with him, I cannot be charged with addressing you from any Motive of private Pique, or personal Resentment: but as a Lover of Truth and a friend to the Disciples of JESUS (tho' I am no Methodist) what-ever name they bear, permit me to put in a Word concerning the controversy between you and Mr. Shirley.
>
> The Kingdom of GOD my friend, is not in WORD but in POWER: you are to be sure sufficiently profuse in WORDS, but Facts remain the same, and will have Weight, with all honest and unprejudiced Men...⁸

If the writer of the letter is Parsons, then this is his important contribution to one of the more significant controversies in Methodism at the time when the Calvinist majority came into conflict with Wesley's Arminian evangelicalism. This gives us a second reason for accepting Parsons as the author, for the letter

---

⁵ Hayden, 1991, 381.
⁶ Gunnis, 1951, 293.
⁷ Cater, 1834, 78.
⁸ Parsons, 1772, 2-3.

reflects a view that focuses away from a wordy, educated argument in favour of the power and authority of God. This was a theme apparent in his 1763 correspondence and would be taken up again in 1774. Rev. John Fletcher of Madeley was one of the few supporters of Wesley's views, yet a vociferous supporter nonetheless and author of published correspondence with Rev. Walter Shirley, a cousin of Selina, Countess of Huntingdon.[9] The writer of our letter, whether Parsons or not, was clearly moved to respond to Fletcher's 1771 published letter titled *Check to Antinomianism*, with its follow-up supplement called *A Second Check to Antinomianism*, in which Fletcher defended the 1770 Wesleyan Conference minutes which appeared to preach salvation by works rather than as a gift of God's grace by faith. The writer defends the traditional Calvinist position with both pastoral and evangelistic passion in a series of queries to his reader:

> 1. Is there not more of a meek and Jesus-like Temper evidenced in Mr. Shirley, thro' the whole of this Affair, than in yourself? And does he not appear to be a Man of Deeds, while you are a Man of Words only?
>
> 2. Does not personal Envy (or Enmity) discover itself, in the Course of your first and second Publication, more than a Love to Christ, and a godly Zeal to promote Truth?
>
> 3. Do you really believe that the Works of a fallen Sinner can appear before the Holy Lord God, in whose Sight the Heavens are unclean, and the Angels charg'd with Folly; as the Matter of the Sinners Justification?
>
> 4. Is not such a Doctrine directly contrary to the Tenor of Scripture? And has it not a Tendency to overturn divine Revelation, establish Heathenism, and rob the Son of God of the expressive Name given him by his Father; Jesus, a Saviour, and a Saviour of his People from their Sins? In what Sense can Jesus save, if Men are justified by their Works?[10]

The writer concludes the letter with a personal plea, that Fletcher moderate his tone and be prepared to change his mind:

> These Thoughts Sir, occurred in reading what has come to my Hand relative to this Controversy: You may perceive an artless Simplicity in them. And be persuaded by a plain Man, to moderate your fiery Zeal in Defence of a Point, in which it is very possible you may be mistaken—to banish from your Mind that unfriendly Acrimony, which is blended with what you have

---

[9] Hempton, 1984, 30-31; Rupp, 1986, 466-7; Sell, 1982, 68-69.
[10] Parsons, 1772, 5-6.

hitherto written—and to write no more, till you can do it with Charity, Meekness, and Love. The Gospel is to be supported without metaphysical Subtilties, much less does it require Sarcasms, Invectives, and Envy.—A dreadful Doom awaits those who offend one of Christ's little ones; and remember that the wrath of Man worketh not the Righteousness of God; but great is the Truth and it will prevail.

I am Sir, An Enemy to no Man, But a FRIEND to RELIGION. BATH, February 3, 1772.[11]

This final appeal to an uncluttered simplicity in letting the Gospel truth have its own way is reminiscent of Parsons' letter to the Western Baptist Association nine years earlier, with its appeal the 'Symple Primitive Glory' of the Gospel. For Parsons, if the Gospel will be preached then the only Gospel that will grow is one where grace is the free gift of God and where righteousness is dependent on faith in the saving power of Jesus Christ.

Education and Ministry

The themes of the sufficiency of God's grace for salvation and the fact that godly truth will prevail occur again in the final known published work of Robert Parsons. In June 1774 Parsons preached a sermon to his own congregation which was later published as *Abilities for the Ministry of the Gospel from God alone: A Discourse on 2 Corinthians iii. 6*. The title pre-empts the text in leading the reader to consider who it is who prepares someone for the ministry of the Gospel. The conclusion intended to be drawn is that God alone prepares his Gospel ministers. 2 Corinthians 3:6 is set in the context of the sufficiency of God, the God 'Who also hath made us able ministers of the new testament; not of the letter, but of the spirit: for the letter killeth, but the spirit giveth life.'[12] It is clear that in the years after the formation of the Bristol Education Society the issue of ministerial education and training was still as contentious as ever. It might be supposed that the condescending tone of the introductory letter written in 1770 had hardly sought to improve the situation:

> The importance of a liberal education, more especially to candidates for the Christian ministry, is so exceedingly obvious, that one might almost think it impossible that any considerate, intelligent person should not be convinced of it. Yet there are, it is well known, some very worthy people who, from a mistaken view of things, not only call in question the importance of such an education, but even seem to imagine it is rather prejudicial than useful. Now, if these prejudices are well founded, every

---

[11] Parsons, 1772, 7.
[12] 2 Corinthians 3:6. Authorised Version.

scheme formed for the education of pious youths designed for the ministry ought to be discountenanced. But if, on the other hand, it should appear that these prejudices are unreasonable, and that a learned education is highly useful, then every institution calculated for that purpose must be deserving of the warmest and most effectual encouragement.[13]

Although there was an attempt to mitigate this by acknowledging that education on its own would be insufficient to prepare anyone for ministry:

> That all the learning in the world is, of itself, by no means sufficient to complete the ministerial character is readily acknowledged; and it is, therefore, a very great absurdity to think of training up young persons to the Christian ministry in the same indiscriminate manner as to any other profession. If a man be not truly religious and furnished with talents adapted to the work of the ministry, let him have as much learning as may be, it cannot be expected that he should be an acceptable and useful minister. And it is much to be apprehended that an abuse of learning, in this respect, hath contributed more than anything to bring it into disrepute. Let it, therefore, be remembered, all that is pleaded for in this introduction, is the usefulness and importance of learning in *subordination* to what is more essentially requisite to the ministerial character. Many persons without any of the advantages of learning, we freely confess, have been very able, laborious, and successful ministers of the Gospel. But not a few of these ministers themselves, so far from decrying learning as useless, have sensibly felt their own want of it, and with an amiable candor acknowledged the disadvantages they lay under on that account.[14]

If Parsons was not the main target of this appeal it is difficult to imagine that he was not at least one of the 'worthy people' to whom the criticism was addressed. The appeal continued:

> We have already observed that no man can be an acceptable minister of the Gospel if he be not a converted man, and furnished with those ministerial gifts or talents which God alone can communicate; but, then, is he not to endeavour, in the use of proper means, to improve these talents?[15]

And yet Parsons was not to be persuaded by the case. It was not that Parsons was against learning and education absolutely, for he was clearly literate and

---

[13] Swaine, 1884, 75.
[14] Ibid, 75-76.
[15] Ibid, 77.

well-educated himself in many ways; and he had ensured the education of his son, Thomas, in a wide variety of disciplines, although the details of how or where remain unknown. Neither was it that Parsons wanted to diminish or hinder the preaching of the Gospel through lack of properly called and thoroughly equipped preachers and ministers, as is evident in the regular practice of the Bath Baptist congregation in calling such preachers in the 1760s and 70s. In regard to education and ministry, however, Parsons was highly convinced that it was under the sovereignty of God alone to empower and equip ministers of the Gospel – and it was to this subject he turned to address in 1774.

In his introductory epistle to the 'Friendly Reader' Robert Parsons addresses his being unaccustomed to employing the press, but that the situation is so serious that he feels compelled so to do. His motive is the number of publications he has read which have 'a tendency to lead from, and not to the bible, the fountain of truth, flowing from the God of Truth', and the 'gradual, yet visible departure of the professors of the present age, from the pure simple truth, worship and ordinances of Christ, as laid down in the new testament.'[16] Again we see Parsons' appeal to the purity of a simple Gospel, pointing towards the unadorned Scriptures. Indeed the object of his opposition is now clearly and specifically the call for the more educated ministry as put forward by the Bristol Education Society and growing pleas for the unity of purpose among the Baptist churches of the Western Baptist Association.[17] Parsons' introductory epistle concludes:

> I expect not applause from men, I seek it not; neither would I designedly grieve one soul for whom Christ died: but in an age when a liberal education is more pleaded for than truth, and a false concord more disagreeable than false doctrine, who would not step forward and cry out Hosannah? lest the stones rebuke our infidelity. If I have therefore been enabled to advance truth, I have the satisfaction of being a feeble witness in my Master's cause; before my tongue is silent in the grave: if I am mistaken, help me in praying, what I know not Lord teach thou me. Amen.[18]

Parsons begins the published sermon by laying down the context for 2 Corinthians 2:6 in a discussion of the sufficiency of God. Directly quoting from John Gill's expository commentary on Paul's Corinthian correspondence, Parsons states, 'none are sufficient but whom God makes so, and those he makes able and sufficient, by giving them spiritual gifts fitting them for the

---

[16] Parsons, 1774, iii.
[17] Moon, 1979, 11-15, 129-134.
[18] Parsons, 1774, iv.

ministry; and these are ministers of the new testament.'[19] This is in line with Parsons' simple thesis that God alone makes those he has called fit for ministry.

It may or may not be significant to this discussion that Parsons used John Gill as his authority, as Gill was one of the London ministers associated, as we have seen above, with a form of hyper-Calvinism that tended towards decline. Although Gill's own church in the Goat Yard, London, was in decline, Tom Nettles suggests this was as much attributable to the amount of time he spent in his study, [20] than to any lack of belief in preaching the Gospel. Nettles argues that Gill's concern in his study and considerable published output was to defend the purity and the clarity of the Gospel as preached – and that in these ways Gill made his 'activist' contribution to the Evangelical Awakening from his study as much as others did the 'the field'. Nettles continues:

> The medium of the Awakening was preaching. Gill viewed the preaching task of the gospel minister with sober delight. One of the major reasons for the decline of the eighteenth century in Gill's opinion was a lack of courage, clarity, and orthodoxy in the pulpit. Just as private Christians might depart from true doctrines, "so may ministers of the word drop and depart from sound words" just when they should show "boldness, confidence, and courage" in preaching "the truths of the gospel."[21]

Gill's writings were widely circulated, read and used during the eighteenth century and beyond, and we see in Robert Parsons' sermon an example of the use of his commentaries for the purpose of preaching, arguing for the purity and simplicity of the Gospel, preached by those of God's choosing and equipping. It could be that there is no other significance in Parsons' use of Gill, other than that Parsons owned commentaries by Gill.

The body of the sermon consists of three sections. In the first he considers 'the sphere in which ministers are to move, or the business God hath employed them in and about.'[22] The text refers to 'ministers of the new testament', which Parsons takes as meaning that the sole business of ministry is testimony to the Gospel of Jesus Christ, the new covenant of grace as opposed to the old covenant of works:

> In our text it is called a new testament, not only intending a covenant compact or agreement, but including the idea of a will; alluding to the practice of men, who dispose of their effects by their last will and testament: the gospel is the will of GOD,

---

[19] Ibid, 8 - a direct and accurate quote from Gill, *Collected Writings*. 2 Corinthians 3:6, 46-47.
[20] Nettles, 1997, 140.
[21] Ibid, 142.
[22] Parsons, 1774, 9.

> declared, published, sealed, signed and delivered by the testator Jesus, who hath appointed the Holy Spirit sole executor.[23]

It is the primacy of truth and doctrine over liberal education that gives Parsons the confidence to advocate the preaching of the Gospel. For Parsons the equipping of God's Spirit is sufficient, whereas human learning is insufficient. This is the central section of the sermon in which he turns to consider 'those things, which according to the scripture, are necessary to ministers of the new testament; or those qualifications which are requisite in a faithful minister of the gospel.'[24] Heavily dependent on Gill's commentary, Parsons' main points can be tabulated as follows:[25]

> 1st. Experimental conversion; or the experience of that change in his own soul, which in the new testament is called regeneration.
>
> 2d. Qualification is a spiritual knowledge of the new testament, without which the heart is not good.
>
> 3d. Things necessary to that character, which is a dispensation from GOD to preach the gospel… A dispensation from GOD, implies or supposes the fore-mentioned experience and knowledge; and may consist of the following things:
>
> 1. An aptness or aptitude to teach
>
> 2. A humble desire to engage in the ministerial work, in GOD'S way, and in his own time; convinced that GOD is a GOD of order.
>
> 3. An experience of the power of religion, together with a knowledge of the gospel, are insufficient without a tongue capable of conveying this experience and knowledge intelligibly to others.
>
> 4. To these we may add, the concurrence of the church, or a call from the saints with whom such a person is in fellowship.
>
> 5. Moreover a minister of the new testament, ought to be free from lucrative views.
>
> 6. The last qualification of the gospel minister is, a life and conversation that honour the new testament: though this is implied in almost all that has been said, yet it is the crowning point of all.

---

[23] Ibid, 13.
[24] Ibid, 18.
[25] Ibid, 19-38.

The fifth section clearly shows how in Parsons' view the matter of education and full-time paid ministry are connected, which will continue to be a struggle for him. This connects with the reputation that is repeated in many of the early accounts, that 'during the whole of [his ministry]...he received no remuneration for his services, gaining his livelihood by working at his trade of stone-carving.'[26] To have received payment, other than expenses, would indeed have been 'lucrative' for Parsons, and crossed the sacred-secular divide.

In the final section of his sermon Parsons turns to 'enquire whence those qualifications come, or who it is that makes men able ministers of the new testament?'[27] Once again Parsons turns to the text and the sufficiency of God, and his argument against the prevailing order:

> Nevertheless the world have sought out many inventions, and impiously wrested the work out of GOD'S hands. Others, as if it was incomplete, are ready to lend a helping hand to finish what GOD has begun...[28]

Parsons' thesis is that the scriptures teach that it is Christ who established the church and provides gifted ministers for it, a fact universally acknowledged by his 'ministerial servants in the new testament', and that it is 'To God and to God alone' that prayer for a continuity and succession of gospel ministers is to be made.[29] Parsons concludes:

> And lastly, it farther appears that it ever was, and ever will be the work of Christ alone to provide able ministers, seeing he hath not left any direction, command or hint in the whole new testament for men to make or attempt to make ministers; or to aid and assist him in making them, or to finish them off for him when made. The Creator of the ends of the earth is the only maker of able ministers of the new testament.[30]

The evidence from this sermon demonstrates why the appeals from the Bristol Education Society for the Baptist Academy received little or no support from the Bath church – something that would be reversed by the beginning of the nineteenth century. Parsons would teach his congregation to depend entirely upon God and upon the Holy Scriptures and their understanding within the context of the local church:

> ...and here we find no school but the house of God, no academy but the church of God, no means but the means of

---

[26] Tyte, 1903, 112.
[27] Parsons, 1774, 38.
[28] Ibid.
[29] Ibid, 40-44.
[30] Ibid, 45.

grace, no teacher but God himself, who only is able to make wise unto salvation...[31]

For the purposes of the church and the Gospel, human learning for Parsons is nothing short of idolatry,[32] and so in the closing section of the sermon he turns to quote from *Christian World unmasked* by a 'worthy minister of the gospel' whom he chooses not to name but who nonetheless has influenced Parsons' own thinking:

> Human science, keeps men out of mischief, trains them up for civil occupations; and oft produceth notable discoveries, which are useful to the world; but never can lead the heart to Jesus Christ, nor breed a single grain of faith in him. They who know most of human science, and have waded deepest in it, know the most of its vanities, and find it but vexation of spirit.[33]

The author of *The Christian World unmasked — Pray come and peep*, to use its full title, was John Berridge (1717-93), passionate convert from Arminianism to high Calvinism, vicar of Everton, and friend of George Whitefield and Selina, Countess of Hungtingdon. A popular book from the start it was first published in 1773, and thus hot off the press when Parsons read it. He was clearly influenced by it, just as the book was clearly influential – a second edition appeared later in 1773, with a third in 1774, and was still being reprinted as late as 1853.[34] The irony is, of course, that the same Parsons who rejected an educated ministry was himself widely read, even in the latest theological works with which he concurs, and also in the liberal classical arts within which world, as carver stone mason with a good reputation and wide success, he lived his professional life. There would seem to be a tension in Parsons' view of education, based on a dualism that separated matters of life in general and faith in particular.

Robert Parsons' life was immersed in learning and the arts, for he was a man of his age and thrived on the culture of the city in which he had made a significant livelihood and reputation. Further he would ensure that his son, Thomas, would receive a classical and scientific education that surpassed his own – and as we shall see shortly, Thomas thrived in this world. Yet for Robert Parsons, the things of Caesar and the things of God were to be kept very separate indeed – a dualism that perhaps reflected the Greek thought of the neoclassicism of the day more than any Christian understanding of the sacred and the profane.

---

[31] Ibid, 46.
[32] Ibid, 51.
[33] Ibid, 47.
[34] *The Christian World Unmasked* was followed in 1792, two years after Parsons' death, with *Cheerful Piety, or Religion without gloom: exemplified in select letters on the most important truths of Christianity*.

Thomas Parsons

In March 1778 tragedy was once again to hit the Parsons household as Robert's second wife Sarah died, aged 69.[35] Yet once again within a very short period Robert Parsons was married. Lucy Atkins, a widow of Bath, became Robert's third wife in 1779.[36] Robert Parsons was at this time sixty-one years old, and it is understood that the thirty-five year old Thomas assisted his father in both business and church. There is also reason to believe that Thomas considered himself as co-pastor with this father, although the church minute books do not indicate any appointment to such a position. Morris West has pointed out that 'it must be extremely rare in the history of any church, certainly a Baptist Church, for a father and son to be co-pastors of one church.'[37] West gives the example known to him: Hugh and Caleb Evans at Broadmead in Bristol. It is possible that here, at least for a short time, is another example. As we have seen above, it was in May 1771 that Thomas Parsons was formally recognised as a preacher within the Bath congregation and elsewhere. His preaching was described as 'judicious' and 'eloquent', but he was apparently not popular with a large section of the church.[38]

In 1788 the church at Somerset Street agreed to appoint an assistant minister to help the ageing Robert Parsons with his preaching and pastoral work. The natural choice would have been Thomas Parsons who had assisted his father and was called upon to preach on occasion. Thomas' assistance would have helped the church during this period, yet he was often absent pursuing other interests. In fact he differed from his father over many issues, and his preaching was not at all popular. Walter Wilson recorded that:

> A difference of opinion from his venerable parent, upon some high point of doctrine, entertained by the good old man, & which was magnified by suspicion & officiousness on the one part, & a refusal to come to explanation on the other, occasioned him to be interdicted labouring in the church.[39]

Instead they called Rev. William Holland, who unfortunately soon became seriously ill; and in the register for the Bath Baptist burial ground it is recorded that the 40 year old 'Baptist Minister originally of London, late from Romsey and Preacher amongst us for one year' was buried on 28 June 1789.

In February 1790 Robert Parsons himself died, aged 71, and was buried at Walcot on 7 March. The *Bath Journal* reported Parsons' death as follows:

---

[35] Wilson, 1948.
[36] Ibid.
[37] West, 1984, 160.
[38] Cater, 1834, 79.
[39] Wilson, nd.

> Sunday died Mr. Robert Parsons, who for 40 years had been pastor of the Baptist congregation in Garrard-street, and to whose disinterested zeal that society owed its origin and establishment.[40]

Within a year the church had lost both its minister and assistant. John Rippon, the London minister who trained at the Baptist Academy in Bristol in the 1770s, and who as 'enthusiastic collector of Baptist news' compiled and edited the *Baptist Annual Register*,[41] issued the following announcement:

> The Rev. Mr. ROBERT PARSONS, pastor of the Baptist church at Bath, died Feb. the 28th, 1790; his amiable assistant, the Rev. Mr. WILLIAM HOLLAND, departed this life a few months before him, viz. on June 23, 1789. But as no biographical traits of them have been communicated either by the church or the families to which they belonged, the Register is under a necessity of passing over both these respectable characters with the bare mention of their names and the times of their exit; a circumstance this which will frequently, and indeed unavoidably, happen, unless the friends of our deceased connections interest themselves in collecting and forwarding in good time, suitable material.[42]

Confusion followed Parson's death, caused amongst other things by the subsequent behaviour of Thomas Parsons.

The process of finding a new minister had already begun and, as we shall see, this period would mark an important transition from an era marked by a strictly structured Baptist community to an era marked by fragmentation and diversity. Soon after Parsons' death the church's attention had been drawn to John Paul Porter, from Wokingham, and his possible suitability for ministry in Bath. At the Somerset Street church meeting on 2 May 1790 it was 'Resolved that Mr John Porter be invited occasionally to preach to us for three months from this time.' It was also 'Resolved that Mr Thomas Parsons be invited to preach occasionally amongst us; and that our Brethren Mr Singers, Mr Jn Evil, Mr Williams & Mr Newport be appointed to request the aforesaid Mr John Porter & Mr Thomas Parsons to comply with those Resolutions'.[43]

Thomas Parsons is the earliest Bath Baptist for whom we have a probable portrait likeness,[44] and we know a little more of his biography. Further extracts

---

[40] *Bath Journal*, February 1790.
[41] Moon, 1979, 15; Brown, 1986, 118.
[42] Rippon, 1790-1793, 142.
[43] SSBC, *Minutes*, 2 May 1790.
[44] Turner, 1977, 68, & 90. In his catalogue for the exhibition on Science and Music in eighteenth-century Bath, Turner includes this description: 'Engraved portrait on paper, inscribed Mr. Thomas Parsons. Drawn and Engraved by N. Branwhite, from a Painting by S. Medley. Size of

from Thomas junior's Bible and copied by his father into his Commonplace Book fill in some of the details. After the references to Robert Parsons we read:

> Thomas his only surviving son was born April 1744. He married Hannah Frances, the daughter of Thomas and Hannah Best of Wyvenhoe near Colchester, September 18, 1770 at St Peter's, Colchester.
> Thomas and Hannah Frances Parsons had nine children, namely,
> Thomas, born August 13, 1771
> Mary, born January 8, 1773 who died May 20, 1779
> Hannah Frances April 13, 1774
> Robert, March 4, 1777 who died May 13, 1779
> Elizabeth April 5, 1779 who died Novr 1, 1779
> Robert April 30, 1781
> Mary November 5, 1783 who died Mar. 10, 1788
> Lucy November 28, 1785 who died Oct. 31, 1788
> Elizabeth March 22, 1788
> Their amiable Mother died November 15, 1788 aged 37 years.[45]

Therefore it needs to be taken into consideration that when Robert Parsons died in 1790 his son Thomas was already a widower and had lost five children in infancy. Thomas was very different from his father, mixed in a different social circle, and would appear to have received a more modern scientific liberal education, whilst he was also skilled in carving like his father. Rupert Gunnis, managed to confuse Robert and Thomas Parsons in his *Dictionary of British Sculptors*, and placed them at the scene of one of Bath's amusements:

> His book of designs is in the possession of the Bath Municipal Library and shows that he copied his vases from drawings by Hoare, Cipriani, Kent, Wedgwood, Mrs. Coade, etc. He made the famous vase for Mrs. (afterwards Lady) Miller into which verses were dropped by the wits of Bath. These she would pick out and read to her assembled guests, an amusement which

---

engraved area approx 5 ¾ in. x 5 ⅜ in. (119 mm x 110 mm). Half length portrait to front. Son of a stone mason from Bath, Thomas Parsons also followed this trade until about 1791, by 1805 however, he had turned to grocery. Fossils and the process by which they occurred were proposed as subjects for the attention of the Philosophical Society early in 1780, and Parsons seems to have been a local collector. It seems likely also that he was the author of a series of comments to *Gentleman's Magazine* and the *Monthly Magazine* on natural history topics between 1781 and 1799, over the signature 'T. P. Bath'. There were however two Thomas Parsons in Bath at this time, and no doubt others with the same initials…Lent by the Municipal Reference Library, Bath.'

[45] Russ, 1925-1959, Parsons.

terminated on the day when a most indelicate ode polluted the urn.⁴⁶

This latter observation conflicts with other known information about the vase. William Tyte tells the story of Lady Miller's vase thus:

> The founders of this entertainment were Sir John and Lady Miller, the former an Irish gentleman, the latter an English lady. They built the house known as Batheaston Villa, and laid out the grounds with taste; but having spent more than their resources justified, the young pair betook themselves to the Continent to retrench...Among the numerous paintings and works of art which they brought back from Italy, was a beautiful vase, found in 1769 at Frascati, near the spot where is supposed to have stood the Tusculanum of Cicero, "and by its workmanship (says a contemporary writer) seems not unworthy of such an owner."⁴⁷

Which of the stories is correct, or whether both come together in the Vase story, is not easy to tell. Thomas Parsons would, it seems, have enjoyed being part of this literary and artistic world. We do not know how or where he received his education, although practically at least no doubt from Robert. He may possibly have been self taught to a large degree, having started life working with his father as a stone carver. Parsons certainly took a wide interest in literary and scientific affairs. It is to be noted that 'Mr. Parsons' was present at the inaugural meeting of the influential group raised by Edmund Rack that was to become known as the 'Bath and West Agricultural Society'.⁴⁸ The minutes and records of the Society give evidence of Thomas Parsons' attendance and contributions for the next twenty years. Later, in December 1779, we again find Parsons entering into association with others as the newly formed Bath Philosophical Society—again formed by Edmund Rack on the suggestion of Thomas Curtis, Governor of the Bath General Hospital.⁴⁹

---

⁴⁶ Gunnis, 1951, 292-3.
⁴⁷ Tyte, 1903, 91.
⁴⁸ Turner, 1977, 81; Williams & Stoddart, 1978, 56. The inaugural meeting of the Agricultural Society is listed as 'John Ford Esqr. in the Chair, Revd. Dr. Wilson, Revd. Mr. Ford, Dr. Wm. Falconer, Dr. Patrick Henley, Wm. Brereton, Esq., Mr. Saml. Virgin, Mr. Richard Crutwell, Mr. Foster, Apothecary, Mr. Cam Gyde, Mr. Benj. Axford, Phillip Stephens, Esq., Paul Newman Esq., Mr. John Newman, Willm Street Esq., Mr. Symons, Surgeon, Mr. Crutwell, Surgeon, Mr. Arden, Mr. Wm Matthews, Mr. Parsons, Mr. Edm. Rack, Mr. Bull.'
⁴⁹ Turner, 1977, 82-83; Williams & Stoddart, 1978, 68-69. A list of the original members of the Bath Philosophical Society (1779-1787) has been compiled by Hugh Torrens: 1. Hon. Hugh Acland (1728-1805), 2. John Arden (1702-1791), 3. Mr. Atwood, 4. Charles Blagden (1748-1820), 5. John B. Bryant (fl 1779-1792), 6. James Collings (c 1721-1788), 7. Thomas Curtis (c 1739-1784), 8. William Falconer (1744-1824), 9. John Henderson (1757-1788), 10. William Herschel (1738-1822), 11. John Coakley Lettsom (1744-1815), 12. John Lloyd (1749-1815), 13. Mathew Martin (1748-1838), 14. William Matthews (1747-1816), 15. Constantine John Phipps (Lord

One of the consequences of the stone working that was going on in Bath was an increased interest in the geological history of the area. Fossils were being found everywhere, and Robert Parsons had delivered fossils to his customers in fulfilment of their orders.[50] John Wood himself had noted in his *A Description of Bath* that

> The Rocks at Twiverton, a Village lying about a Mile and a half to the West of the hot Springs, and so on Westward to Cainsham, produce Stones ribb'd and coil'd up like an Adder, which the credulous, as Mr. Camden takes notice, formerly believed to have been real Serpents turned into Stones by an imaginary devout Virgin, that bore the Name of Keina: I myself have found the like Stones in several Beds of Gravel under the Body of the City; the outside Scale of such spiral Fossils abound in the marly Soil about two or three hundred Yards to the Eastward of the hot Springs, but in a kind of Ore that looks like Silver; and in the very Freestone Rocks of the Hills on the North, East and South Sides of those Springs, I have often seen the Moulds of Serpentine Stones, but covered with little Stalactites, or sparry Icicles, of divers Shapes, as though Water congealed had made the Vacuum.[51]

Fossils and their origins were discussed at a meeting of the Bath Philosophical Society, following a paper given by Thomas Parsons on 21 January 1780. This was the fifth paper of the Bath Society, in consequence of which Edmund Rack himself took up a greater interest in fossils, which he was later to reflect upon in his paper to the Royal Society in 1782.[52]

It would be interesting to surmise whether Thomas Parsons was more interested than his father in the liberal education offered at the Baptist Academy in Bristol. If so, this would certainly have increased the tension between father and son in the last years of Robert's life; and if this tension was also reflected within the Bath Baptist community, then the stage would be set for challenging the earlier antipathy towards an educated ministry. Certainly within a decade Bath Baptists were openly supporting the Academy. Hugh Torrens notes that:

Mulgrave) (1744-1792), 16. Caleb Hillier Parry (1755-1822), 17. Thomas Parsons (1744-1813), 18. Joseph Priestley (1733-1804), 19. Samuel Pye, 20. Edmund Rack (1735-1787), 21. Rev. Samuel Rogers (1731-1790), 22. Benjamin Smith (fl 1779-1807), 23. John Staker (c 1731-1784), 24. John Symons (died 1811), 25. John Walcott (1755-1831), 26. John Walsh (1726-1795), 27. William Watson (1744-1824). Williams and Stoddart continue: 'Comparison with the list of founder members of the Agricultural Society shows that several people were members of both. A remarkable feature of the list is that no fewer than eleven members were, or became, Fellows of the Royal Society, London and ten are featured in the *Dictionary of National Biography*.'
[50] A large collection still exists in the possession of the Bath Scientific and Literary Society, Queen Square.
[51] Wood, 1765, 61.
[52] Torrens, 1978, 222-223.

> A museum was set up in Bristol in 1784 at the Baptist Academy there and certainly contained fossils and other geological material by 1799, but the first reference to such a collection on public display in Bath is not found until 1809 when the large Natural History Museum at 21 Union Street was open.[53]

Furthermore Torrens suggests that it was probably Thomas Parsons who contributed the following letter to the *Gentleman's Magazine* in 1788, signed 'P.T.', about the 'thousands of petrifactions of once living animals' to be found in the excavations then in progress on the slopes of Lansdown:[54]

> Mr. URBAN, So much has been said in your entertaining Magazine relative to the petrifaction of human bones, I ask, whether, if the bones of an animal will completely petrify, can there be any doubt that human bones will petrify also? Now I have before me one joint of the backbone of some large animal, which is not crusted over with stony matter, but which is throughout as perfect stone as can be possibly found, and as solid, and near as heavy, as a flint stone. It was found among the stones and rocks dug up on Lansdown Hill, where the new Crescent is building, and where may be seen thousands of petrifactions of once living animals, both marine and terrestrial. P.T.
> P.S. The petrifaction in my possession is an inch and three quarters wide, and seven inches in circumference.[55]

There is furthermore a surviving bill for ornamental stonework presented to the Corporation of Bath that links Thomas Parsons to Thomas Baldwin's 1783 rebuilding of the Cross Bath. The bill from Thomas Parsons dated August 1783 is signed as examined by Thomas Baldwin.[56] The account is as follows:[57]

Augt. 13 *1783*	*The Chamber of the City of Bath to* *Thomas Parsons*	
	1 Door-head including Architrave freeze	
	Tablet & Pilaster Caps, Stone masoning & Carving	2.13
	12 ½ feet Vitruvian Scroll D(itto) @ 2/3	1.8.1 ½
	8 Pateras, Stone masoning &c @ 12/	4.16
	6 Corinthian Capitals @ 1.11.6	9.9
	Carving Bladud & Vases in Relievo	10.10

---

[53] Ibid, 226.
[54] Ibid, 242.
[55] *Gentleman's Magazine*, 1788, lviii, 793.
[56] Manco, 1988, 72-73.
[57] Ibid, 84, Appendix 2: Stonemasons' Accounts.

Stone for the three Niches	2. 5
1 large Stone with 3 Pannels	2.12
72 feet of Festoon Freeze @ 4/	14. 8
2 pannels, festoons & flowers	2.10
1 Central Oval Pannel & Cross	<u>1.15</u>
Exd. Ths Baldwin	£52. 6. 1 ½

Until recent redevelopment as part of the Bath Spa Millennium project scheme the Thomas Parsons carving of 'Bladud' and the 'Vases in Relievo' were clearly visible through the openings or windows in the Cross Bath walls. The source for the carving of Bladud was clearly William Hoare's illustration printed by John Wood in his *A Description of* Bath. The story of Prince Bladud had become elaborated during the eighteenth century into the essential foundation myth of the city of Bath,[58] and was an essential adornment to the bathing facility. Consequently it seems, even before the death of his father, Thomas Parsons had carved out a varied and influential career and was himself active at the heart of Bath's industry and creativity.

Figure 19. Bladud by Thomas Parsons alongside its source

---

[58] Borsay, 2000, 49-58.

An Uneasy Succession

The Somerset Street church minutes for 13 March 1791 record:

> resolved...that after a trial of more than Eleven months, to give our Call and appoint our brother Jn Paul Porter to be the Pastor of this Church, Judging him to be a proper person for that solemn office being an Advocate for the truths of the Gospel.[59]

Thomas Parsons was not at all happy with the arrangements to continue the pastorate at Somerset Street. He considered that the church had compromised the wishes of his late father. When in 1791, therefore, the church meeting called John Paul Porter to be pastor there was some opposition, mostly centred on Parsons. Cater tells us that a number of members left to join another denomination, and Thomas Parsons published a letter against the church and new pastor.[60] In this letter dated March 1791 'To the Members of the Baptist Society, Meeting in Gerrard-Street, Bath', Parsons outlined some of the objections he had which forced him to terminate his 'professional connection' with the church that had lasted for more than twenty years, eighteen of which had been as Clerk. There was clearly a difference with the church as to whether he had voluntarily left the church, or whether they had excluded him. Although addressed to the whole church, Parsons' grievances are clearly towards those who were in leadership, the active deacons, 'who have been considered as principals in the management of your concerns', whose behaviour has been, he insists, 'consistent neither with the temper of the Gospel, friendship, or good manners; on the contrary, it has been expressive of incivility, affront and ingratitude.' He attacked the church as 'unscriptural' and relinquished all connection with it. He denounced John Paul Porter as 'ignorant of his profession' and a 'hot-headed Zealot', 'distgustful by his vulgarity'. And as for the services of worship, he said that 'in order to attract the multitude' they had converted 'the house of God into a place of amusement':

> ...instead of the long-established method of singing old-fashioned solemn tunes, once or twice in a service, you admitted the formation of a band, sung three times every service, and introduced a considerable number of tunes, new to most of you, in quicker time, with repeats, and of that light and airy kind which my Father really did, and which you pretended to abominate.

At its heart, Parsons' letter is an appeal to the simplicity and order of the church under his father. 'You had boasted', he continues, 'during a long period of time, of your plainness and simplicity in worship, and often censured with acrimony the modes of worship in other societies, as artful.' He cites other examples of

---

[59] SSBC, *Minutes*, 13 March 1791.
[60] Cater, 1834, 82; Parsons, 1791.

the way things had changed over the year since his father's death: the reports of a number of 'neighbouring Ministers' who had preached at the chapel and were 'disgusted' at 'your insulting manners' and subsequently declined to visit again; that church meetings 'as I am informed, begun without prayer, carried on with the most intemperate abuse and virulence, and ended in tumult and confusion', including the meetings that appointed Porter as pastor; a prayer meeting from which intended members were locked out; a new form of raising money by adopting pew rents; and so forth. Two personal criticisms are particularly worthy of note. Firstly,

> By the overbearing and impetuous exertions of a few, a party was formed, amongst which some of my Tenants and one of my Servants were included, the latter being very unjustifiably appointed to the Offices of Sexton and Gravedigger, although the discharge of the duties annexed to them must necessarily interfere with my service.

Some indication is given here of the social structures within the church fellowship, and the position of Thomas Parsons, as his father before him in the latter stages of his life, as someone of considerable means—an employer and landlord; and the degree of authority and respect that Thomas expected to receive. Thomas was clearly not his father, although there were certain similarities in their expectations. With the changing context there was increasing conflict and tension within the church, which had come to the surface at such a significant time as appointing a new pastor to succeed the pastor who had founded the church. Robert Parsons could never be replaced and in practice Thomas Parsons could never succeed his father.

That this change, and the break down of the old Baptist covenant community, was so significant is brought out in the second personal example cited in the letter:

> Your behaviour to Mr. Singers, your senior Deacon, and if I mistake not, your senior Member, who had preached to you and buried your dead gratuitously for some years, and to whose steady worth, all who knew him will bear testimony; is such as deserves sincere censure: for such a Man to be told on the face of the Church, *'that his name stank all round the Country,'* is such an instance of brutal indignity as degrades the reviler beneath contempt, as he knew at the moment he asserted it, that he was asserting a gross, self-invented calumny. Other instances of savage manners I could exhibit were it necessary.

Tempers were clearly heated by the events, such that it is difficult to discern what was actually going on beneath the surface. That Thomas Parsons was seriously affronted and upset by a community to which and to whom he had been passionately committed is clear. That the first years of John Paul Porter's pastorate were going to be difficult with Thomas Parsons on the scene is evident:

> you have on some occasions boasted that the late Mr. Holland was a learned Man; you have now elevated a Man to the Pulpit, the most ignorant in language that ever yet disgraced it: I wished for a Minister who would have disdained to have been made the tool of a party, who would have abhorred the promotion of strife and division in a Church, and whose reverence for the Scriptures would have preserved him from prostituting them to gratify his own resentments, or from torturing them to express what their divine Author never intended, but who would in meekness instruct those who opposed themselves: the reverse of all this you have chosen, for a very obvious reason, his ignorance impertinence and self-sufficiency were consecrated to your service, and through that medium your enmity and ill-will might operate with greater force against others, and with more safety to yourselves.

Although he concludes, 'I entertain a very good opinion of, and esteem for, many of the individuals who compose your Society', Parsons barely mitigates for the slanderous accusations made against the church and in particular its new minister. A number of important comments need to be made. Firstly, the reflection still in Parson's writing of the issue of learning and education alongside the call and empowerment for ministry. For Parsons, father and son, there are two different issues which they understand to have been confused. Learning is good, whilst ignorance is bad; the sufficiency of the Gospel in ministry is good, whilst self-sufficiency (or a reliance on worldly education and knowledge) in ministry is bad—this would seem to be a fair summary of what was at issue.

Secondly, the grace with which the Baptist community seemed to have received and accepted Thomas Parsons' attack is astonishing. Save the bare facts, there are no acrimonious references in the minute books. The period 1790 to 1791 would be one in which shock waves would travel through the Bath Baptist community, which from this point on would exhibit itself as increasingly fragmented. It might be suggested that it was necessary for there to be a break down of the old strictly controlled and regulated church under the covenant agreement and authority of the pastor for there to be any room for growth in the next period of its life. It might also be suggested that the composition of the church and its ability to respond to changes in its local context made apparent chaos and disorder inevitable. As we shall see, the next forty years were certainly marked by conflict and momentous change of one sort or another in the Bath Baptist community, but that remarkably this can be seen to have sprung out of rather than completely overturning the formative years of the church's life.

Thirdly, the degree of animosity thrown at John Paul Porter at the start of his ministry, and the criticism contained within the written record, makes it easy to understand why on his death John Paul Porter's widow should want the record set straight and asked Philip Cater to write his biography. Cater went to great pains to describe Porter's early life, his evangelical conversion, his early experience in preaching, and his acceptance by the dissenting church in Wokingham in June 1787.[61] It was in Wokingham that he was finally convinced about believers' baptism and was subsequently baptised by his friend T Davis, a Baptist minister in Reading.[62] Cater continues:

> Though Mr. Porter had now for some time been engaged in the exercise of preaching, he had never received a call to the ministry from any of his brethren according to the usual practice of dissenting churches, and being little disposed to defer to what he considered mere human opinion, he had never applied for one…He was afterwards however convinced that such a practice was consistent with Scripture, and conducive to the dignity and order of the Christian Church. He was now therefore regularly called to the ministry by the church of which he was a member, and to whom for some time he had preached the gospel.[63]

The emphasis is the familiar one of a ministry called by God, confirmed by the church, experienced, but nonetheless uneducated for the purposes of the ministry. In recognising John Paul Porter as their minister in 1791 the Bath Baptist community were confirming that they had indeed taken to heart many of the principles of the previous generation. Born on 16 December 1759, Porter had in his early life 'received a common education suited to that sphere of life in which it appeared he was destined to move.'[64] His preparation for ministry was experiential, through a great struggle of conscience and soul, until in 1787 he 'now felt that he should be willing to engage in the ministerial work, could he be persuaded that in so doing, he should act agreeably to the divine will.'[65] From the commencement of his ministry in Bath, Cater's account of Porter's ministry is one of great business and success, punctuated by times of anxiety but nonetheless productive. And from the start his views over the trouble with Thomas Parsons are described in tactful terms and with great diplomacy, revealing nothing of the acrimonious correspondence:

> Mr. Thomas Parsons was a man of strong mind and of liberal education: his pulpit exercises were generally very judicious, and even eloquent…He was a man far removed from dogmatism,

---

[61] Ibid, 25-47.
[62] Ibid, 53.
[63] Ibid, 55-56.
[64] Ibid, 25-26.
[65] Ibid, 45.

and was cautious lest he should avow any sentiment that was unsupported by the strongest evidence. His orthodoxy, whether well or ill founded, was certainly doubted by some of the people in Somerset Street Chapel. Whilst we maintain that an inquisitorial power in a church is utterly to be condemned, as inconsistent with mental freedom on the one hand, and mental imperfection on the other, yet it cannot be concealed that in the present case there was not in Mr. T. Parsons that candid avowal of his religious sentiments which could have been wished...The people being dissatisfied with his ministry, a separation between him and the church ensued. Some time afterwards he became afternoon lecturer on the Lord's day in the chapel occupied by Mr. Green, near St. James's Parade. This service was however only continued for a twelvemonth.[66]

But this wasn't the end of the situation.

On receipt of Thomas Parsons' letter the church decided to reply, again in print. *Remarks on a Printed Letter (Lately Published) and Addressed to the Members of the Baptist Society, Meeting in Gerrard Street, Bath, By Mr. Thomas Parsons* was issued in May 1791. It was issued anonymously by 'A Member of the Baptist Society' on behalf of the whole community, but it is clear from the minutes of the meeting that approved its publication that it was largely the work of Porter. At this same meeting the church excommunicated Parsons 'in consequence of his letter published to the world with an intention to injure the Church' and because he 'renounces all communion with us as a Religious Society'.[67] Lucy Parsons, Robert Parsons' widow by his third and final marriage, also absented herself from meeting with the church, as did Richard Singers, and after six months' notice to return was 'cut off'.[68]

The church's reply to Thomas Parsons' letter was written so that 'its abominable falsities may be set in a fair light.'[69] Its twenty-two pages go through each paragraph of Parsons' letter, point by point, demonstrating the false accusations and the truth as they saw it:

> The first paragraph informs us of the determination of the Author; which is, to "relinquish a professional connection which has subsisted more than twenty years."
>
> Strange, indeed, that a man possessed of such profound wisdom and deep penetration as Mr. Parsons, should be so extremely ignorant of church relation and discipline, as to imagine, that he

---

[66] Ibid, 79.
[67] SSBC, *Minutes*, May, 1791.
[68] SSBC, *Minutes*, November, 1792.
[69] *Remarks*, 1791, 3.

> can take that power to himself, which belongs to the whole community: as receiving members into a church is the act of the church, certainly the power of excommunication is lodged in the same hands.

The pamphlet continues:

> An individual may lay himself under the censure of the church, by his bad conduct, as you have done by your publication, which will plainly appear to all that are acquainted with the matter; and all religious societies that are desirous of taking the word of God for their rule will be careful to put the laws of Christ in execution (impartially) against all delinquents. [70]

It is unnecessary for the purposes of this study to go through each of the accusations in detail, only that each of the points was answered at some length. Yet the conclusion of the church is that Parsons had misunderstood or been misinformed about what was going on. The pamphlet supposes that Thomas Parsons' intentions were mainly for the purposes of self-publicity, as the following paragraphs illustrate:

> But we suppose Mr. Parsons was fearful that the populace would not know that he was in possession of some houses, in the city and suburbs; and therefore thinks it necessary to inform them, that *some* of his Tenants, and *one* of his Servants were of that party.

> What an impertinent lord-like declaration is this!—What can this have to do with church relation?—If all the members had been your tenants, that could not, nor at least *ought* not, in any sense, to affect them as members of society; for, however men may be situated in common life, whether in affluent or indigent circumstances, yet, in matters of Religion and Conscience, they are all upon a level; neither doth it reflect on the characters of the persons to whom you allude—rather it redounds to their honour, thus to hazard their interest for conscience sake; and, though you may be their Landlord, you have no right to lord it over their consciences.[71]

And in conclusion:

> Mr. Parsons seems to be thirsting for human applause, and we suppose him desirous that his name should be immortal: you have hit upon the means to accomplish your design; for we really think, that, in consequence of your *wonderful* performance,

---

[70] Ibid, 3-4.
[71] Ibid, 10-11.

> your name will be enrolled in the annals of Slander, when you are no more![72]

Thus the Bath Baptist community put the matter to rest publicly, and dealt with the resultant disciplinary matters within the confines of the community. The rift was healed in time and the church was keen to record in its minutes in April 1799 that

> it was unanimously agreed, consonant with similar Resolutions made nearly 4 Years since but omitted to be then inserted that the Widow Parsons, Mr Thos Parsons, Mr Richd Singer, at their Decease, be interred in the Burial Ground free of the usual Fine and that in future no person shall be buried without the usual Fines except those who have a legal right & that no Minister shall officiate at the interrment of any Person in that Ground but our own, without his & the Church's Consent.

Their burials were later recorded in the burial register: Lucy Parsons on 11 May 1812, aged 70 years; Richard Singer of St James's Parade on 16 May 1813, aged 90 years; and Thomas Parsons of Claverton Street on 24 September 1813, aged 69 years.

On departing the Baptist community Thomas Parsons was to move his attention to the Independent Congregation meeting at Argyle Chapel, where William Jay had built a highly reputable ministry. Here Parsons remained active until his death. The writer of Thomas Parsons' obituary paints a very different picture from the one painted by the details of his acrimonious dispute with the Baptist congregation:

> It has seldom fallen to the lot of any journalist to record the decease of an individual so deeply lamented, or so universally beloved. Few men possessed a more extensive acquaintance, and fewer still combined such rare qualifications.

> His knowledge of the Arts and Sciences was general; and, in the departments of Sculpture, Drawing, Chemistry, and Astronomy, he certainly excelled.

> His literary attainments were considerable. Possessed of a most acute understanding, he frequently employed his pen in defending the religious and civil rights of his fellow men; and his publications abundantly prove, that while his opponent had much to fear from his keen mode of investigation, he had nothing to dread on the score of personality or unfair conclusions. As a Poet, he was lively, humorous, and inclined to good-natured satire.

---

[72] Ibid, 21.

> In his domestic life, as Husband, Father, and Master, he was truly exemplary and endearing.
>
> As a Friend he was kind and sincere: to the young particularly easy of access, and communicative. His advice was much asked, and his sentiments always conveyed in that manner, which displayed at once the correctness of his judgment and the sincerity of his heart.[73]

Thomas Parsons' literary output was most pronounced in the period after his disconnection from the Baptist community, and so is strictly outside the detailed concern of this study. Yet it demonstrates in part some of the substance of the obituary account and the importance of his place in the wider Baptist community at a time of fragmentation and transition.

Parsons' Public Voice

In 1799 Parsons published an extended poem, *Effusions of Paternal Affection, on the Death of a Lovely Daughter*. The following year he issued his *Letters to a Member of the British Parliament, on the Absurdity of Popular Prejudices; The Causes of the Present High Price of Food; The Means of Speedy Alleviation; and The Measures Most Proper for Securing Future Plenty*, in which he argues profusely against the high taxation for the purposes of war which were increasing levels of poverty and prices of food, effecting the poor the most. As a vociferous advocate of peace, Parsons states persuasively:

> This is not a time for empty ceremony and false delicacy; everything momentous and essential to our well-being demands the acquisition of Peace. War provides neither "seed for the sower, nor bread for the eater:" Peace supplies both; cheers the glad earth with plenty, and renovates every charm of nature. To this object may all your energies be devoted![74]

Parsons' pacifist views were further developed in a series of letters to Thomas Falconer published in 1804. On 25 May 1804 Rev. Richard Warner, Rector of Chelwood and Great Chatfield, had preached a sermon entitled *War Inconsistent with Christianity*. This would have been less controversial were it not for the fact that the country was twelve years into a war, and there were a company of Bath Volunteers on parade with their officers in the congregation. A local battle raged, that through the power of the press became significantly greater. Rev. Thomas Falconer had published against Warner, so Thomas Parsons rallied to the defence of Warner with two substantial letters to Falconer which were published later in 1804. The first, *Christianity, a System of Peace: A Letter to the Rev. Thomas Falconer; in which a Vindication of the Subject of the Rev. Richard Warner's*

---

[73] *Bath and Cheltenham Gazette*, 22 September 1813.
[74] Parsons, 1800, 38.

Sermon, entitled "War inconsistent with Christianity," is attempted; the second. *A Second Letter to the Rev. Thomas Falconer; in which The Arguments adduced in Support of Defensive War are examined; and a further Vindication of the subject of Rev. Richard Warner's Sermon, is attempted.* The local debate had clearly been raging in the pages of the *Bath Chronicle* and other newspapers,[75] but Parsons' contribution clearly had more lasting and far reaching consequences for the campaign against warfare and violence. In his study of European pacifism, Peter Brock quotes the nineteenth-century Quaker, Joseph Crosfield, as commenting that up to this time 'there was nothing presented to the public so replete with sound argument, and in so mild, so polite, and so appropriate a style',[76] and argues that Parsons' was an influential and persuasive argument, making the point that warfare in whatever guise was inconsistent with 'the placid genius of the gospel'. As a Baptist voice in the public arena, Thomas Parsons eloquently makes his case quoting widely works of Biblical scholarship, theology and moral philosophy in ways which would have been quite unknown to his father, Robert. Yet like his father, at the end of his sophisticated argument in which he is adept, Thomas focuses on the simple straightforward truth of the Biblical text as he sees it. For example:

> Can it be imagined, that our Lord and his apostles, by their silence on this head, connived at or countenanced the passion of the Romans for extending their arms, and subjugating the whole human race? It is rational to suppose, that he, who preached deliverance to the captives, would lend even the slightest encouragement to a haughty people, whose potent legions kept in slavish subjection the greatest part of the world, to persist in their sanguinary progress, and to detain their ill-gotten conquests?[77]

Further, Parsons argues:

> Cornelius and his connections under the instruction of St. Peter, received the extraordinary gifts of the Holy Ghost; they spake with tongues, and magnified GOD. Now is it credible, that supernatural powers were communicated to these soldiers, for the purpose of their continuing in the same situation and employment as before? Is it not more reasonable to infer, that these miraculous gifts, by which they were qualified to propagate the Gospel, should lead them to engage in that service; and, relinquish the weapons of war, induce them to become the heralds of salvation?[78]

---

[75] Parsons, 1804b, 26.
[76] Brock, 1972, 372.
[77] Parsons, 1804b, 22.
[78] Ibid, 23-4.

As his father had welcomed peace at the end of the Seven Years' War some forty years earlier, Thomas was now commenting at the height of the Napoleonic Wars. There was a great deal of consistency between father and son, yet enormous differences – mainly in the area of their own education and learning. Parsons' final publication appeared in 1808 under the title *High Church Claims Exposed, and the Dissenters and Methodists Vindicated*, in which he again rallied to the defence of a cause that was close to his heart. Here he betrays that despite his sojourn with the Independent congregation under the ministry of William Jay, and his extensive intellect, he is truly an eighteenth-century Baptist in the strict but evangelical Calvinistic mould of his father. An extended quotation from the final section of the pamphlet demonstrates this well, and ties together much of what we have already discussed above about the nature of church, ministry, education, understanding of Scripture and the propagation of the Gospel:

> That there are many individuals who sincerely believe that religious establishments are not favourable to the promotion of the christian religion, I admit; but I deny that such a sentiment is connected with any want to loyalty, or an inclination to resort to any arguments but what the New Testament and sound reasoning will supply and sanction. Such an opinion may very naturally arise in the mind, not of an *idiot*, but of a man of seriousness and sound intellect, and may as naturally coalesce with a knowledge of the *real church of Christ*, much superior to that which many pretend to have acquired. If you will indulge me with a moderate degree of patience, I will tell you why I think so. I suppose then, a sober intelligent person, free from any strong previous bias, to read and study the New Testament, for the purpose of obtaining a clear knowledge of the subject. The New Testament being written before the formation of established national churches, it is very obvious to suppose, that, unless they correspond exactly with the description there given, he must discern the difference. He will learn from that pure source of information, the principles on which the primitive church was formed, and the construction of the society so denominated. It will be totally impossible for him to find there the superfluities you have specified, because they had not then an existence. He will see there a concise, but succinct account of the voluntary associations of believers, united together in the same faith, professing subjection to the Lord Jesus Christ, and cherishing mutual love, and personal holiness; but not a word of creeds, and articles of faith. He will see Jesus Christ to be an high priest over the household of God, but not the most distant hint of an order of priests under him, and over them. And instead of the church being national, and protected and

supported by the civil government, and incorporated with it, that it was extended through a great part of the world, in direct opposition to all the established religions existing at that period, destitute as christians then were of the countenance and aid of the civil power. I really hope that there are many sufficiently capable of understanding their bibles, and very warmly attached to them, who may have formed such notions of a gospel church, as the New Testament suggests, without being subjected to the charge of ignorance, or of being factious. Nor is there anything criminal in the supposition, that a person, having acquired a settled standard idea of the primitive church, may compare therewith churches now existing, and very properly estimate the proportionable excellence of each, as it appears to approximate, or recede from the original pattern. And if in the exercise of a benevolent principle, he make liberal allowances for early prejudices, long-established customs, and even surreptitious appendages, which time and venerable names have combined to sanction, and so supply the term—church of Christ as to comprehend christians of all descriptions, yet he deserves no reprehension for preferring that society, which appears to him most nearly to resemble the first christian churches as described in the New Testament, from whence we have supposed his ideas to be derived.[79]

The view of church expressed here in this important passage is directly connected with the Baptist church community Robert Parsons had established in the city, had defined with a covenant document, and defended on every available opportunity: a 'voluntary association of believers' based on the simplicity of the Gospel under the sovereignty of Christ and no other authority – a gathered Gospel community. Wherever his temporary home, Thomas Parsons was spiritually at home in the Baptist fold, and whether consciously or not was advocating its principles and expressing his Baptist identity to the wider community. Indeed the fact that he was never truly at peace amongst the Independents was hinted at by William Jay in his funeral sermon, *The Loss of Connexions Deplored and Improved*, which he preached for Parsons on Sunday morning 26 September 1813.[80] After commenting on and illustrating Thomas Parsons' 'good, though not a learned education' and 'early discovered very superior powers of mind, which he constantly cultivated by reading and exercise'[81] Jay focused on those things in which Thomas seemed so similar to his father:

---

[79] Parsons, 1808, 80-82.
[80] Jay, 1813, 33-4.
[81] Ibid, 24.

> He loathed indeed every thing that bordered on the spiritual coxcomb; and scrupled not to make free with inflated academicians, and all those, who by their confident and self-conceited manner, seemed more than satisfied with their own performances, and defied rather than depreciated criticism. But he always esteemed grace more than talent. He often remarked, that stirling and elevated piety, in the simplest character, is far superior to the finest intellect, and the most extensive acquirements unassociated with the fear of God.[82]

In commemoration of his passing, Thomas Parsons earned a monody from the pen of John Thomas, printed in the *Bath and Cheltenham Gazette*. It included amongst its fifteen verses the following:

> I see thee, heav'n-sir'd maid, in tears deplore
> That PARSONS' great solicitudes are o'er,—
> Or when the public weal his precepts fir'd,
> Or chaste religious zeal his pen inspir'd.
>
> Now in dark caverns found, or from yon field
> Etherial drawn, thy griefs, bright Science, yield;
> To thine let Wit and Learning join their woes:
> Where fire celestial dwelt corruption grows.[83]

There is a sense in which this melodramatic gesture heralds the end of an era, an era in which the neo-classical muses and the providence of old Calvinistic Dissent were merged; and from which things were to become more chaotic albeit productive.

---

[82] Ibid, 25-26.
[83] *Bath and Cheltenham Gazette*, 24 November 1813. 'Monody on the Death of Mr Thomas Parsons' by John Thomas.

Chapter 5: Growth and Fragmentation

Gospel Propagation in Twerton

The significance of the changes that the passing of Robert Parsons, the removal of his son Thomas, and the new ministry of John Paul Porter brought about should not be underestimated. Although Porter was still keen to hold tightly onto the reigns, the gates of the strictly walled community had at least been opened sufficiently in the turmoil of succession to allow for new possibilities. This is best illustrated by reference to what was happening at Twerton, the industrial village on the Bristol side of Bath along the Avon that was by the early nineteenth century fully annexed as part of the city. The early history of the Baptists in Twerton has not previously been fully told, yet the story is significant for it practically demonstrates the spreading of the Gospel by Baptists in the villages around Bath, and shows the transition from a small village preaching station dependant on its mother church and a supply of itinerant preachers to a fully fledged Baptist community in its own right. Twerton was one of the destinations around Bath for the itinerant preachers who continued to emerge from the Baptist community in the city, and who we have identified above.

There had been Baptists living in the Twerton area in the seventeenth and early eighteenth centuries, Twerton being immediately adjacent to Haycombe. On 15 January 1754 Robert Strudick, a member of the Baptist church in Bath, licensed his house in the village for 'Anabaptists'.[1] The Bath Baptist burial register names several others living in the village, one of whom 'was drown'd in Newton River' and buried at Walcot on 24 August 1792.[2] For their Sunday worship, throughout the course of the eighteenth century, Twerton Baptists had to make the regular and often difficult journey into Somerset Street Chapel in the city. In 1804 members of Somerset Street took over a house in Twerton belonging to Walter Tanner so that they could worship in the village, and regular preachers were supplied from the 'mother church' in Bath.[3] On December 25 1804 the minister at Somerset Street, Rev. John Paul Porter, recorded in his diary, 'Preached at Twerton, opened a new place of worship, may the Lord bless the attempt.'[4]

It must be assumed that during the first few years things went smoothly, because it is four years before the Baptist group at Twerton were brought to the attention of the church at Somerset Street. The Twerton members had written a letter to Somerset Street, and two of the deacons, Opie Smith and Robert Goldstone, were in January 1808 sent to investigate. What the content of the

---

[1] SRO, Q/RRW 1. Clerk of Peace Returns, 1852.
[2] TNA, RG4. *Bath Baptist Burial Register*, 24 August 1792.
[3] *Baptist Magazine*, i, 38; SRO, D/D/RM. *Dissenters Certificates*, 26 December 1804.
[4] Cater, 1834, 100.

letter was, and what Smith and Goldstone were to investigate is not totally clear, although it had something to do with the arrangements at Twerton becoming more permanent, and were associated with them building their own premises. This was causing the church at Somerset Street some concern, so in May 1808 Opie Smith was sent, this time with James Thomas, to visit their fellow member and local builder Richard Harris regarding 'his views and designs concerning the Meeting House intended to be built at Twerton'.[5] Reporting back to the church, Harris emphasised that the Meeting House he was helping to build was to be 'fully under management of this Church, and is a branch of the same — And that no individual shall have any ruling power either as to filling the pulpit or otherwise, but as approved and appointed by this Church.'[6] So Somerset Street would be in control. It transpires that the Twerton congregation had outgrown their original hired meeting room and they had decided to build a more suitable and larger place for worship—demonstrating their initial success.

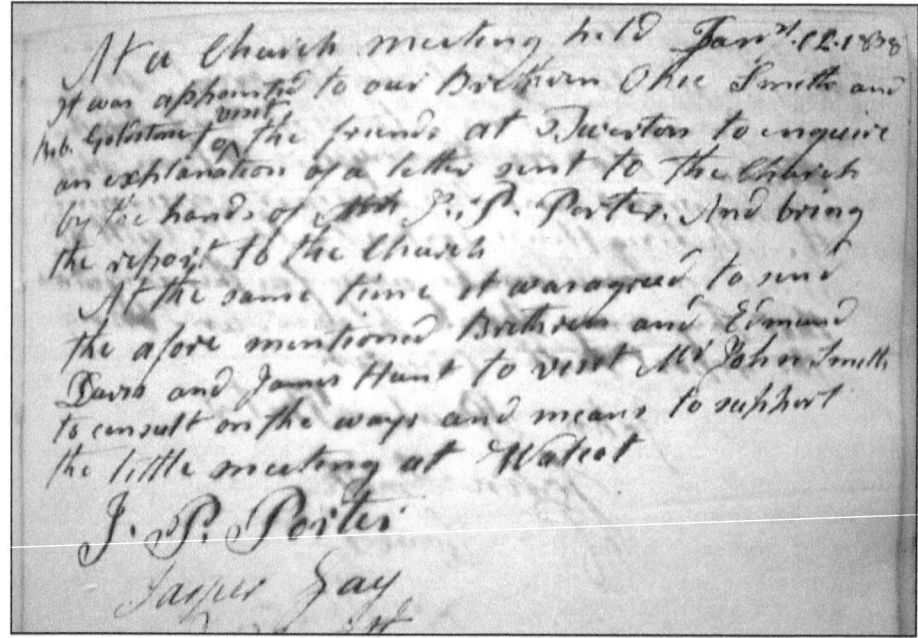

Figure 20. Opie Smith and Robert Goldstone sent to Twerton

James Thomas was appointed secretary and treasurer, to organise subscriptions for building the meeting house, and on 6 September the completed building was opened, seating 300 hearers![7] Richard Harris, who had been called to exercise a preaching ministry by Somerset Street in 1805,[8] was appointed to supply the

---

[5] SSBC, *Minutes*, 3 May 1808.
[6] Ibid, 15 July 1808.
[7] *Baptist Magazine*, i, 38.
[8] SSBC, *Minutes*, 22 October 1805; 17 December 1805; 22 December 1805.

pulpit at Twerton on a regular basis. As we have seen, it was common practice to approve local preachers in this way. Originally this arrangement was for three months, but it was renewed so that when, in 1812, the account books were audited they 'found them very correct, and balanced within three pounds — they declare that much praise is due to Brother Harris for his unwearied exertions.'[9] However, in 1814 Richard Harris relinquished his oversight of Twerton, and after careful examination Henry Crook was in 1815 chosen to replace him.[10] Like Harris, Crook had been called by Somerset Street to the preaching ministry in 1814.[11]

With Richard Harris as overseer, Twerton had been safely under the control of Somerset Street. With the newly appointed Crook at the helm things were not so certain. He had been responsible for 'the concerns of the place both as to Spirituals and Temporals' for only a year when in December 1816 Somerset Street received a letter from the members at Twerton asking to be formed into a separate church, or to be permitted to receive the ordinance of the Lord's Supper at Twerton. Twerton members had all this while still been obliged to travel into Bath for communion. Their request was swiftly rejected by Somerset Street on the grounds that 'The Title Deed forbids the former — and the latter is repugnant to the mind of the minister.'[12] There is no record of the original Title Deed for the site, so no indication whether there really was any bar on independence. It certainly wasn't an issue a decade later. Why communion should be objectionable to Porter is equally curious, save that there was an understanding that Somerset Street was a 'closed communion' church, which ensured that the communion table was open only to members. The mother church maintained control, and in her view there was really only one community—so the proper place for communion was at the Somerset Street table. Unless the appropriate safeguards were in place at Twerton, there could be no communion there. Yet for the members at Twerton all hope was not lost. Since Henry Crook could no longer supply the pulpit every week, a team was appointed to preach at Twerton, which included Opie Smith, Henry Crook, Richard Harris, Thomas Langdon, and Rev. John Paul Porter himself.[13] The Twerton members were grieved, not having intended their request to upset the city church. They appealed to Porter, arguing that either he or another person could administer communion at Twerton. Porter appears to have agreed to this arrangement—it was not so repugnant an idea after all—and other arrangements were also easily dealt with. Richard Harris was again given charge of the pulpit, and James Thomas was appointed as treasurer, with power to 'appoint a Sexton to open the doors from time to time, and to keep the house

---

[9] Ibid, 20 August 1812.
[10] Ibid, 30 March 1815.
[11] Ibid, 3 April 1814.
[12] Ibid, 5 December 1816.
[13] Ibid, 19 June 1817.

aired &c. &c.'[14] The Twerton community had started to take on its own character and identity.

Although formally attached to Somerset Street Chapel as a preaching station, the young church at Twerton was active and successful in its own right. The meeting house was regularly in use. Not only was there regular preaching, and now the occasional Lord's Supper, but from early on they had considered work among children to be a priority. From now on their work with local children accelerated. The Baptist Sunday School, the first to be formed in the village, started in 1810. The Annual Report for the year ending 24 June 1817 describes why this work was so important to them:

> GRATUITOUS Religious Instruction of Poor Children is now acknowledged to be so universally important, that any attempt to prove its utility might be deemed superfluous. The Conductors of the Twerton Sunday School therefore humbly submit to the inspection of their Friends and Benefactors the Annual Report of the Baptist School, and while they retrace with pleasure the liberal Contributions which on past occasion they have received from their Friends, are encouraged to hope that the present appeal on behalf of the Poor Children now under their care will not be made to a Benevolent Public in vain.
>
> Amidst the general gloom which once overspread the Poor of this our highly favoured Country, the Children of Twerton lay buried in ignorance;
>
> > For Knowledge to their eyes her ample page,
> > Rich with the spoils of Time, did ne'er unroll;
>
> until a few friends of the Baptist connexion, deploring the destitute condition of the benighted Children of Twerton, established this Sunday School, which has since been taken under the auspices of the Bath Sunday School Union; to the Committee and Secretaries of which Institution the Conductors return their most grateful thanks, and acknowledge the obligations they are under for the very kind assistance which they have repeatedly received. [15]

The remainder of the report is worth quoting in full because it highlights not only the pioneering nature of the educational endeavour of the Baptist community in Twerton, but also because it explicitly connects the general education of their local children with the planting of Gospel ideals and virtues that were so lacking in the village. As we have seen above in our discussion of

---

[14] Ibid, 29 July 1817.
[15] TBC, 1817. *Sunday School Annual Report.* The report was framed and was recently still seen hanging in the vestibule of the now closed Twerton Baptist Church.

various reactions to itinerant preachers, such as were active in Twerton, the Bath Sunday School Union founded in 1813 played an active part—and Twerton was an active member from early on. Philip Cliff's study of the Sunday School movement would suggest that the Twerton experience was fairly typical of what was happening across the country at this time.[16] Yet amongst Bath Baptists the Twerton Sunday School was the first. Somerset Street Baptist Sunday School didn't begin until 1812, when on 25 June it was 'agreed to commence a Sunday School on a small scale which we hope to enlarge as the Lord shall enable us.'[17] A girls' school was started in the Somerset Street vestry in February 1813, with a boys' school meeting at 73 Avon Street. Starting on a 'small scale' they soon grew, such that in 1814 a purpose built Sunday School was erected in Milk Street. Opie Smith and Thomas Langdon, names associated also with Twerton, were among the committee of the Somerset Street Sunday School, although there is evidence that it continually struggled so that 'the Church feels the pressure of debt on the School Building in Milk Street', and it was sold to the Methodists in 1844.[18] The 1817 Annual Report of the Twerton school continued:

> Although the present report cannot boast of an increase during the past year in the number of Children receiving instruction in the School, yet, when it is considered that during the past year two new Schools have been opened in the Village, one by the Wesleyan Friends at their newly erected Chapel, and the other by the respected Members of the established Church, it is a pleasing reflection, for every liberal mind, as well as cause for great thankfulness, from the Managers and Teachers, that (while the number of Children attending this School for Instruction have diminished) they have been, under God, the honoured instruments of provoking their fellow Christians to "Love and to Good Works."
>
> The Conductors and Teachers of this School, in common with Benevolent Christians, rejoice at every attempt made and every Institution formed, for promoting the Circulation of the Sacred Scriptures, the overturning of Ignorance and Vice, the establishing of Knowledge and Virtue, the good of Society, and the glory of God; and thank him who is the "Giver of all good," that their existence is placed in a land where, at a time when, Christians of various denominations around them are zealously employed in "Training up Children in the way they should go," and accomplishing the pious wish of our beloved Sovereign, by

---

[16] Cliff, 1986, 72-93.
[17] SSBC, *Minutes*, 25 June 1812.
[18] *Centenary Record*, June 1912.

> first placing the Bible in the hands of Poor Children, (without distinction as to sect or party,) and then instructing them to read its sacred pages, which, by the blessing of God attending the perusal, are able to make "wise unto salvation."

Yes, the Twerton Baptist community were motivated by religious and spiritual values, but it is also apparent that they were as much concerned to transform the behaviour, prospects and usefulness of their young people in the community as a whole. As the report continues the Baptist community was keen to demonstrate that it was a valuable and significant part of the wider community, as well as improving the employment prospects of the young people of Twerton:

> Much pleasing information might be adduced concerning the readiness manifested, and pleasure experienced, by some of the Children, in committing to memory various portions of the sacred volume; but the limits of this brief statement will not admit it. Neither can the Conductors enter into any detail of a MISSIONARY ASSOCIATION lately formed at the request of the Children, but must refer their friends for particulars respecting it, as well as respecting the Sunday Evening Religious Meetings, account of a fund raising by the Teachers for the Relief of Sick and Destitute Children, &c. to the ANNUAL SERMONS.
>
> In order that the Children may, as much as possible, during the week reap the benefits of the Instruction imparted to them on the Sabbath, a Library has been formed for the sole use of the School, which at present contains nearly one hundred volumes, of such Religious and Moral Publications as are considered most likely to prove instructive and entertaining to the Children. By means of the Teachers and Children the greater part of these books are circulated through the Village every Sunday.
>
> During the past year, many of the elder Boys and Girls, who had received that Instruction which it is the design of this Institution to afford, have left the School, grateful for the pains bestowed on them by their Teachers. Most of them are now living in places of servitude, and several are occupying, with credit to themselves and satisfaction to their employers, various situations in the adjacent City.
>
> On reference to the statement of accounts, it will be seen that a small balance is due to the Treasurer, for the liquidating of which and defraying the necessary expenses of the School, during the ensuing year, the Conductors deem it useless to say anything more, by way of recommendation, than that the

Institution for which they are now soliciting support, may justly be considered the PARENT OF THE TWERTON SUNDAY-SCHOOLS.

Attached to the Annual Report was a statement of accounts from 24 June 1816, to 24 June 1817, which illustrates briefly some of the Sunday School activities described.

Dr.	£	s	d
Amount of Subscriptions, Donations, & Collections,	17	16	0
Books sold to Children,	1	1	6
Balance due to Treasurer,		13	7
	19	11	1

Cr.	£	s	d
Balance of last year's account,	2	16	9
Printing,	1	8	6
Given to Bath Sunday School Union,	2	0	0
Carpenter's Bill,	1	1	1
Library,	2	6	10
Books, Paper, Pens, Ink, &c.	6	15	7
Sundries, including new pipe for Stove, Coals, &c. &c.	3	2	4
	19	11	1

Examined and approved by James Cadby, John Hayter, John Wadham.

Although Smith, Crook, Harris and Langdon were the committee from Somerset Street responsible for Twerton, it is clear from this rare surviving record that Twerton was for the large part looking after its own day to day affairs. Local members James Cadby, John Hayter and John Wadham had examined and approved the accounts—although of course all Twerton members were still first and foremost members of the mother church at Somerset Street. What is significant is that from this point forward it is the names of locals such as Cadby, Hayter and Wadham that feature as important figures in the church at Twerton—and constitute its embryonic leadership—further demonstrating a move towards independence. Account books survive for activities between 1814 and 1816 that give greater detail to the stationary bill highlighted in the 1817 Annual Report. Paper, pens and ink were constantly needed; and also quills, copy books, writing books, arithmetic tables, and a good supply of coal for the stove. There is no record of actual numbers of pupils, although the relative size can be estimated as the accounts record that in April 1816 £1.13s.4d. was spent on 400 buns for the Easter treat.

John Paul Porter's Success

The hiatus caused in the Somerset Street church around the death of Robert Parsons and the appointment of John Paul Porter was reflected in a slight dip in the membership figures around 1791, some of which is accounted for by Thomas Parsons and those associated with him leaving to worship elsewhere. **Figure 21** plots the membership of Somerset Street from 1789 until 1837, and it shows that far from the disaster that Thomas Parsons had indicated John Paul Porter's was a most successful period of ministry. From his appointment in 1791 until 1818 when it reached its peak, a period of nearly thirty years, the church continued to grow year on year. We have already seen this trend in the figures plotted for the Western Baptist Association. In the Bath church the trend is particularly pronounced. For the following two decades, however, the record shows an equally pronounced decline in membership, and a gap in the records until 1835.

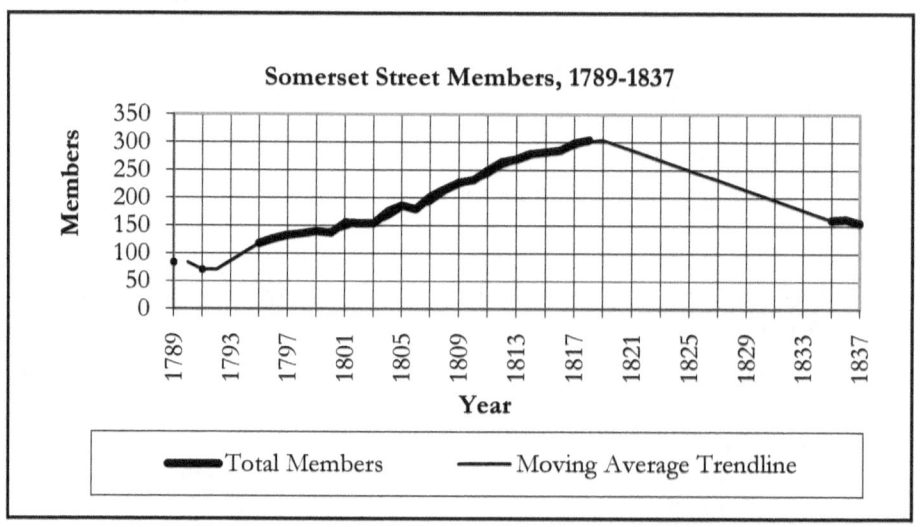

Figure 21. Somerset Street Members, 1789-1837.

It is possible to compare the growth pattern seen at Somerset Street with firstly the Western Association churches together, and secondly with national trends for Baptists and other Dissenters during the eighteenth and early nineteenth centuries. In each case the pattern discovered by A D Gilbert can be observed: steady growth, where there is growth, throughout the eighteenth century until 1790 when there is rapid growth until the 1830s.[19] At Somerset Street growth was remarkable, with an increase of about three hundred percent in a little

---

[19] Gilbert, op. cit, 32-42. See also Currie, Gilbert & Horsley, 1977. The main national growth factor is the delayed influence of the Evangelical Revival; among Baptist churches additional impetus came from the theology of Andrew Fuller countering the effects of high Calvinism and the new missionary movement inspired by William Carey and others.

under twenty years. There was a major crisis within Somerset Street around 1828, preceded and surrounded by a number of secessions and the dismissal of members to form other churches, such as at Twerton – thus in 1835 Somerset Street's membership was diminished for some considerable time.

One of the major positive factors towards growth at Somerset Street was John Paul Porter himself. Philip Cater's biography of Porter shows that his early ministry was energetic and busy. He was engaged not just in Bath, but involved in projects further afield, such as the formation of the Aged and Infirm Baptist Minister's Society — a momentous step in an era without pensions and extreme poverty.[20] Porter was also involved in the formation of the *Baptist Magazine* of which he was a founding proprietor, and he was busy in the life of the Western Baptist Association which Somerset Street had since rejoined.

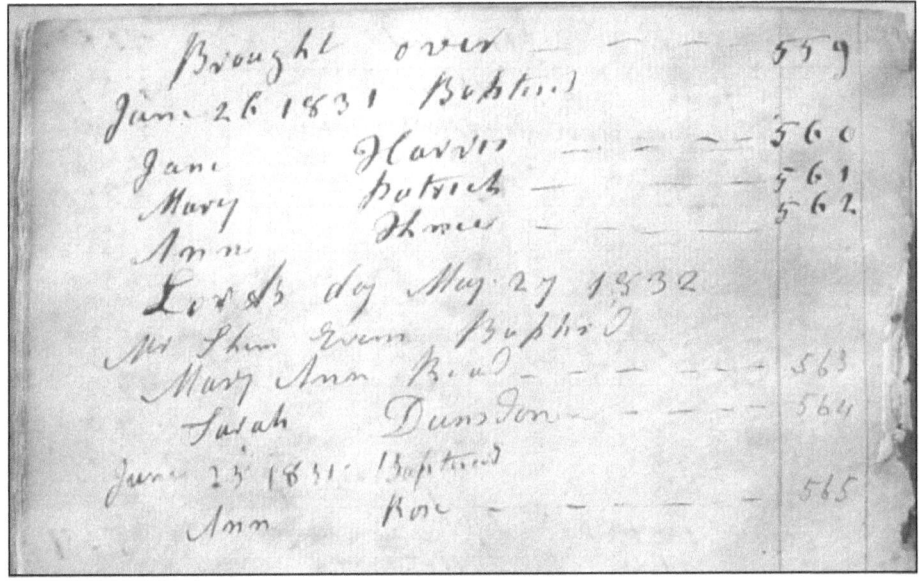

Figure 22. John Paul Porter's Baptism Record

As a preacher, John Paul Porter not only filled the pulpit in his own church but also travelled within the Association, and occasionally further away. Yet his primary commitment was to Somerset Street, and the preaching of the Gospel there. In the surviving Somerset Street archive is a notebook with the heading 'The Names of the Persons baptiz'd by John Paul Porter at Bath & the time when they were baptiz'd & join'd the Church'. It is clear from the evidence of

---

[20] Sherring, 1908. John Paul Porter was first Secretary from its formation in 1816 until his death; likewise Opie Smith was first Treasurer, succeeded by his nephew James Grant Smith in 1837. Douglas Sparkes' comment that this was 'frequently known as the "Bath Society"' springs from the fact that for the first twenty years of its life this benevolent society was run from the vestry of Somerset Street Baptist Church. Sparkes, 1996, 5.

the book that there was no separation of baptism from membership – those baptised through Somerset Street were baptised into membership of the church, and this was and continued to be their customary practice. **Figure 23** shows the number of people baptised by Porter during the course of his ministry, and it can be seen that there were a number of baptisms each year. There were more baptisms some years than others, and the fifteen years between 1805 and 1820 were most fruitful. It is possible from the list of names to analyse the numbers according to gender, and thus is can be seen that more women were baptised than men, although there were years when that was reversed. At the end of the list the totals are given. John Paul Porter baptised 621 people, of whom 554 were from Somerset Street and 67 from other places. There is no indication when or where these other places were, although Hetling Court and Dunkerton are named as accounting for eight baptisms between them. The remarkable record shows that John Paul Porter made a considerable evangelistic contribution through his ministry in this way.

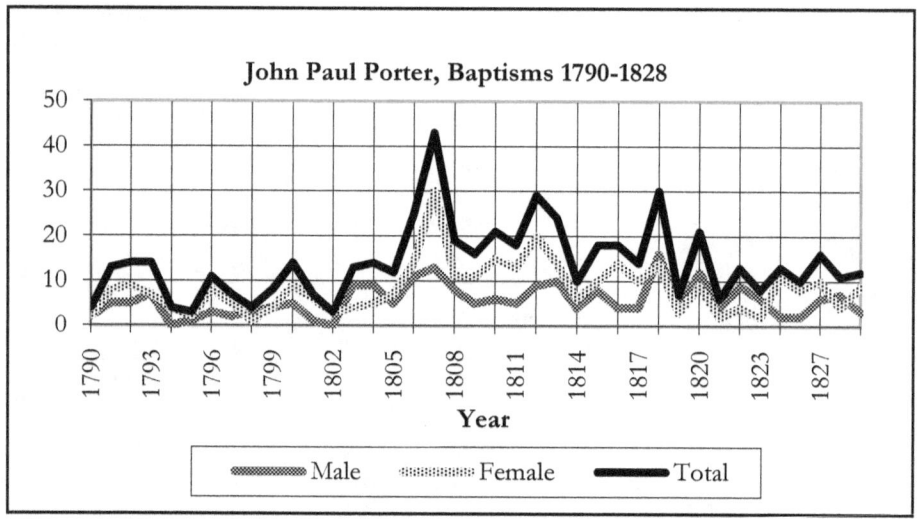

Figure 23. John Paul Porter, Baptisms 1790-1828

Yet there were negative factors too in the early years of the nineteenth century leading to the fragmentation and eventual diminishing of Somerset Street's membership. Philip Cater recalls how on one occasion in 1792, early in his ministry at Bath, Porter had been called by one of the deacons to meet William Huntington, 'one of the most singular characters of his day.' Cater continues:

> In the interview between Mr. Porter and this singular character, no invitation was given to Mr. H. to occupy the pulpit in Garrard Street. To some of the members, this was a very serious and even sinful omission on the part of Mr. Porter, not easily to be forgiven or overlooked. One of the usual effects of Mr.

Huntington's preaching, was to make the people to whom he addressed himself, dissatisfied with their own minister.[21]

This indeed happened in Bath, and several members of the congregation followed Huntington to Bradford on Avon where he was preaching next. As a leading high Calvinist Huntington's preaching would have appealed to a number of the Bath congregation who were still in the early days of transition from the strict Calvinism of Robert Parsons to the clearly evangelical Calvinism of John Paul Porter.[22]

There is considerable material in Cater's *Memoirs* of Porter to piece together other times in Porter's ministry when similar things happened. In 1809 Porter recorded in his diary:

> Jan. 11. "A friend introduced a minister in the vestry wishing me to ask him to preach in the evening; but this I declined because he was a stranger.
>
> 15th. "This evening our prayer meeting was thinly attended: the aforesaid minister preached at a house in Walcot; he insinuated that I did not preach the gospel, and some of our people were busily employed in persuading the people to leave the chapel to hear him. I felt grieved, but the Lord supported me.[23]

There is little clue in Cater as to who this minister was, although Oliver suggests that he was from Manchester and subscribed to the teachings of William Gadsby.[24] It may well have been William Warburton, the Lancashire weaver and early convert of Gadsby, who was touring the West Country at this time and was later minister for forty years at Trowbridge.[25] Another clue to the identity of the preacher comes from the letters of William Gadsby. In a letter from Manchester in March 1809 to Mr Robins, minister at Gower Street, London, Gadsby writes:

> I am truly sorry for the Bath friends, and wish it was in my power to assist them; but I do not see a way at present. For me to go to London or go there without a view of getting a supply would be wrong. Could I see a way I should like to go to Bath a Lord's day or two; but as you seem to think you cannot come to Manchester this year, I see no way at present of either being at Bath or London.[26]

---

[21] Cater, 1834, 86.
[22] For Huntington see Dix, 2001, 6-29.
[23] Ibid, 109.
[24] Oliver, 1968, 86.
[25] Underwood, 1947, 186. For Warburton see Broome, 1996.
[26] Gadsby, 1884, 431. Until recently this clue was lost, for the letters appended to the original published volume of Gadsby's sermons have been omitted from the 1991 reprint.

Gadsby continued to encourage his 'Bath friends' as best he could. A C Underwood explains how the followers of Gadsby were accused of Antinomianism, but continues:

> They were not Antinomians, though they preached so much about being no longer under the law but under grace, that they gave their opponents some pretext for charging them with that heresy.[27]

Whoever this preacher actually was, feathers were ruffled at Somerset Street, and the disappearance of some members to form another meeting with the stranger caused a great strain. The Somerset Street minute book records that in 1809 and 1810 various members were brought before the church meeting for disaffection. One was 'saying that our Minister does not preach the gospel insinuating that there is much hidden evil in the church',[28] and another suggesting 'Mr Porter's ministry defective in as much as he does not insist on the various operations of the Spirit in the special application of the Word and that the Church is too easy of access in the admission of members.'[29] One member even reported 'that Mr Porter's ministry was not any longer profitable to him and as it was starving his soul to come here he thought he had a right to go elsewhere to seek food'.[30] On the one hand Porter's ministry at this time was visited with much success, and the church thriving; on the other the clash of high Calvinism against his own evangelicalism caused Porter great anxiety. Such was the crisis that Porter wrote in his diary:

> The Antinomians are litigious and impudent; but I am determined not to answer them a word: if they curse may I bless, if they do ill may I do well; if they preach error, may I preach truth; if they breathe their own spirit, may I breathe the spirit of Christ…This afternoon excluded thirteen persons from the church, ten of the Antinomian party and three others. This was trying, but needful. May this painful piece of discipline be blessed to the offending party and to the Church at large.[31]

This was 20 May 1810. From what we have already said about Porter's involvement in the *Baptist Magazine* it is significant that the 1810 and 1811 volumes both contain long articles against Antinomianism.[32]

The excluded members took rooms in Parsonage Lane which they converted for worship,[33] which *The Original Bath Guide* describes as follows:

---

[27] Underwood, op. cit, 187.
[28] SSBC, *Minutes*, 17 October 1809.
[29] Ibid, 31 October 1809.
[30] Ibid, 7 November 1809.
[31] Cater, 1834, 112-113.
[32] Cater, 1834, 111.

A part of Mr PORTER'S congregation has recently seceded from his meeting-house, and assemble in a large room in Parsonage-lane, fitted up for a chapel, where prayers and preaching take place at the same hours as at the chapel in Somerset-street. Mr Thomas Dobney is the preacher.[34]

Figure 24. Portrait of John Paul Porter

---

[33] SRO, D/D/RM. *Dissenters' Certificates*, 28 November 1809.
[34] *The Original Bath Guide*, 1811.

In 1811 they moved to a newly built chapel in York Street, which was opened by William Gadsby.[35] This new building was described as 'a neat building, with galleries round the walls'.[36] There were a short succession of ministers, a number of them unknown, including Edmund Robbins from 1811 to 1815, and David Denham, the hymn writer who later settled in Plymouth, in 1815. Gadsby was always keen to visit Bath, but was seldom able. He writes from Plymouth to Manchester in January 1822 that 'The friends at Bath wanted me to promise to stop there one Lord's day; but I told them I could not do so.'[37] For a short time York Street was the centre of a missionary drive into Wiltshire which would result in a network of Gospel Standard Baptist churches.[38] John Broome describes the contrast between Somerset Street and York Street in terms of acceptance or rejection of the 'Modern Question' or teachings of Andrew Fuller.[39] Although York Street's presence was felt strongly at the time of its formation and for a few years afterwards, this congregation did not last long in Bath, unlike some other cities,[40] which was becoming a strong evangelical centre. The Strict Baptist churches that did survive in Bath did not emerge until well into the nineteenth century. By 1828 the York Street building was empty, at which time it came to be used by another seceding group from Somerset Street.

The Somerset Street of John Paul Porter in the nineteenth century was now very different from that under Robert Parsons in the eighteenth. Along with an expanded congregation came a new participation in the Western Association, as has been shown above. The Bath church's membership of the Association had ceased soon after Robert Parsons' critical letter of 1763, but Somerset Street joined again in 1795 when the Association met at Frome.[41] In 1797 the Association was invited to meet at Bath, and for the two days of meetings on 7 and 8 June the chapel was whitewashed and the windows painted.[42] In addition there was accommodation and an Association Dinner provided at the

---

[35] Oliver, 1968, 87; Broome, op. cit, 63 & 141; Ramsbottom, 2003, 101; *Dissenters' Certificates*, 27 November 1811.
[36] *Gibb's Bath Visitant, or New Bath Guide*, 1835.
[37] Gadsby, op. cit, 407.
[38] Broome, op. cit, 107. 'A solid group of churches was building up in the Wiltshire area, radiating out from York Street, Bath initially, under William Gadsby's influence; taking root under Warburton and John Dymott in the Trowbridge, Hilperton area; spreading out to Devizes under William Gadsby's influence; and moving across to Melksham, Studley, Calne and Grove, near Wantage, through the influence of John Warburton. This was the beginning of the Baptist churches in the West Country, that were later to identify themselves with the Gospel Standard after its inception in 1835.' For Gospel Standard Baptists in the West Country under Gadsby, Warburton and others, see also Dix, op. cit, 44-58.
[39] Broome, op. cit, 104. 'The 'Modern Question', as the teaching of Andrew Fuller was called, was all the talk of the times. Warburton was a noted preacher against it, attacking the offer of the Gospel, duty faith and duty repentance, and denying that the Law was the Believer's Rule of Life, but rather the Gospel. This was the difference between Somerset Street in Bath, and York Street.'
[40] For a different view of high Calvinism in Manchester and London at this time see Shaw, 2002.
[41] SSBC, *Minutes*, 14 May 1795.
[42] Ibid, 13 May 1797.

Christopher Inn, run by Methodists and where Wesley's Chapel often held their meetings. Contrasted with the plainness and simplicity insisted on by Robert Parsons in his day, the Somerset Street congregation were now used to making elaborate preparations for their Association visitors. Indeed, the question had come full circle by 1815 when the Association was planning to meet at Bath in the following year. At their meeting at Salisbury it was

> Resolved—To hold the next Association at Bath, on the Wednesday and Thursday in Whitsun-week...

As a codicil to the Association letter of 1815 appears the following notice in small print:

> Our friends in Bath are earnestly requested, from a regard to the future prosperity of the Association, to avoid every thing superfluous in the provision they make for the Ministers and Messengers, at the next Meeting. They may rest assured, that the feelings of their brethren will be much more gratified, by an example of plainness, which, if followed, will relieve the Association from the difficulties under which it labours, than by the most costly fare that generosity and kindness could procure.[43]

From references to the number of letters received from absent churches needing to be read, it would seem that cost was at least one factor in reducing the number of churches actually in attendance at Association meetings, something which we noted above about the Association in the mid-eighteenth century. Perhaps if the church at Somerset Street would offer more modest hospitality, more member churches would be induced to attend, and the Association would be saved from additional cost.

Opie Smith

Opie Smith was born in 1751 or 1752.[44] We know when he was born from the trail of property deeds and other documents recorded during his lifetime. He was a Gentleman Brewer,[45] who used his successful business to lubricate a life of Christian devotion and service. A prominent member of the Baptist church in Bath, his generosity was familiar to many Baptist congregations in the West Country and as far afield as the Baptist missions in India. At the time of his

---

[43] Association Letter, 1815.
[44] Where Opie Smith was born, or to whom, is as yet unknown. The estimated years are derived by working backwards from later documents.
[45] Opie Smith made his fortune from the brewing industry at a time well before temperance became fashionable, and before adequate clean water and sanitary arrangements made safe alternatives to small beer an option. Smith, James Evill and George Cox were among the contemporary Baptists who were now establishing themselves successfully in business in the City, to one degree of success or another.

death in 1836 Opie Smith was the senior member of an influential Baptist family in Bath, and his passing marked the end of an era in the life of the Baptist church in Bath. Contrary to P T Phillips' argument cited above, that the Baptist denomination in Bath lacked men of much substance, Opie Smith represented a substantial presence within the Bath Baptist community. The purpose of reconstructing what can be known of his life is to demonstrate his substantial influence, and his significance, and to restore his place within the story of Bath Baptists—and, as will be clear, his place within the story of the wider Baptist community too. The value and importance of the Bath Baptist story and its mission is illustrated well in the person of Opie Smith.

Little is known about Opie Smith in his earliest years, until about 1779 when he and his brother John became members of the Baptist church meeting in Somerset Street, Bath. Neither can we certain when he was first married to his wife Mary.[46] His first daughter Mary was born around 1781[47] followed by Mercy around 1783.[48] By 1783 they were resident in Bath, where it is recorded: 'Opie Smith of Bathwick, Brewer, age abt 31 years'.[49] In the following year Opie Smith became 'late of the Parish of Bathwick in the County of Somerset but now of the said City of Bath Brewer'.[50]

For about fifty years the rising fortunes of Opie Smith can be traced through the surviving deeds to properties he leased from the Corporation of Bath between 1783 and 1830. On 14 April 1783 he leased number 18 Horse Street for £50 at a yearly rent of 10 shillings. The other people quoted in the lease are very interesting: John Palmer the elder, tallow chandler, aged about 80 years, and his son John Palmer the younger, aged about 42 years. This was probably the John Palmer who was soon to be influential in reorganising the postal system by mail coach, as well as in theatrical and other business enterprises. Born in 1742 he was 'the only son of a rich tradesman', John Palmer Senior, who 'owned a brewery and a chandlery and was a partner in the Bath theatre.'[51] Evidence thus strongly suggests a relationship between these Palmers and Opie Smith in Horse Street during the early part of Smith's Bath brewing career. Number 18 Horse Street was evidently inadequate, so on 19 April 1784 Smith annexed the neighbouring property to his own, and numbers 17 and 18 were incorporated into one lease for an additional £34 and a yearly rent of 11 shillings.[52] The life of John Palmer the younger, 'of the said City of Bath, Gentleman, age abt 43' is again quoted in the lease, alongside James Grant

---

[46] There is a record of a marriage on 28 July 1778 at St Mary Major Church, Exeter, between one Opie Smith and one Mary Punchard which could refer to the same Opie Smith of Bath.
[47] BRO, DP 2728.
[48] Ibid.
[49] BRO, DP 2725.
[50] Ibid.
[51] Davis, 1984, 4.
[52] BRO, DP 2725.

Smith, 'son of William Smith, mealman, of Hinton St George, Somerset, age abt 10.'[53] In later years James Grant Smith would also become influential in Bath Baptist life, following the family business as brewer at the Horse Street or 'Albion Brewery'. He was referred to as Opie Smith's nephew, making his father William Smith a brother of Opie Smith, along with the aforementioned John. The premises in Horse Street were still expanding two years later when on 10 April 1786 the lease on number 19 Horse Street was taken out for £228 and a 9 shilling yearly rent. The lives of Martha Milsom, 'widow, age abt 46', and his daughters Mary and Mercy are quoted in the lease.

Working his way down Horse Street, Opie Smith was gradually taking over a series of properties. A reconstructed schedule shows that 10 April 1786 saw a further lease of numbers 20 to 23 Horse Street to Opie Smith. On 8 August 1803 Smith also took out the lease further up the street at number 12.[54] In his topographical study, Mike Chapman concluded that 'Much of the lower half of the street belonged to the Southgate Brewery and the Bath Arms belonging to Opie Smith, a wealthy and influential Baptist'.[55] Elizabeth Holland, his colleague on the *Survey of Old Bath*, commented that 'In pictures we have seen of the district, a massive building which must have been the brewery stood about there.'[56] There was, in other words, a substantial business occupying rapidly expanding premises. Other properties within the city were also leased for business purposes. On 25 February 1793, for example, he purchased the lease of number 2 Frog Lane from the Corporation of Bath for £47.18s.4d. and an annual rent of 13s.4d. There were almost certainly inns and public houses distributing the produce of the main brewery in Horse Street.

The same documents also help fill in the particulars of an expanding family and its connection with the business. For example, Opie's brother William, who in 1784 was at 'Hinton St George, Mealman', was by 1797 working alongside his brother at the Horse Street (or Southgate) Brewery.[57] Also at the turn of the century a Robert Smith was working with them in Horse Street;[58] whilst also connected with them was a John Smith, Brewer, of the Walcot Brewery.[59] Robert and John are both recorded in the Baptist Registers, along with their wives, Elizabeth and Sophia, and the thirteen children born between them. James Grant Smith and his wife, Mary, are recorded with their five children, along with the three children of James' brother, Henry, and his wife, Deborah. Family connections with the Horse Street brewery were strong well into the nineteenth century.

---

[53] Ibid.
[54] BRO, DP 2721, 2724, 2725, 2728. Root, *Schedule*.
[55] Chapman, 1997, 26.
[56] Holland, 1997, *Correspondence*, 8 October 1997.
[57] BRO, DP 2725.
[58] BRO, DP 2602B.
[59] BRO, DP2728.

Whilst his expanding business serves as the context to the growing financial stability and increasing economic and social respectability of Opie Smith, it is as a generous and mission orientated Baptist that Smith is most remembered, as we shall see, by contemporaries such as Benjamin Godwin and Frederick Trestrail. His connection with the Somerset Street congregation began around 1779,[60] when he appears as a subscribing member. It was common for some of the male members to sign the church meeting minutes: John Smith's name first appeared on 28 June 1779 whilst Opie Smith's name didn't appear until 14 May 1788. We can only speculate that in these early years of membership Smith's primary preoccupation was with his business. In any case 1791 was a transition year for the Bath Baptists. After the death of Robert Parsons, whose strong character and reputation, as we have seen, had dominated the scene since the church's founding in 1752, the church had appointed John Paul Porter from Wokingham to succeed him as pastor. In time a more moderate and more openly evangelical Calvinism would characterise the new ministry, providing a new context within which the gifts of Opie Smith and others were to thrive. It was also around 1791 that Opie Smith provided for himself a comfortable residence outside the city called Westfield House, which was probably built especially for him. R E M Peach describes the house thus:

> Westfield House. On the ancient Fosse Road. A house of the Georgian period about 1791. An admirable type of mansion, well built, equally well proportioned, internally as well as externally, commanding on the south a sweep of well-timbered undulating park-like scenery; to the north parts of Lansdown; and to the west that vast combe or valley extending almost to Bristol, the foreground of which is exceedingly lovely...[61]

This house was Smith's retreat for the rest of his life, to which he would return from his travels, and where he would welcome visitors. The occupant became as much a local landmark as the house, as this 1823 guidebook reference illustrates:

> On the old Wells road betwixt the house of Opie Smith, esq. and Capt. Grose, on the right there is a charming sequestered ride, which leads to the foot of Englishcomb Round-hill...[62]

Elsie Russ, former Bath local history librarian, described the house as follows:

> Westfield House. The earliest entry it has been possible to trace in the Bath Directories is in 1829 O. Smith, Esq., 1837 James Grant Smith, Albion Brewery and 1862-3 Lt. Gen. Hewitt. The original deeds of the house should give some information but

---

[60] SSBC, *Minutes*, List of Subscribers 1779.
[61] Peach, 1893, 146-7.
[62] Meyler, 1823, 38.

we have been able to trace no record of the building of the house.⁶³

Figure 25. Westfield House

A few surviving deeds to the Westfield estate do give more information, but little relating to the building of the house. Opie Smith was becoming comfortable in material terms, and his commitment to the church was undiminished. In December 1796 he was called to serve as deacon. The terms of the appointment were open-ended, with no specific period of office specified. From this time onwards Smith seems to have developed a specific interest in preaching the word of the Gospel. His gifts were so recognised, that on 17 May 1801:

> It is agreed to Call our Brother Mr Opie Smith (who is a Deacon of this Church) to the work of the Ministry. He having been engaged some time in speaking a word of exhortation and have also repeatedly addressed this Church and Congregation from the pulpit – We do hereby give him a call to preach the Gospel wherever the Lord may succeed his labours.⁶⁴

As we have amply demonstrated, this was a usual practice amongst Baptists. Yet for Opie Smith this was no mere recognition of gifts to be used within the local

---

⁶³ Russ, *Local Index*.
⁶⁴ SSBC, *Minutes*, 17 May 1801.

church alone, but a call to exercise his preaching gifts wherever he might be called. He set about pursuing his call with evangelical zeal and enthusiasm. The Somerset Street congregation benefited from his service, practically and spiritually,[65] as did the connected Baptist preaching stations in the villages around Bath, such as Combe Hay, Walcot and Twerton.

Yet amongst all this success, Opie Smith also suffered his own personal tragedies. In 1792 Opie and William Smith buried two of their young servants in the Baptist burial ground at Walcot.[66] Furthermore, there is no further reference in any of the records to Smith's daughter Mercy, who appears not to have survived infancy. His daughter Mary later married her cousin James Grant Smith, and they later benefited from Opie Smith's substantial estate. Then on Thursday 2 July 1807 the *Bath Chronicle* reported the death on the previous Friday of 'Mrs. Smith, wife of Mr. Opie Smith, brewer, Horse-street.'[67]

At the same time it was becoming more apparent that Opie Smith's gifts were being used in a far more wide-reaching way. It is possible that as a new widower Smith threw himself into a ministry for the Gospel with increased passion. Certainly at a church meeting on 15 November 1807, at the end of the year in which his wife had died, the church resolved to convey to Opie Smith a most peculiar honour and calling, as the full text of the resolution demonstrates:

> For several years past many of the destitute churches in the Baptist connection, have expressed an earnest desire that our Brother Mr. Opie Smith might be permitted to administer the Lord's Supper unto them, as well as to preach the Gospel. This has been made known to several Ministers in the connection. They also acquiesce in their Request, and have repeatedly expressed the same desire.
>
> After consulting with Dr. Ryland and others on the subject, it was thought by him and them as the most scriptural and orderly way to recommend to the Church of which Mr. Opie Smith is a Member, to call him to the office of a Teaching and Ruling Elder in that Church. And on Lord's Day Nov. 8 1807 At a full Church Meeting the following Entry was read to the Members for their consideration, until the next Lord's Day. When if approved by them it is to be ratified.
>
> Whereas our Beloved Brother Mr. Opie Smith has not only been for many years an active, useful and honourable Member of this Church, but also for near Eleven years discharged the office of

---

[65] Ibid. 8 June 1807.
[66] TNA, RG4. *Bath Baptist Burial Register*, 1 February 1792 'buried James Osborn, age 28 years' and on 25 April 1792 'an unnamed servant aged 29 years'.
[67] *Bath Chronicle*, Thursday 2 July 1807.

Deacon well; and likewise has been encouraged and requested by us to engage in the public work of the Ministry: in which he has engaged Seven years, and his labours have proved acceptable and useful in many places. We therefore having made so long a trial of him and found him faithful, do now by a vote of the Church call him to the office of a Teaching and Ruling Elder in this Church (That he may if illness or urgent call should require administer the ordinances at home for our beloved pastor) And also we hereby, express our approbation of his administering the ordinances of the gospel in any of our Sister Churches, that may need his assistance.

We think the case of our Brother Mr. Opie Smith to be very peculiar. His long standing in the Church, his office as a Deacon, his being called by this Church to the Ministry: and as God has given him zeal, acceptance in the eyes of the Churches, and Worldly property, and Influence, by which he is enabled to carry the gospel into many places where others cannot, destitute of these advantages. We think it right to encourage him therein, We do not mean to establish this our conduct as a precedent, nor do we wish to draw this to example. But if any of our Sister Churches, or ourselves at any future period, should meet with a similar Character connected with similar circumstances: they have a right to do as we have done.

The above was ratified at a full Church Meeting immediately after the administration of the Lord's Supper, Lord's Day Nov. 15 1807.[68]

It was clear that the church considered Opie Smith's position to be unique, hence the uncertainty as to how to proceed without the advice of Dr Ryland of Bristol – his ministry was to be somewhere between local preacher and fully recognised minister. The esteem in which Somerset Street members and their minister held Opie Smith is obvious and he in return remained loyal to both minister and church throughout his life.

Outside Somerset Street he took part in the opening devotions of Twerton Chapel in 1808,[69] to which, as we have seen, he and others had been appointed to oversee;[70] and he was instrumental in encouraging the building of a Baptist meeting house in Limpley Stoke, a village not far from Bath, around the same time.[71] He was also a member of the new Milk Street Sunday School Room

---

[68] SSBC, *Minutes*, 15 November 1807.
[69] *Baptist Magazine*, i, 38.
[70] SSBC, *Minutes*, 12 January 1808; 3 May 1808; 15 July 1808; 5 January 1815.
[71] *Baptist Magazine*, xiv, 161.

building committee in 1814.[72] Opie Smith loyally represented his church at many occasions and meetings, including an experimental formation of a Baptist General Union in London. Records show that Opie Smith represented Bath at a meeting at Eagle Street on 22 June 1815, chaired by Dr. Ryland, which began at eight o'clock in the morning![73] Furthermore he was also a regular subscriber of 2 guineas to the Bristol Education Society, which formed the basis of the Bristol Baptist Academy, each year from 1802 until his death.[74] It would seem that the Bath church in general, and Opie Smith in particular, were as keen supporters of education for ministry in the early nineteenth century as the church had been in opposition during the 1770s.

Opie Smith's loyalty to Somerset Street and John Paul Porter was to be particularly tested in 1828 when a dispute led to a split in the church's membership. We shall consider this dispute in more detail in due course. However, briefly, the church had invited Owen Clarke from Silver Street, Taunton, to preach on probation as co-pastor with the ageing John Paul Porter.[75] Differences in opinion about his suitability, the terms of his appointment, and the procedures by which he had been appointed, led to two years in which Porter and others were locked out of Somerset Street. They were forced to meet in the former Catholic chapel in Corn Street, obtained by Opie Smith and their supporters. Two years later in July 1830, after the case had been dismissed from the Court of Chancery, a committee of arbitration consisting of five experienced deacons from other local Baptist churches returned John Paul Porter to his pulpit in Somerset Street. Yet by then the damage had been done, the membership of the church had been depleted and Opie Smith and John Paul Porter were elderly men. Porter was certainly in very bad health when he died, a broken man, only two years later on 10 October 1832.

Opie Smith's property dealings also showed a concern for the needs of the wider Baptist family, as the history of the Southcot House estate demonstrates. Southcot House was built in about 1777 by John Evill, one of the Bath Baptist deacons and also a brewer. On John Evill's death in 1791 his sons John, a brewer and maltster of Bathwick, and Luke, an attorney of Walcot, appear to have let the house out for several years.[76] In 1799 or thereabouts it was sold to Opie Smith.[77] Not needing to live in it, for his own Westfield House was much larger and grander, Smith started to divide and develop the Southcot estate for residential building whilst retaining ownership and letting the house and its still sizeable garden. In 1810 Opie Smith set aside the lowest northerly part of the estate, backing on to Gibbs's Mill and Claverton Street, for a new Baptist burial

---

[72] SSBC, *Minutes*, 6 January 1814.
[73] Price, *Baptist Quarterly*, iv, 171.
[74] Bristol Education Society, *Annual Reports*.
[75] SSBC, *Minutes*, 13 March 1828 to 3 July 1830.
[76] *Bath Chronicle*, 22 September 1796. Advertisement.
[77] *Bath Herald*, 20 April 1799. Advertisement.

ground, to relieve pressure on the crowded space out at Walcot. We shall consider this second burial ground in due course. On the land to the west and south of the burial ground were built the various terraces on Lyncombe Hill, and the modest but stylish Southcot Place in about 1817, and Richard Harris the Baptist builder was also involved in this project.[78] Here, in one of the first houses to be completed, John Paul Porter came to live.

Figure 26. Southcot House

As we have seen, Opie Smith always took an active interest in spreading the Gospel. He was particularly encouraging to young people who were keen to test their fledgling gifts. An early challenge of Opie Smith's was remembered many years later by Benjamin Godwin. Benjamin was the son of a poor Bath Baptist family that had come into the church under the influence of Robert Parsons. Benjamin had run off to sea as a young man, returned to Bath in 1802, and would much later be pastor at New Road Baptist Church, Oxford and principal of the Baptist academy in Bradford. Godwin recorded his biography in a series of letters written to his son, John.[79] They tell of his early experiences as a boy in Bath, his dramatic and traumatic experiences at sea—which nearly cost him his life—and his call into the ministry of the Gospel. Some of the early letters testify to the influence of Opie Smith on Benjamin Godwin's life and his lifelong cause to be grateful. Opie Smith had been a good friend of Benjamin's father George, who was seventy years old when he died—having had an active

---

[78] Peach, 1893, 130.
[79] Godwin, *Letters*.

life, including a period of time living in America where he had heard George Whitefield preach.[80] George Godwin died on 15 September 1796 and was buried in the Baptist burial ground at Walcot, where John Paul Porter 'preached his funeral sermon to a crowded audience.' Being born on 10 October 1785, Benjamin was just eleven years old when his father died. He attended the Blue Coat School, and then was apprenticed to a shoe maker, before escaping the poverty of home by travelling to Bristol with a friend and going to sea aboard the Mohawk, just before his fifteenth birthday in 1800.[81] The dramatic experience of the young man included first hand experience of navel warfare, as the first Napoleonic wars were in full flight. It was a much relieved seventeen year old Benjamin who finally returned home in August 1802, 'to the unbounded joy of my mother and the great satisfaction of my old friends'.[82] Godwin confesses to his son:

> This was the start of a critical period of my life as my course into the future now hung in the balance. On the one hand, there were those circumstances that promised to exercise a very ungodly influence on my life.

These circumstances included a group of 'ungodly' friends. On the other hand, there were good influences – and it is here that Opie Smith re-enters the story. As Godwin continues in his letter of October 1844:

> Under the influence of this group of friends, I was embarking on a mundane course of life from which it was likely I would never have escaped except for the influence of my step-sister, Mrs. Cooper. Mrs. Cooper was the daughter of my father's first wife and had been a member of the Baptist Church for some 30 years, she was older than my mother and I looked up to her. She kept a lodging house and I spent much time there and often lodged with her. In her youth, she had been gay and spirited but was now more sober and full of zeal for religion. Through her, I met several warm hearted and pious people and I went with her to chapel several times when the memory of my father, in the place he used to worship, influenced my mind with thoughts of his strength and peace in God and helped endow my spirit with a longing for religion. One week on coming out from evening service, Mr. Opie Smith saw me, took me by the hand and said "I am glad to see you here my young friend, there is joy in the presence of the angels of God over one sinner that repenteth so think of the rejoicing of your father now that he knows that his son is seeking the Saviour".

---

[80] Godwin, *Letters*, October 1839.
[81] Ibid, February 1840 onwards.
[82] Ibid, October 1844.

This was a major turning point in Godwin's life from which he never looked back. During 1803 Godwin had to hide at a house in King Street for several weeks from a press gang that was targeting Bath in an attempt to bolster a depleted navy. This gave him time to think, and on 12 July 1803:

> I wrote to Mrs. Cooper from this place of seclusion, in which I refer to my desire to join the Baptist Church under the care of Mr. Porter. I took this step after much self-examination and with apprehension lest I should be unable subsequently to sustain a Christian character. On Sunday, August 27th, 1803 I made a public avowal of faith in Christ and devotion to His service, and was baptised with five others, including Dobney. The others were John Davis, Mr. and Mrs. Hayward and a daughter of Mr. Opie Smith, all of whom have now entered the next world.[83]

Opie Smith's encouragement was not confined to words alone; he was willing to put practical assistance into place. On 21 March 1806 Benjamin Godwin met with Opie Smith, who suggested that Godwin's gifts weren't suited for ministry at home but might be suitable for overseas missionary work. Godwin later wrote that:

> My discussion with Mr. Opie Smith seemed to open for me a door to usefulness as I had a deep interest in missionary work and there now appeared to be a good prospect that I would engage in this field of work: yet when I considered the full import, my mind was greatly agitated.[84]

After a bungled attempt at preaching with a friend in nearby Englishcombe, which earned him the rebuke of John Paul Porter and others, Benjamin Godwin discovered that there were those who were willing to take him more seriously. After deciding that after all Godwin would not make a suitable missionary, Opie and his brother John, who by now owned an estate in Ailburton in Gloucestershire, came up with a solution. Godwin, who had preached successfully before the church on three occasions, agreed to move to Ailburton to 'introduce evangelical preaching among the villagers' and find 'opportunities to preach and spread the gospel.'[85] He also persuaded Betsey Hall, a member at Somerset Street, to become his wife. They were married on 14 August 1806. Although their time in Ailburton was not easy, Godwin preached successfully and with appeal. Yet the Anglican authorities led serious attacks on the couple, so after much struggling they returned to Bath. With the continued support of Opie and John Smith, Godwin was able to remedy his biggest weakness: his lack of proper supervised training. Through Opie Smith's offices and connections

---

[83] Ibid, November 1844.
[84] Ibid, September 1846.
[85] Ibid.

with the Cornish Baptist churches, Godwin was offered the oversight of the small Baptist congregation at Chacewater, whilst receiving further education from the Baptist minister at Redruth, Mr Rowe, a friend of Opie Smith. Opie Smith had been instrumental with the Bristol Education Society in settling Rowe, who was from Salisbury, into this position at Redruth.

The arrangement with Rowe was a simple one but not overly successful. Benjamin Godwin found Rowe patronising and heavy handed, and he was often humiliated in front of Rowe's school pupils. Despite this Godwin was encouraged by the overall experience, his confidence increased, and he made many lasting connections. On returning home on 3 June 1808 he knew that the preaching of the Gospel, 'the Gospel Ministry', was from now on to be the centre of his life. As Godwin looks back in his letters to his son:

> My future line of life was now fixed and the objective of my most fervent desires was now in a fair way of being accomplished. I had given up my trade, for which I was never fit and had the prospect of consecrating my entire life to the sacred work of the Christian ministry.[86]

Godwin would never ever forget the generosity and influence of Opie Smith and his brother John.

Just a few years later we catch another glimpse into the relationship between Opie Smith and his friend Rowe. Rowe had cause to visit Bath for his health in 1813, spending time with Opie Smith, and on 10 April he wrote to another friend and pastor, John Saffery, in Salisbury:

> I inform you I have no reason to regret my Journey to Bath as I have reason to believe that God has so far blessed the means made use of as to lead me to entertain the most sanguinary hopes that I shall ultimately obtain a radical cure which may be speedily affected so as to render my stay in Bath unnecessary after the early part of next month. The wound in my leg is completely cured and the eruptions which have shewn themselves begin to disappear.

He complained bitterly about how intolerably uncomfortable staying in Bath was for him, and continues:

> There are very few who obtain a real cure, many go away much better, but I think the greater part who leave derive little or no benefit…Mr Opie Smith has shown me great kindness. I have frequently been at his house. He has given me an unlimited invitation. He heard from Cornwall about three weeks ago. Sister is better but the Case of the Child is still considered

---
[86] Ibid, August 1847.

> dangerous—I have been to Twerton two or three times and partly agreed to spend a Sabbath with them before I leave.

Before finishing the letter he lodged a curious query with his friend, following up his comments on visiting Twerton. He asks whether there might be

> ...a way whereby I may obtain either the sanction or refusal of the church as a village preacher as I have long formed a determination that I will not engage in any thing which comes under the cognisance of the church without its consent.[87]

Opie Smith had a growing reputation as a friend of many churches in the West of England. Interest in this area had been sparked towards the end of the eighteenth century with the introductory forays of the infant Baptist Missionary Society into Cornwall in 1795, and two years later with the Baptist Society in London for the Encouragement and Support of Itinerant and Village Preaching.[88] Frederick Trestrail, who was born and brought up in Falmouth during this period, wrote in his reminiscences that

> The Baptist churches in Cornwall owe their existence partly to the labours of a few distinguished ministers who, towards the close of the last century, occasionally visited the county on evangelistic tours, but mainly to the liberality of the late Mr Opie Smith of Bath.[89]

This is presumably the source of S J Price's description of Opie Smith as 'a Bath layman and benefactor of churches in Cornwall'.[90] That Opie Smith is singled out in numerous accounts indicates that there was something unique about the patronage he extended.

This liberality showed itself not only in the interest, care and encouragement shown to those engaged in the work, but also in the financial contributions he was to make. He had contributed, along with his brother, John, the sum of £20 towards Benjamin Godwin's expenses after all.[91] He also used his skills to raise funds from others for the important task of the evangelising the farther reaches of the West Country. In a passionate letter to his 'dear friend' John Saffery on 5 February 1807 from his home at Westfield House in Bath, Opie Smith wrote,

> I have for some time past been hesitating in my mind whether or no I shd ask a favor of you – for knowing your many engagements in the Church Family and Business – I felt my mind a little discouraged – but on the other hand considering

---

[87] Reeves Collection, R11/8.
[88] Lovegrove, 1988, 24-25.
[89] Trestrail, nd, 11.
[90] Price, *Baptist Quarterly*. iv, 171.
[91] Hancock, 1991, 24.

> your readiness to serve the Cause of Jesus Christ as well as to Assist and Oblige Me Caused me to take the liberty of sending you this – beging it as a favor you will take up the Helstone and the Redruth cases Making together About £120 – and beg it for them being Assured you will get twice as much as almost any one else – but knowing it will be attended with much loss of time…[92]

From Cornwall, up into North Devon, the cares and concerns of Opie Smith were indeed very wide. David Thompson in his 1885 *Short History of the Baptist Churches in North Devon* recalls about the Baptist cause at Great Torrington that

> Opie Smith, Esq., of Bath, must have had his attention drawn to the spiritual condition of Torrington; for we find that he sent Mr Pulsford to labour there. His settlement was in the summer of 1819. Never could there have been a more appropriate choice.[93]

Smith's attention may have been drawn to Torrington a year earlier in July 1818 whilst visiting nearby Bideford with Charles Sharp, pastor at Bradninch, and Charles Ferris of Barnstaple. Their mission was to 'ascertain if there was an opportunity of commencing a Baptist cause', which they did in finding three people who were to form the core of a new Baptist community.[94] In 1821 Opie Smith was involved with Rev. John Cocks, later to become minister at Twerton, in setting up the Baptist chapel at Crediton, Devon;[95] yet home in Bath was not forgotten when he donated £100 to help build the new Baptist chapel in Thomas Street, Walcot.[96] The Baptist cause at Pill, Bristol, also had much for which to be grateful to Opie Smith. The *Baptist Magazine* report of the formation of the church at Pill on 27 November 1815 includes the following tribute:

> The labours of the students from the Bristol academy, together with the kind attention of Mr. S. of Bath, have principally contributed towards this good work. The people have now a stated minister, and hope, through the blessing of God, and the encouragement which the friends of religion may afford, to see this wilderness soon become as the garden of the Lord.[97]

The Baptist church in Bath was from the start a missionary church, and took a personal interest in many of the early Baptist missionaries who were often well known to the church. Opie Smith featured strongly in this, and the influence he held in his family as well as among Baptists in general is evident in the correspondence. James Grant Smith, Opie Smith's nephew, received regular

---

[92] Reeves Collection, R20/96.
[93] Thompson, 1885, 32.
[94] Ibid, 52-53.
[95] *Baptist Manual*, 1851, 42.
[96] *Baptist Magazine*, xxii, 395.
[97] Ibid, 1816, 263; Hart, 1987, 7.

correspondence from the mission field to his home at Westfield House. William Ward, for example, added his own personal greetings to his amanuensis copied circular letter from Serampore on 5 February 1822. Two years later on 15 November 1824 Joshua Marshman wrote to James Grant Smith from Serampore that the college was flourishing, that he was working night and day, and that he sent his love to all at Westfield House.[98] One month later on 16 December 1824 Joshua Marshman again had cause to write to James Grant Smith, who was looking after his daughter in Bath. She received hospitality,

> …so affectionate and tender in your excellent family as would make her almost forget home.

Marshman then continued in reminiscent vein. We have encountered the second part of the following quotation from the letter affectionately referring to Robert Parsons earlier in this study, but here again in its fuller context:

> I exceedingly rejoice that you are likely to perpetuate the memory of your worthy Uncle Mr Opie Smith in the happiest manner by being like him a blessing to your denomination and the cause of God in general. I never had the pleasure of seeing him; but his character has for many years endeared him to me, and I beg you to present to him my most affectionate regards. Mr Porter I know; I heard him preach thirty two years ago; — and Bath I assure you was ever endeared to our Christian friends at Westbury Leigh. Old Mr Parsons was every thing but adored there. He baptized (if I recall it rightly) my Father at Westbury Leigh in 1763, and the veneration my Father had for him I can scarcely describe. He and Mr Hains the Baptist Minister at Bradford in 1762 and two others, supplied the church at Westbury Leigh quarterly at that time…[99]

Opie Smith would have warmly received the greetings and sentiments expressed as they melted away the years that had passed since he had first entered the church at Somerset Street some time before 'Old Mr Parsons' had died. He remembered, too, his Gospel zeal. It was presumably the strength of this personal relationship between Opie Smith and friends in Bath with the missionary friends at Serampore that lay behind their continued support for the Serampore Mission when it separated from the Baptist Missionary Society in 1829.[100] It was important for Marshman that the story of these pioneering Bath Baptists and their contribution to the spreading of the Gospel was remembered. As they highlight the themes of this study it is significant that their combined lifespans bridge the entire period of this study. For, on Thursday 30 June 1836

---

[98] Reeves Collection, R4/13.
[99] Reeves Collection, R4/12.
[100] Carter, 2000, 245.

the *Bath Chronicle* reported amongst the other deaths in Bath on the previous Saturday:

> June 25, at his residence, Westfield House, near this city, much respected and deeply regretted by his family and a numerous circle of friends, Opie Smith, esq; in the 85th year of his age.[101]

He was presumably buried in the new Baptist Burial Ground on Lyncombe Hill, which he had provided at the bottom of the Southcot House estate, although no corroborative record of his burial survives because the relevant burial register was not submitted to the Registrar General and has since been lost.

Figure 27. Stone Vase in front of Westfield House

---

[101] *Bath Chronicle*, Thursday 30 June, 1836.

The New Baptist Burial Ground

In May 1810 the Somerset Street church meeting minutes first record the acquisition of their new burial ground in Widcombe:

> This concerns the right of burial for Members of this Church and their Children in the new burying ground at Widcomb.
>
> I Opie Smith of the Parish of Lyncomb and Widcomb, County of Somerset, A Member and Deacon of the Baptist Church of the City of Bath, County of Somerset, have by my Last Will and Testament secured in the hands of Trustees to the Members that now are or may here after be in full communion with the said Church, and their children to the age of 15 years, a right of burying in unwalled and uncovered graves, free from any expense more than 2s.6d. each and the expense of digging or opening the grave, In a piece or parcel of ground being part of an Estate called South Cot House Estate in the Parish of Lyncomb and Widcomb, and set aside by me for the purpose of a burying place. May 9 1810. Opie Smith.[102]

The church received the Trust Deed for the ground from Opie Smith at the end of 1813, and it was immediately placed 'into the Church Chest'.[103] The deeds and burial register for the land have since been lost, so it is difficult to work out precisely what was happening – but it would seem that Smith was keen that the church be able to begin using the burial ground right away, as the church was in need of the burial space. Indeed the loss of records makes some of the story difficult to reconstruct. Yet the questionnaire, completed in 1837 to accompany the submission of the church's registers to the Registrar General, refers to an unsubmitted book. It 'contains register of burials from 1807 to 1837 and relates to a burial ground situate in the parish of Lyncombe and Widcombe in the County of Somerset called the Baptist burial ground.' It was not submitted, 'as it contains a general scheme of the burial ground and is an index to interments.' The trustees of the Somerset Street chapel and the Walcot burial ground, as we have seen above, now had charge of the ground at Lyncombe Hill; although by October 1827, some members having in the meantime deceased, their number now consisted of Arthur Tozer, William Stockham, William Evill, Opie Smith — brewer, James Evill — silversmith, William Taylor, Jaspar Gay — gent, James Grant Smith, Thomas Horsey, William Day Horsey, John Passmore — gent, Thomas Pike, James Salter, Joseph Tapp — cordwainer, Edward

---

[102] SSBC, *Minutes*, 9 May 1810; TNA, RG4/1790. *Bath Baptist Burial Registers*; Scott, 1993, 78. Maurice Scott describes the burial ground: 'Lyncombe Terrace…At a gap in the Terrace there was, until 1970, an attractive arched entrance to the (Manvers Street) Baptists' Burial Ground (see picture in Coard). Now there is a short walk to padlocked gates at the entrance to the cemetery. This burial ground has been purchased by the Bath Preservation Trust.'
[103] SSBC, *Minutes*, 11 November 1813.

Hancock, John Marshman Hill, John Buck — taylor, James Dyer, Thomas Gunning — basket maker, and Robert Leonard.[104]

Bounded on the north by a high wall above Claverton Street, the site was very soon to be screened on the west by the new houses on Lyncombe Hill and on the south by Southcot Place, the building development in which we have seen that Opie Smith was involved with Richard Harris and others. The burial ground, approximately 180ft long by 90ft wide, was approached from Lyncombe Hill. In January 1827 the winter climate persuaded the church to send Jasper Gay and Thomas Langdon to approach Opie Smith, and 'solicit him to build a shed in the burying ground to shelter the people attending funerals in bad weather.' A temporary 'shed' may have been built, but before long the burial ground was entered through a grand Gothic style archway built between numbers 5 and 9 Lyncombe Hill.[105] It was more than a mere entrance, for the building incorporated accommodation in an upper room, which was presumably intended for the Sexton or keeper of the ground. It was about 25ft long by 12 ft wide, there was a gateway at either end, and plenty of space underneath to shelter for prayers and readings, before the committal outside. There is reference to the continual tenancy of the 'cottage' up to the 1950s. A report in 1963 described the 'two communicating rooms accessible by [an] external stone staircase off Lyncombe Hill'. However, complaints of infestation and decay, and the mounting cost of maintenance, led to a decision to demolish the structure in 1970. This led in turn to a 'row' over the fate of this grade three listed building, considered as 'particularly charming...a splendid link to grade two buildings up the hill' by The Bath Preservation Trust, and as 'a dangerous building and of no particular architectural merit' by the trustees of the ground.[106]

From the entrance porch, the pathway led towards the far end of the burial ground. Small rounded stones to the north side of the path, and letters and arrows carved into the upper and lower boundary walls, marked the rows A-B-C, and so on, the first row beginning close against the backs of the terrace on Lyncombe Hill. From the fifty one[107] surviving stones, it seems that most were buried in unmarked graves. The number of burials is unknown although probably considerable, for a correspondent in 1958 noted from the register that between 1807 and 1853 there were 324 children interred in the ground, and 204 of these were under 2 years of age. It is equally difficult to ascertain when the final burial took place. Orders in Council dated 31 December 1886 and 7 March

---

[104] *The Case of the Baptist Church meeting in Somerset Street, Bath*, 1829, 1-5.
[105] *Bath and Wilts Evening Chronicle*, 26 February 1970 - Letter to the Editor; Coard, 1972, 5 & 62.
[106] Ibid, 24 February 1970.
[107] In 1963 the number was recorded as fifty. A survey of the stones conducted in 1990 by the present writer transcribed thirty of the stones. At that time the burial ground was completely overgrown and many of the graves were covered. A subsequent revision of the list of burials by the Bath Preservation Trust lists 51 graves containing 103 burials, although many more are buried in unmarked graves.

1887 closed the ground from 1887, although the last burial recorded on a headstone is that of William Hayman in 1907.[108]

Further details of individual burials may be found in a small number of published obituaries. Rev. John Paul Porter was able to use his influence as a founding proprietor of the *Baptist Magazine* to publish an extended obituary of his wife Jane in the first volume.[109] It describes in detail her spiritual experience and condition, and her eleven year suffering and affliction which led to her death on 18 August 1808, aged 47. She died childless for their son, Ebenezer Paul Porter, died after only thirty days and was buried at Walcot on 18 August 1800. 'Some friends used to meet every Lord's day evening in her chamber to spend an evening in social Prayer. These meetings were profitable to herself and others, as the recollection of many testifies.' It was intended that the obituary serve as an example, for although 'She well knew that her death was approaching... The fear of death was entirely removed, so that she could meet it as a friend to conduct her to Glory.' In her last days she was heard to apply to herself the lines, 'Now I am dead to all the Globe, And all the Globe is dead to me', taken from a verse of Isaac Watts's hymn, 'When I survey the wondrous Cross':

> His dying crimson like a robe,
> Spreads o'er His body on the tree;
> Then am I dead to all the globe;
> And all the globe is dead to me.[110]

Her last words were also recorded 16 hours before her silent but apparently painless death:

> Thou dear Redeemer, dying Lamb,
> I love to hear of Thee,
> No music like Thy charming name,
> Nor half so sweet can be.

She was buried on 23 August in the Lyncombe burial ground, just below the house in Southcot Place where John Paul Porter was later to live with his second wife, Martha Cross, whom he married on 25 September 1809 at Bathwick Church. Mr Barnard of Bradford on Avon officiated at the committal of Jane Porter, and preached on the following Sunday from her chosen text, Job 19:25-27:

> For I know that my redeemer liveth, and that he shall stand at
> the latter day upon the earth: And though after my skin worms
> destroy this body, yet in my flesh shall I see God: Whom I shall

---

[108] Bath Preservation Trust revised list of burials.
[109] *Baptist Magazine*, 1809, i, 27; Cater, 1834, 106-8, 111.
[110] Manning, 1942, 125. This verse, Manning suggests, has 'passed from memory'.

see for myself, and mine eyes shall behold, and not another; though my reins be consumed within me.

Continuing the connection of the Porter family with the burial ground, we are told by Philip Cater that John Paul Porter died exclaiming the words 'peace— peace— glory— glory', and was buried on Thursday 18 October 1832, 'in the presence of a multitude of spectators'. He was carried to his grave by John Owen, minister at the Countess of Huntingdon's Chapel in the Vineyards; Philip Cater, minister at York Street and later Porter's biographer; Shem Evans, who as we shall see was Porter's assistant at Somerset Street; and J Jackson, probably James Jackson, who had preached for Porter on previous occasions and had interests at Twerton, Thomas Street and later at the new Baptist chapel at Bathford. The address at the graveside was given by William Jay of Argyle Chapel:

> who after some general remarks on the subject of mortality, proceeded to bear honourable testimony to the character of the deceased: and alluded in a very affecting manner to the circumstances of his standing over the grave of one who for so many years had been his fellow labourer in the vineyard of the Lord, and with whom he had commenced his ministerial career in the City of Bath.[111]

The precise location of the above burials is unknown.

One of the remaining headstones in the burying ground, however, records a nineteenth-century Baptist who lived within the time period of this study and made a significant contribution to improving the lives of Bath's poor. These were years when Nonconformists were making a large contribution in the city to the process of political and social reform. The radical face of Baptist life is best represented in the burial ground by George Cox, whose funeral was described as 'one of the most remarkable demonstrations of popular affection and regard the city has ever known'. Cox's biographer, Rev. David Wassell, was also later buried in the Lyncombe ground. Cox's father had died when he was eight, and his mother when he was eleven; so, being sent to Bath, he was brought up by his eldest sister. She found him a job in a hat factory, where he worked hard and his employer kept him until two or three o'clock on Sundays. He was often ill, and was sent to Weymouth for a short while. On returning he entered the Countess of Huntingdon's Chapel at the Vineyards to hear the preacher point out 'the awful effects of drunkenness.' As Cox later recorded, 'this, to me, was very alarming, for I felt sure that it was through God's mercy I also had not perished, having been frequently in the same state.' From that time he attended the chapel, and the seven o'clock prayer meeting. He said, 'my conduct and cleanness on the Sabbath, and my attending the early prayer

---

[111] *Baptist Magazine*, 1833, xxv, 288; Cater, 1834, 157-8.

meeting, so annoyed the men, that they agreed to do my work if my master would allow me to be away from them on that day.'[112]

Figure 28. Headstone of George Cox

Cox worked hard for the Bath Sunday School Union, which, as we have seen and Cox reminds us, was formed by 'Baptists, Methodists, Independents, and Lady Huntingdon's people', and as a Sunday School teacher was active in founding schools at Radstock, Limpley Stoke, and Bath: Vineyards, Rush Hill, Tyning Lane, Guinea Lane, Bedford Street, Avon Street, and the Baptist school in Milk Street. It wasn't until 1812 that he attended a baptismal service and felt called to follow the example himself. From this time, as a Baptist, he felt that his duty was among the poor, and was called 'to speak to poor sinners, in the city, and elsewhere, in Avon Street, Milk Street, Bath Quay, Little Corn Street, Gibb's Court, Mark's Hill, Snow Hill, Larkhall, Upper and Lower Bristol Road, Holloway, Dolemeads' and other places. In George Cox can be seen the Bath Baptist determination to live out the Gospel, particularly in those places where the church was not usually found. His Christian concern and sympathy extended to 'many whom neither dissenting nor Church agencies effectually reached', who lived in these neglected parts of Bath. Concerned with the spiritual and physical condition of those he encountered, Cox became active in the reform movement, fighting with those who were striving for the abolition of the Corn Laws and seeking religious equality, associated with Chartists from 1841, and worked hard to sustain the Peace Society. Although outside the

---

[112] Wassell, 1862, 17-40.

timescale of this study, Cox's life spanned another transition in the life of Bath Baptists to an era of increased political involvement, as demonstrated at the turn of the nineteenth and twentieth centuries by Manvers Street's significant involvement in the city council. This is seen also in David Wassell, Cox's biographer, who was engaged in passive resistance against church rates[113] and was also buried in the Lyncombe burial ground. Cox's involvement in the Peace Society also reflects an earlier period, and the pacifist trend in Baptist thought which we have above identified in Robert and Thomas Parsons.

George Cox, the Master Hatter of Stall Street, became a popular hero; he spoke with modesty, and conscientiously advocated temperance among 'so many homes where poverty, and misery, and crime, were to be traced to strong drink.' At a public meeting in 1859 those gathered heard Dr Tunstall's testimony:

> Mr Cox has won the admiration of his fellow citizens because he has shown them an example of virtue and integrity; and though some of the good seed he has in his life time scattered, has fallen among thorns, much of it has descended into good ground, and must bring forth fruit. A man's deeds do not rest with the generation in which he lives, because it is impossible to rescue a man from vice without the better feeling generated in his breast, descending to his successors, and thus a grandchild is blessed by a grandfather's reforms.[114]

He died on 1 January 1861, and his funeral procession was witnessed by thousands who lined the roads between Stall Street and the Baptist burial ground on Lyncombe Hill. And such was 'Bishop' Cox's popularity that a public memorial was erected by his fellow citizens in St James's burial ground on Lower Borough Walls, 'to mark their sense of his self-denying and unwearied labours for the temporal and spiritual welfare of the poor in this city, for more than fifty years'. That memorial is now gone, but his headstone remains as a reminder of the radical political participation of Bath Baptists in the 1830s, a period when the country was seeking considerable political reform. 1831 and 1832 saw the Reform Bills passed through Parliament, followed soon after by Poor Law legislation. The use of George Cox by later historians gives another example of how Baptists have often been airbrushed out of the story – in their recent book Graham Davis and Penny Bonsall refer to Cox considerably, without once mentioning his Baptist connections and excluding all but one reference from the index.[115]

The story of the continued use and then disuse of the Baptist burial grounds is one example of how the story of the Bath Baptist community has largely been

---

[113] The local parish still had the authority to issue a local tax on residents until much later in the century, which was often strongly opposed by Nonconformists in this period.
[114] Ibid.
[115] Davis & Bonsall, 2006, 208, 229 & 323.

lost, but also an example of how some of the story began to be recovered at the end of the twentieth century. The Baptist burial ground at Walcot has long since disappeared. It became full early in the nineteenth century, and was used for a variety of other purposes including as a coach yard. By the mid twentieth century the surrounding tenements had become quite derelict; and in 1949 the land 'at rear of Myrtle Place, used as garages and storage space — formerly disused burial ground' became subject to a Clearance Order on grounds of health under the 1936 Housing Act, and the ground was purchased from the Baptist trustees and cleared[116] – any human remains being removed to a mass unmarked grave in the municipal cemetery at Haycombe. Since that time considerable redevelopment at Snow Hill has changed the shape of the site; but its approximate location can be identified on and to the west of the ground now occupied by Walcot Church Hall, with its western end covered by the much realigned access to Snow Hill from the London Road.

Figure 29. Lyncombe Hill Baptist Burial Ground Restored

Yet the Baptist burial ground at Lyncombe Hill remains. For many years the Baptist church in Bath, which in 1872 moved from Somerset Street to Manvers Street, had tried to find other uses for it, including several attempts to persuade the Bath City Council to take over ownership. Maintenance had become difficult, and the necessary additional cost of removing human remains prohibitive. Various suggestions were made for recreation, car parking, and

---

[116] BRO. Records of 'Clearance under Housing Act 1936, on grounds of health, of Snow Hill No. 2 Area, 1949-51.'

building on the disused ground; and it was the city council's view that the site could make a suitable small park for local residents.[117] The Council's refusal to purchase the site, and their rejection of an application to build sheltered housing, led to the Secretary of State for the Environment calling for a public inquiry. This was itself halted at the last moment, when it was concluded that 'the council will buy the overgrown land which does not appear to be of much use to anyone following past decisions.'[118] This did not happen but in the 1990s ownership of the ground was transferred to The Bath Preservation Trust who have cleared the undergrowth, repaired walls and memorials, and engaged in a scheme of sympathetic replanting – their stated aim being to maintain the Baptist burial ground on Lyncombe Hill as a garden and a peaceful haven for people and nature together.

Somerset Street in Trouble

By mid-1825 the Baptist church at Somerset Street, Bath, was increasingly conscious that their pastor, John Paul Porter, was plagued by age and illness, and weighed down with his pastoral duties. There were an increasing number of Sundays when Porter was unable to fulfil his pastoral obligations. The church meeting held on 11 August was mainly taken up with their concern to fill the pulpit on Sundays during their pastor's frequent absences. The matter equally troubled Porter himself, who wrote to the church a letter which was discussed at a 'general and special Church Meeting' held on Monday 29 August 1825. Porter makes it clear to his friends at Somerset Street that:

> My earnest desire is to promote your peace and real prosperity, and being brought from the gates of death contrary to my expectation, am willing to demonstrate my readiness to remove every obstacle that might prevent the desirable blessings.
>
> First. From this time I shall not consider myself engaged to preach three times on Lord's day.
>
> Secondly. That I shall willingly accept any assistance that the Church may procure by different ministers till the ultimate object of their wishes may be obtained – which is, to procure an assistant minister – and when such person shall be found of good character, sound in the faith, of suitable talents and acceptable to the people, such person will be acceptable to me.
>
> Thirdly. That from Sept 29 1825 (My usual Salary being paid) I will subscribe £50 per annum towards the support of such assistant, which with that which has previously taken place will

---

[117] Bath City Council, 1978, 97.
[118] *Bath Evening Chronicle*, 18 July 1981.

> be relinquishing £70 per year – which I shall feel to be a great sacrifice.
>
> As I am about to leave home for a few weeks in hope that my health will be established by such means – I hope to have an interest in your prayers, and I will endeavour to repay in kind.
>
> In what I have hereby expressed, I have no innuendo, no covert expression, nor mental reservation; but have expressed what I mean and mean that which I have hereby expressed, and remain your afflicted but affectionate Pastor.[119]

Porter was clearly feeling the strain and considered it wise that he have assistance. The final paragraph is significant in the light of the controversy and misunderstanding with which the church had been plagued and which it would experience again within a few years. It was indeed the church's desire that Porter should have an assistant, and through the deacons they decided to seek a suitable candidate. William Mearsell, a student at the Bristol Academy, was invited to supply the pulpit for one month, although it seems the appointment was not extended. John Paul Porter's continued illness meant that a lot of church business would be conducted in his absence, a situation necessitating the need for deacons Thomas Langdon and Jasper Gay to visit their minister 'for the purpose of requesting the production of the Book containing the names of the Church Members.'[120]

The following January a Mr J Davis was invited to preach at Somerset Street.[121] He was thereafter appointed on a short trial, and on 2 March 1826 awarded a salary of £100 per annum for the course of his engagement. As agreed on 13 April, a special meeting was held on 21 April to discuss extending Davis's appointment:

> The period being nearly expired for which Mr Davis was called as an assistant minister to our pastor, we well take the sense of the Church relative to calling him for a longer period, to appoint what time: three, six, nine or twelve months, hoping that the friends in general will find pecuniary assistance to answer the purpose. A motion was made by Mr Jasper Gay seconded by Mr Langdon that Mr Davis be further called as an assistant to our pastor for six months, after the expiration of the first call, and that Mr G Evill and Mr T Langdon inform him of the same.[122]

John Paul Porter subsequently signed the minutes of the meeting. He would from now on have an assistant he approved of. Davis accepted the call for a

---

[119] SSBC, *Minutes*, 29 August 1825.
[120] Ibid, 1825.
[121] Ibid, January 1826.
[122] Ibid, 21 April 1826.

further six months from 15 May 1826,[123] and this was extended indefinitely 'by a great majority' at the church meeting held on 14 September. For a short time, at least, the records demonstrate that the arrangement was acceptable to all concerned. Yet within a year this position would alter considerably.

In October 1827 Davis was in London, and wrote to the church at Somerset Street about the possibility of being appointed co-pastor alongside John Paul Porter.[124] The church considered this possibility seriously, and time was given for Porter to consider the matter himself.[125] In the event, however, the church decided that they could not support this financially,[126] and the answer would have to be negative. It was at this point that Davis's reason for visiting London became evident, as Somerset Street received a letter from Davis begging leave of the church to take up an invitation from the Baptist church at Tottenham to be their pastor. Things were not as simple as they seemed.

Although the church had communicated its financial inadequacy to support a co-pastor, there were those who believed the primary reason was John Paul Porter's personal opposition. Without an assistant minister, and fewer services being preached at by Porter, the deacons were increasingly obliged to find other ministers to supply the pulpit on Sundays.[127] Yet the church's respect for their ageing pastor put John Paul Porter in a strong strategic position. The 17 January 1828 church meeting recorded the reaction of some of its members:

> Some of the members were highly offended because Mr Porter could not comply to have a co-pastor. They sent a letter in print to our Deacon Mr J Gay addressed to the Church, saying that they had agreed to unite themselves together to form another Church on somewhat different principles from us, and that they withdrew themselves from our communion, and if any communication should be sent to them that it may be communicated care of Mr G Evill.[128]

This they did, and twenty three members were dismissed to form the meeting at Hetling House, opened for that purpose by Robert Hall.[129] That the twenty three members were disappointed is clear; what the 'different principles' refers to is not so clear from the minutes. Philip Cater later confirms that the issue was over 'open communion', which York Street would practice,[130] whereas at the Somerset Street church the communion table was closed to all but members.

---

[123] Ibid, 15 May 1826.
[124] Ibid, October 1827.
[125] Ibid.
[126] Ibid.
[127] Ibid.
[128] Ibid, 17 January 1828.
[129] Cater, 1834, 148.
[130] Cater, 1858, 6.

We will recall that this is consistent with the first Bath Baptist church's constitution around a strict bounded covenant – and also the reticence of John Paul Porter to allow communion at the new community at Twerton.

Hetling House contained a number of public rooms that would hold a small gathering, yet this congregation soon expanded and moved into the premises in York Street that had been occupied by the now disbanded group that had formed a separate congregation after the visits of William Gadsby and John Warburton. The premises needed renovating, so a grant was obtained from the Baptist Building Fund.[131] Lease documents for the site in York Street, which was later owned and redeveloped by the city council, show the 'present' and 'intended elevation' of the new chapel as it was planned in 1829.[132]

There was little antagonism between the York Street and Somerset Street congregations, partly it seems because there was very little actual difference between the parties, and George Evill was a senior second-generation member of the family with which Porter had fond associations. By this time there were a growing number of Baptist churches in Bath, so the concept of a single Bath Baptist community was long since past.[133] Whether it was a matter of growth by friendly division, or that memories were short and the original issue was soon forgotten, Baptist witness to the Gospel continued as new congregations were planted. Yet there was still, as we shall see, the tension within Somerset Street to maintain its own dissenting community tradition. John Paul Porter preached at York Street at least once,[134] and by 1850 York Street was a thriving, busy congregation, and the chapel 'a neat edifice with galleries round the walls.'[135] Philip Cater, the author of Porter's biography and memoirs, was the first minister appointed in 1831 and he served the church until 1841 when he moved away. Cater returned to York Street and was their last recorded minister from 5 July 1857 until his retirement on 25 December 1858. Suddenly, without any known reason, the congregation dispersed, with only a few words recorded in the Membership book: 'In 1859. March 3rd the last meeting was held & the church dispersed. The proceeds of the sale of the Chapel being divided among 5 existing Societies.'[136]

John Davis, who was at the centre of the controversy, did not go to Hetling House with the other members, but moved to Tottenham, London. Almost immediately, Owen Clarke was invited to Somerset Street from the Baptist church at Taunton. It was debated whether Clarke should be invited as co-pastor, and he was under the impression that he had been when leaving his

---

[131] Price, 1926-8, 276.
[132] BRO. DP 2441B. *Lease of a Plot of Ground and a Chapel built thereon situate in York Street.* Illustration reproduced by kind permission of Bath Record Office. See Figure 30.
[133] For further discussion, see pp.174, 218.
[134] Cater, 1834, 149.
[135] S Gibbs, *Gibbs' Bath Visitant, or New Bath Guide*, 1850.
[136] MSBC, *York Street Membership Roll*, 1828-59.

former pastorate. Porter disagreed, and would not sanction Clarke's ministry, eventually withdrawing from the church himself. He later described this period as 'the season of anarchy; while the Rev.d O. Clarke, and his friends, asserted authority over all'.[137]

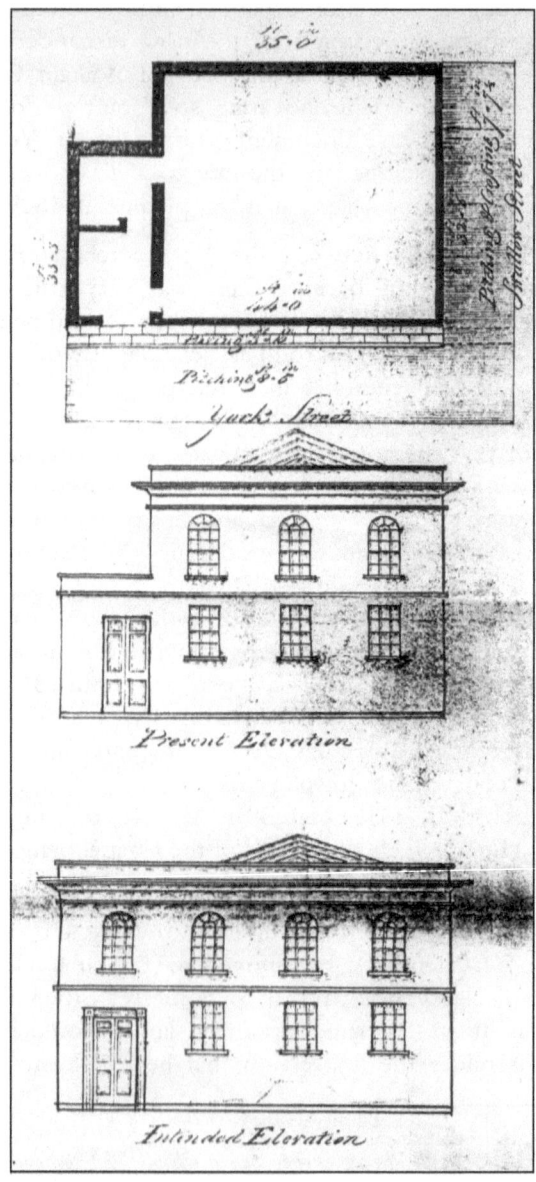

Figure 30. York Street Chapel, 1829

---

[137] SSBC, *Minutes*. A remark added to the book in 1830 describing the period from 5 June 1828 onwards.

The church split in two: those supporting Porter, and those in favour of Clarke. Only a few members supported a motion that Clarke's invitation was irregular.[138] Porter's supporters would not co-operate, nor would they add their names to a letter sent to implore Porter to reconsider.[139] In his reply, Porter accused members of disaffection: 'you have denied me the character of a pastor of the Church' and he complained of the 'utter contempt in which you hold me';[140] he threatened action against any who disrupted his ministry again. What Porter meant by 'the character of a pastor' is difficult to discern, although from the context of the dispute it would seem to refer to a lack of respect and deference to his pastoral authority as a minister of the Gospel. There was, of course, great surprise that John Paul Porter should have so misunderstood their intentions; both groups were certain that they were right – after all, the whole controversy began from the desire of both sides that Porter should have assistance in his infirmity.

On one Sunday in the autumn, Clarke and his friends arrived to find the chapel locked. Porter could not be found with the keys and so they had to worship in the Sunday School room in Milk Street until the locks could be changed.[141] On another occasion Porter entered the church to find Clarke already in the pulpit, and the stairs guarded by constables.[142] This was 9 November 1828. Only three days previously Clarke had hesitatingly accepted the call as sole-Pastor. Such was the antagonism that Robert Hall wisely advised Clarke to seek legal representation in case the worst should happen.[143] The worst did happen, and John Paul Porter opened a suit in the Court of Chancery in an attempt to regain control of the chapel in Somerset Street. A search of Dissenters' Certificates in the Bath and Wells Diocesan collection has unearthed an interesting detail about this period. According to the law, the Somerset Street chapel should have been licensed as a place of worship in 1771, but a certificate does not appear to have been taken out until October 1828. Clearly Porter had himself taken legal advice, and it was thought wise to remedy the licensing error before taking the matter to court.[144]

While this was all happening the members at Twerton again requested to be dismissed to form a separate church.[145] Porter gathered some members together for a meeting and an equally respectful letter was sent in reply to Twerton.[146] Twenty-nine members were formed into a separate church, and the

---

[138] Ibid.
[139] Ibid.
[140] Ibid.
[141] Ibid.
[142] *Proceedings in Chancery*, 1829, 7.
[143] SSBC, *Minutes*.
[144] SRO, D/D/RM. *Dissenters Certificates*.
[145] TBC, *Correspondence*, 1816-53.
[146] TBC, *Correspondence*.

circumstances explain why less than one third of the Somerset Street membership signed the letter of dismissal.

Owen Clarke's supporters were surprised that this could have taken place, considering Porter no longer their minister and invested therefore with no authority. Both groups considered that they were the true mother church. So, seeing that 'Twerton have been long desirous of being separated and as they possess a sacred right to the enjoyment of their Gospel Liberty',[147] the church group led by Owen Clarke also dismissed Twerton to further the Gospel separately. It is somewhat ironic that soon afterwards Porter recorded in his diary: 'Preached at Twerton with pleasure; but in returning home with Mr Harris met with an accident: the night being dark and the rain heavy we fell down and were severely hurt. Great pain in my left arm.'[148] It is possible to trace their route for the two miles from Twerton along the Lower Bristol Road on the south side of the Avon all the way into Widcombe, turning into Lyncombe Hill where Richard Harris lived a few doors up on the left, then past the entrance to the burial ground, and left into Southcot Place, where John Paul Porter had his residence.

It might be supposed that this accident set the tone for the months to follow. The Winter of 1828 to 1829 was involved in collecting pleadings to present before the Vice Chancellor. The Plaintiffs — John Paul Porter, Opie Smith, James Grant Smith, James Evill, and others — gave evidence concerning the rights of the trustees in governing the church, and the procedure for electing a new minister (including the evidence of Joseph Ivimey of Eagle Street). The Defendants — Owen Clarke, Thomas Langdon, George Cox, and others — based their case on Owen Clarke's positive offer of a co-pastorship, the offer of living accommodation from Opie Smith, and put forward a set of quite different procedures for electing a minister![149] Several remarks can be made about this, in what it demonstrates about Baptists in Bath at this time. There were present within the Baptist community at Somerset Street a variety of experiences and expectations regarding the appointment of a pastor, and these were dividing the congregation. No longer was this church an isolated, protected unit, bound together by such strong relationships as had been defined by the church covenant and as we have seen demonstrated in practice sixty or seventy years earlier. Furthermore, there were now a number of Baptist churches in Bath[150] — Somerset Street was no longer the main focus for Baptist worship and witness amongst the Baptists of Bath. This diversity is further reflected in the evidence collected, the witnesses cited, and even in the resolution and final outcome of the dispute.

---

[147] SSBC, *Minutes*.
[148] Cater, 1834, 149.
[149] *Proceedings in Chancery*, 1829, 7.
[150] For further discussion, see p.185.

As it turned out the court action was useless, for the Vice Chancellor could find no grounds on which to interfere. The trust deeds related to the worship of God by Particular Baptists holding five quite specific doctrines, and said nothing about discipline, government or choosing a minister. Porter was the church's second ever pastor, and the first actually to have been appointed – and then amid controversy, as we have seen – so there was no real longstanding precedent to bind the congregation.[151] Meanwhile, John Paul Porter proceeded to preach at the old Roman Catholic chapel in Corn Street, acquired by Opie Smith for the purpose,[152] and Owen Clarke continued to occupy the pulpit at Somerset Street. The case was left in the hands of local Baptist arbiters who met in the Spring of 1830:

> The parties at variance after considerable time spent in the Court of Chancery mutually agreed to submit the business to arbitration. Five very honourable deacons of Baptist Churches engaged in the affair. After examining the witnesses in Bath during the space of eight days at the White Lion Inn. and brought the business to a conclusion and restored J.P. Porter to his pulpit.[153]

This was 3 July 1830; the following day the Lord's Supper was celebrated and the church covenant reaffirmed. Later that month the church made a point of copying the covenant into their minute book whereupon it was signed by those members present at the meeting:

> The undersign'd members of the particular Baptist Church, meeting in Somerset St in the City of Bath, under the pastoral care of John Paul Porter after having been depriv'd of the place of worship from November ye 9th 1828 to July the third 1830, at that period restored to them by arbitration; – do hereby avow their attachment to each other as in the sight of God to walk together in Church fellowship and sign the covenant which has been in the Church more than seventy years, from its first formation[154]

This is significant; for it demonstrates the base line upon which the church considered that it had been built. As we have seen above, the covenant had set out the relationships and the mutual accountability of each of the members to each other and the church. The garden wall, to use the imagery they were familiar with, had been breached and there were other more open enclosures in the vicinity. Furthermore, the 'bonds of love' had been broken, as one group after another had questioned, challenged and then acted against the authority of

---

[151] Ibid, 81.
[152] SRO, D/D/RM. *Dissenters Certificates*.
[153] SSBC, *Minutes*, 3 July 1830.
[154] Ibid, 25 July 1830.

the church. Members felt able to speak openly and unkindly against each other, and they had significant precedent for this from the time of Thomas Parsons, who was still actively promoting his cause, as we have seen, into the first decade of the nineteenth century.

The church was tired and worn out, and this is, as we shall see, reflected in the membership figures. The members of the church who had followed Owen Clarke continued to meet elsewhere, and Somerset Street began to look seriously again for assistance for John Paul Porter – in fact the church was now looking for a co-pastor. There was therefore still some practical difference between the Somerset Street members and their pastor, for although by the end of 1831 an acceptable co-pastor was found in Mr Shem Evans,[155] Porter only considered him to be his assistant.[156] The church, however, had a more practical purpose in mind in calling a co-pastor. Yes, Evans would work with Porter, 'but in case of the death of Mr Porter then on probation for the Pastoral office'![157] The seventy-two year old John Paul Porter died on 10 October 1832, having completed over forty-one years as Baptist minister in Bath, and was buried in the burial ground in Lyncombe within sight of the back window of his home in Southcot Place.

---

[155] Ibid, 1831.
[156] Cater, 1834, 153.
[157] SSBC, *Minutes*.

Chapter 6: A New Community

Twerton Separates

During 1828 whilst the Baptist church at Somerset Street was embroiled in its crisis of leadership and ministry the members at Twerton, as we have seen above, took the opportunity of seeking their independence and again requested to be dismissed to form a separate church. Their letter dated 5 November 1828 still exists amongst the collection of letters and papers that had been rediscovered and written about by R G Naish in 1934. Naish was the first really to appreciate the value of the letters for telling the story and did so as his own voyage of discovery through the box of papers that had not been looked at for nearly a century. Although Naish's short series of articles in the *Bath and Wilts Chronicle and Herald* in the late summer of 1934 brought these letters to light nothing more was done with the letters until 1978 when they were included in an exhibition to celebrate the ter-jubilees of Twerton and Oldfield Park. Naish was pressed for space, and only includes selected quotations from the letters in his articles. Furthermore, as we have seen, he does so for the purposes of demonstrating the pioneering nature of the Twerton Baptist Sunday School, the significance of James Cadby in leadership of the Baptist church at Twerton, and important for our purposes here, to highlight the 'How Twerton Baptists Broke Free from Bath' – or the liberation of the Twerton community from the tyranny of their bondage to Somerset Street.[1] The letters have not been published or used for any purpose since 1934, and as substantial extracts in this study will demonstrate, form a significant collection of correspondence – telling the story of the Twerton community from its early days to the middle of the nineteenth century. The letters are also unique as a collection, illustrating the workings and management of a small Baptist chapel, the issues that were its major concerns, and the importance of a small network of itinerant preachers and neighbouring ministers in the counties around Bath. The letters not only address the local, but illustrate the regional context within which the Twerton church was placed.

The letter written from Twerton to Somerset Street in 1828 was addressed to Rev. John Paul Porter in the most respectful of terms:

> Twerton Novr 1828
>
> Reverend Sir,
>
> With feelings of unfeigned veneration, love and gratitude, we whose names are underwritten, being the humble members of your Church residing at Twerton, desire with all lowliness of mind to give thanks and bless the Name of our Lord and Saviour, by whose grace and providence you have been upheld

---

[1] Naish, 1934, 30 August.

so long his faithful minister, and beloved Pastor of our Church, and by whose Holy Blessings you have been made the highly honoured instrument of bringing many poor sinners to His blessed Feet, and Sir we desire ever to cherish in our memories how you have instructed and comforted and warned us even as a Father doth his children.

And now Dear Sir, believing that you will not deny us anything that you judge will be for our spiritual increase, and for the glory of God, we humbly present our desire before you that it may be your pleasure to dismiss us from your Church for the purpose of our being formed a separate Church of the same Faith and Order, and being encouraged Sir, by your fatherly indulgence, if you will please to favour us with your kind aid in our formation of a little new community, we hope reverend Sir, we shall always remember to pray for you, which must remain our indispensable duty and heartfelt Obligation.

The Somerset Street congregation had been divided by their own crisis, and those that had left with Porter were at this point still meeting in the disused Catholic chapel in Corn Street. The meeting that John Paul Porter gathered had called 'on the Lord's day following they were driven out of the place of worship',[2] had dismissed thirty of the Somerset Street members to form into a separate Baptist church community at Twerton. The letter of dismissal also survives:

Mssrs John Cadby, John Wadham,
and others, Twerton.

The Baptist Church meeting in Somerset Street Bath, under the pastoral care of John Paul Porter, to the members of the said Church residing in the village of Twerton.

Beloved Brethren and Sisters in the Lord.

We have known you long, esteem you highly, and earnestly desire to promote your best interest — you have respectfully and affectionately applied to us by letter to dismiss the persons whose names were recorded, in order that you may be formed into a separate Church — We cheerfully comply with your request, and affectionately dismiss you for that purpose, and pray that the Spirit of the Lord may rest upon you, to influence your minds to all that is lovely in his sight, impart a spirit of prayer and supplication, judgment, and discretion, a living faith and living hope, that you may walk in Communion with God,

---

[2] SSBC, *Minutes*, 8 November 1828.

and in love toward each other that you may increase in number, and in gifts, and in grace, as ripe for glory you may enter into the presence of the Saviour in the World of Glory. Thus pray your affectionate Brethren in the Lord.

Signed at our meeting…

Sixty members of Somerset Street signed the letter, and then followed the names of the thirty members dismissed to the new church at Twerton.[3] On Sunday 16 November 1828, John Paul Porter, Opie Smith and Richard Harris visited Twerton to recognise formally the separation and to regularise the formation of a separate church. As we have seen, Owen Clarke's followers also responded to Twerton, and so the new independent Baptist congregation at Twerton was doubly constituted by both parties of a divided church!

The first church meeting of the members at Twerton was held on 19 November 1828, at which they fixed subsequent church meetings for the 'first Wednesday of calendar month', and agreed that the ordinance of the Lord's Supper should take place 'every two months, or within that time'. There was singing and prayer, and significantly it was decided to write to Richard Harris, expressing thanks, and requesting that he continue finding supplies until the end of the year:[4]

> Baptist Chapel Twerton
> 20th of November 1828
>
> Kind Sir
>
> Pursuant to a resolution passed at our first Church meeting held last evening being the 19th day of November we humbly embrace the earliest opportunity to present to you the respectful thanks of our Brethren and Sisters the members of our little Church for all your kind services and Charitable assistance during so long a period and present our humble desire before you that you will please to continue to occupy our pulpit or provide some other supply as hereto fore until the 31st day of December 1828 during which time we entreat Dear Sir that you will join with us in our prayers to the Great Head of the Church for his direction to guide our future steps.
>
> Signed on behalf of the whole
> John Wadham

---

[3] The twenty nine names on the original draft letter with the addition of Ann Clapham.
[4] The contribution of Richard Harris to the early welfare of the congregation should not be underestimated—his concerns were both spiritual and practical. An odd account (TBC, *Receipts and Vouchers*, 23 January 1826), for example, survives addressed to 'Mr Harris' for building supplies for Twerton purchased from 'W Tanner' between 26 November and 21 December 1825.

James Cadby[5]

John Wadham and James Cadby were elected deacons at the meeting on 13 December 1828. If Richard Harris was unable to fill the pulpit, and the church was 'destitute of a supply', it was agreed that John Butterworth, one of their own members, should preach. The question of a pastor arose early on but was dismissed, for on 31 November a meeting decided 'that our pulpit be in future occupied by supplies'.

The freedom of the church to make its own decisions was not taken lightly, and a firm but loving discipline maintained within the fellowship from the start, perhaps reflecting the practice of the mother church at Somerset Street in its early days, as the business of the church early in 1829 reveals. For example, on 4 February it was resolved 'that the afternoon service shall in future begin at half past 2 o'clock'; on 4 March it was decided that surplus money collected at the Lord's Supper 'shall be applied to the aged and afflicted members of this Church'; On 1 April James Harris was 'requested to take the superintendence of our Sunday School as a relief to John Wadham'; and 6 May John Wadham and John Butterworth were sent to visit James Tucker who had requested that the church 'strick my name out of the Church Book and not to consider me any more a member'. Ann Adams was also to be visited. All these isolated matters illustrate a church that although newly separate had been well established for two decades, and was used to the ongoing maintenance of Baptist church life.

It is fortunate that such a remarkable and significant collection of letters has survived to enable the reconstruction of the day to day story of the Baptist community at Twerton for many of them had become damp and were beginning to disintegrate, even in 1934.[6] The letters are now in the safekeeping of the Bath Record Office, and it is hoped that by including them in this study, their survival might not only be ensured, but that they might be of further use to other scholars exploring more than just the local context addressed by this study. By far the most correspondence concerns the appointment of preachers to fill the pulpit and preach on a Sunday. One such preacher, who had clearly supplied on previous occasions, was William Eacott of Chapmanslade who replied to John Wadham's request to preach in 1829.

> [Mr John Wadham
> Twerton Near Bath]
>
> Chapmanslade 9 May 1829
>
> Very Dear Friends
>   I am very happy to hear that you have not forgotten our very poor people or of poor me. Respecting our

---

[5] TBC, *Minutes*, 20 November 1828. This copy of the letter sent was added to the minute book.
[6] Naish, 1834, 24 August.

Company of very poor Children, and can safely say that I felt grateful when I received your very kind Epistle, But on the other hand I felt very sorry that it should happen on such a Sabbath, Which renders it impossible for me to come on that Day for in the first place I am engaged and cannot alter it on the 2 Sabbaths Before, the first at Trowbridge and the 2 at Calne, & also the Very Day you fixed on is our Ordinance. But this I would dispenced with if it had not been for my being out the 2 Sabbaths before so I hope you will see the propriety of our excuse & if God Willing & all Agreable on your side I will come June 14th or 21st or July 5th Which you and My Dear Lord shall see Best of his glory & our good.

Should thank you for a line as soon as possible and then I will Not make any other engagements if you will be so good as to let our friend Dregg have your letter he Will Send it at any time and May the good Lord Bless preserve and keep you and Water you Every Moment with the Dew from above is the Desire of your unworthy friend

In the Best Bonds

Wm Eacott[7]

Such preachers were busy not only with their own congregations, but also with the widespread itinerant ministry they were called upon to undertake. The Twerton letters uncover a local network of Baptist preachers supplying churches in the North Somerset and West Wiltshire area. We have already explored the significance of local itinerant preachers during the late and early nineteenth centuries, and it was due to such people, and the dedication of some members, that the church at Twerton received the regularity and quality preaching which almost certainly underlay their time of initial encouragement. That encouragement certainly included the baptism of new Christians and their entry into membership of the church community. The cycle of preaching the Gospel, people coming to faith in Christ, and their baptism and incorporation into the community, demonstrates the effectiveness of Baptist witness throughout this period. Together the letters and minute books show this story of growth. On 8 July 1829 it was agreed that John Savage, James Davis, Joseph Batten, Maria Savage, Hester Huntley and John Wadham junior be invited into membership by baptism, and 'that Mr Porter be applied to take their experience' – that is, to interview them and agree their suitability.

---

[7] All the otherwise unreferenced letters in this chapter are in an extensive and previously unpublished collection relating to Twerton Baptist Church preserved in the Bath Record Office. Acc. 373.

The monthly meeting on 5 August agreed that from 16 August the school, which was still thriving, should meet from 9 o'clock until quarter to 11; that from the same date preaching should take place on Sunday mornings; and that John Butterworth should preach on that occasion. Mr James was due to preach then, so it was proposed 'that a letter be written to him not to attend or supply our pulpit any more from the present'. It was also agreed to invite John Paul Porter 'to administer the Ordinance of Baptism'. A general meeting the following week, 9 August, agreed to appoint John Butterworth to preach each Sunday morning for a trial period.

At the end of the month, 30 August, another meeting was held for the purpose of 'taking the particulars and experience of some friends as candidates for Baptism'; and on that occasion James Batten, James Davis, Hannah White, Hester Huntley, and Maria Batten 'came forward and was examined and approved of by the members of the Church'. For some reason John and Maria Savage were not present, but were examined on 1 September, when it was agreed to receive them into full membership after believers' baptism on the following Sunday, 6 September. John Wadham junior's name dropped from the record at this point. Evidently also John Paul Porter at the age of sixty-nine had declined the opportunity of baptising in the cold waters of the Avon at Twerton, for James Cadby sent a letter requesting William Eacott to attend on this occasion – Eacott was younger than Porter by about sixteen years:

> Chapmanslade Aug 23 1829
>
> Very Dear Friends
>
> I received yours this morning and was glad to hear from you for I have been ill. Every time I received friend Perces Letter for as my Brothers family left on Saturday I could not go with them therefore my Brother took my place. But I am Still of the Same Mind as when Pearce was here that God Willing to be With you 1st Sab of Sept this is this Day fortnight and as to the privileges of the Day I should feel thankful to you to prevail upon Mr Porter to Speak at the Water & preach in the Morning or else get a friend to preach a short Sermon in the afternoon if you have any preaching. But in taking in the people & Breaking of Bread Will take up the time for to baptise and preach 3 times & take in the people Will be too much therefore I hope you will spare me as I have been very poorly. My kind love to all friends & believe me to Remain your affectionate friend
>
> W Eacott

All seems to have gone according to plan, for on Sunday 6 September 1829 John Savage, Joseph Batten, James Davis, Hannah White, Maria Batten, Hester Huntley and Maria Savage 'was Baptized in the River at Twerton by Mr Wm

Eacott of Chapmanslade and received into the Church in the afternoon of the same day'. This was the first public baptism in the river at Twerton, which is why the church wanted John Paul Porter to be involved on this occasion, further ratifying Twerton's existence as a community.

The surviving record indicates that although John Butterworth was now preaching regularly, supplies for the pulpit were still necessary. The replies to James Cadby's letters of invitation were not always helpful.

> Sept 10th 1829
>
> My Dear Brother
>
> I am sorry to say that on account of many engagements I shall not be able to visit you on the appointed day. I promised to visit another Church for months since but have not been able to yet accomplish it hoping that the best of blessings may attend you
>
> Him yours in the love of the Gospel
>
> H Burgman

For the most part locally an invitation accepted in one place meant a pulpit to be filled in another, although there were also an increasing number of itinerant preachers called from within each of the Baptist churches. Yet the arrangements for any one Sunday could be quite complicated.

> Dear Sir
>
> I shall be able to be with the friends at Twerton next Sabbath week, on one condition, if you would have no objection to remove a trifling expense, which I shall incur, by another individual performing an engagement, which I am expected to fulfil. The expense will only be 10/6; which I shall lose, if I come to Twerton, without any recompensation. I am most unwilling to mention this, but in making any engagement, I like to be explicit and positive. I shall, therefore, be happy to be with you, if you can raise this trifle, so that another gentleman may fill the place, which I was expected to supply. I respect the Twerton friends very highly; I like the cause much, and wish it all prosperity. If you can, without any in-convenience, accede to the request of this note, I will make arrangements for being with you, and can announce it next Lord's day; only I shall be much obliged, if you will let me know as speedily as possible. I wish you every blessing, and considerable prosperity. May God be your portion — Christ your deliverer — and heaven your inheritance.
>
> I remn Sir

Yrs respectfully

Thomas Wallace

11 Northumberland Place, Bath
October 22 1829

It was not only Sundays that needed supplying with preachers, for there was also a regular evening conference meeting to which preachers were invited. It seems that the best laid plans were subject to last minute alteration, particularly in the winter months.

> My Dear Sir
>
> I much regret to say, that, in consequence of personal disposition, over which I have no control, I shall be prevented seeing you this evening, as I anticipated, a severe cold, which much affected my chest, is the cause. I hoped this morning, that I might be able to see you, but my friends advise me, by no means, to persist in going.
>
> Regretting these circumstances, and wishing you every blessing
> —
>
> I remn Yrs. very truly,
>
> Thomas Wallace
>
> Tuesday Feb 7th. 1830

Yet despite such administrative complications, from the surviving record it appears that the church was both active and encouraged. On 2 December 1829 a further two members, Isaac and Priscilla Pearce, were unanimously received by letter dismissing them from the Baptist church at Melksham:

> From the Particular Baptist Church Meeting at Zion Chapel in Melksham to the Baptist Church in Twerton near Bath in the same faith and order
>
> We the friends of the former Church Certify that our friends Isaac Pearce and his wife Priscilla Pearce Stand with us full members Walking from their first making a public profession unto this drawing us in all things according to the Gospel and save we are Depart from them
>
> Deacons   Richard Rue
>   T Small
>   Abraham Little
>   George Knee
>   Jasper Holder
>   William Mail

Thos Cleverly
John Tuff

An important factor influencing the growth of the Baptist community at Twerton was the growth of the village itself during the early nineteenth century, mainly due to its industrial development. There was a great deal of migration from West Wiltshire and further afield as the cloth industry expanded.[8] During the 1960s and early 1970s many of the older Twerton cloth mill buildings were demolished and a significant part of the evidence for the story was lost.[9] It was largely due to the work of local historians Cynthia Turner and Michael Messer that some good photographic and documentary record survives in the Bath Record Office, and they also pointed to the importance of the earlier work of Twerton historian R G Naish in the 1830s. Their pioneering work was followed by others who were able to restore the significance of Twerton to the history of West Country woollen cloth manufacturing, including J de L Mann, Kenneth Ponting and Kenneth Rogers.[10] In 1972 John Wroughton edited a book of essays of topics of Bath social history by his students at King Edwards School, one of which was a valuable study by Wroughton himself on 'Bath and Its Workers' – as part of which he considers working conditions at Charles Wilkins' mill in Twerton, at which many of the Twerton Baptist members were employees, as reported by the Factory Inspectors.[11]

A more recent study by Nicholas von Behr, 'The Cloth Industry of Twerton from the 1780s to the 1820s', is particularly important in that it brings together much of the story from the earlier studies and paints the industrial context of a village rapidly expanding as working opportunities increased,[12] a population into which the Baptist community would live out their faith by providing for religious and other social needs, along with Methodist and other groups. What none of these studies do is to explore the religious life of the community and its workers, a world into which the valuable collection of Twerton Baptist letters gives insight, making the connection between church and community, as we shall see below. Much of the reason for this lack of exploration is that the story has not been told consistently, and the records hidden for so many years, despite the fact that the religious community played a considerable part in the development of the local Twerton community.

The connection between the Baptist church in Twerton and its local community can also be demonstrated in other ways. **Figure 31** plots the membership figures for the Twerton Baptist community throughout the whole of the

---

[8] Confirmed by 1831 and 1841 census returns showing places of birth and occupations.
[9] For example, there is no reference at all to the Twerton clothing industry in *Industrial Archaeology of the Bristol Region*. Buchanan & Cossons, 1969.
[10] Mann, 1971; Ponting, 1971, 1975; Rogers, 1976, 1986.
[11] Wroughton, 1972, 5-20.
[12] von Behr, 1996, 88-107.

nineteenth century. It can clearly be seen that membership increased over fourfold during the first two decades of its life, reaching a peak around 1851 before declining towards the end of the century when the move to Oldfield Park was being planned and organised:

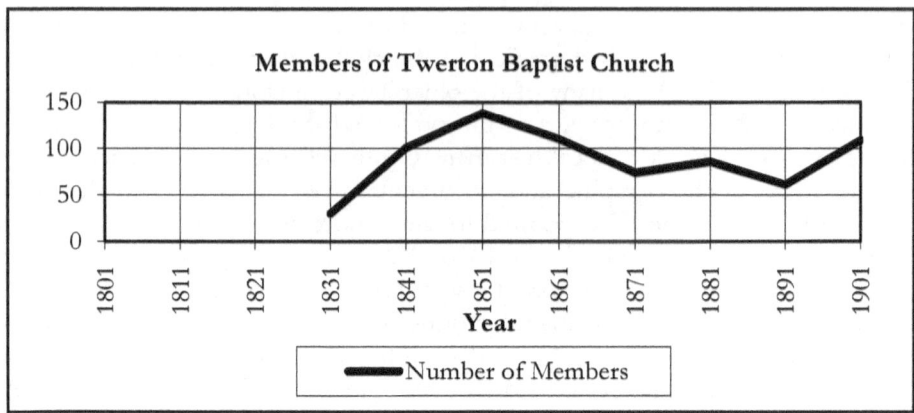

Figure 31. Members of Twerton Baptist Church.

This can be readily compared with the rising population of the village itself as reported in the annual census reports and plotted in **Figure 32**:

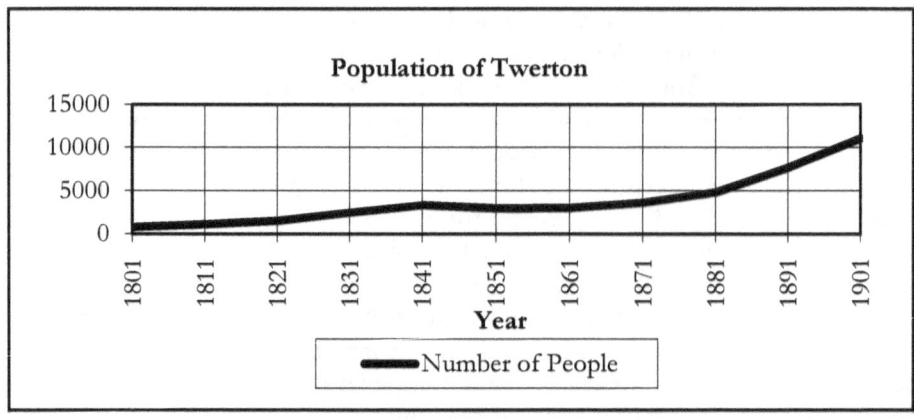

Figure 32. Population of Twerton.

Nicholas von Behr connects this growth with the woollen cloth industry, based on the mills which had been founded on the upper and lower weirs during the eighteenth century, and later developed by Francis Naish, Ebenezer Brown, Charles Wilkins, and the Carr family:

> Under these enterprising manufacturers the two eighteenth-century mill sites on the south bank of the River Avon at Twerton village were transformed into factory premises, where by the mid-1820s the foundations for the emergence of the

internationally-renowned superfine cloth industry had been laid. The parish of Twerton became a growing industrial suburb which was absorbed into the city of Bath in the early twentieth century. Cloth manufacturing continued at Twerton until its demise in the 1950s, in the face of competition from Yorkshire and abroad.[13]

When population figures are plotted together with the Twerton Baptist figures, to show Baptist members as a percentage of the Twerton population, as in **Figure 33**, another story begins to emerge.

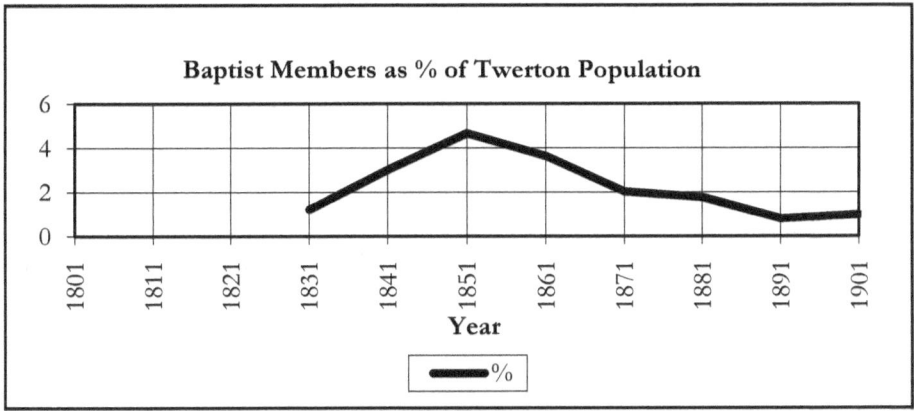

Figure 33. Baptist Members as % of Twerton Population.

The growth in Twerton's population in the second half of the nineteenth century was on the eastern side, infilling the space between the village and the city, and producing a new suburb. The chapel at the west end of the new enlarged parish no longer provided for the main centre of the population which now focused on Oldfield Park, where in response the Twerton Baptists planned to build their new chapel. Although this later development at Oldfield Park is not part of the detailed concern or timescale of this study, it has its roots in a Baptist congregation keen to remain connected to the heart of their local community. In the early nineteenth century this connection can be most strongly seen in the relationship between the Twerton Baptist community and the woollen mills, its major employer.

As we have seen, the Particular Baptist chapel in Twerton was built in 1808, on a plot of land leased from mill owner Francis Naish. In the two decades since, the mills had changed hands, as had the ownership of the land. At the monthly meeting of the Twerton Baptists on 6 January 1830 it was made known that Charles Wilkins, now owner of the woollen cloth mills in which many in the congregation worked, had made available to the church an additional 16 feet of

---

[13] Ibid, 103.

adjacent ground, and there was much discussion about possible enlargement. Up to now there were no formal trust deeds for a Baptist chapel as the land had been made freely available by Naish, so on 25 March 1830 Charles Wilkins incorporated the whole site and assigned the lease of the chapel and ground to John Wadham, described as 'the Elder of the Parish of Twerton', for 500 years and with an annual rent of £1.[14]

In a subsequent deed dated 1 April 1830,[15] John Wadham assigned the property to trustees on behalf of the Baptist community for the remainder of the 500 years. This trust deed provides a wealth of information about the church at this time. The trustees consisted of two groups of men. The first were all members of Somerset Street Chapel in Bath: namely James Grant Smith esquire, of the parish of Lyncombe and Widcombe; Richard Harris, builder, of the same parish; Ebenezer Smith, printer, of the city of Bath; James Dyer, tailor, of Bath; Thomas Shepherd, cabinet maker, of Bath; Joshua Arthur, baker, of Bath; and Benjamin Arthur, baker, also of Bath. The remaining trustees were all members of the Baptist church at Twerton, and all resident in that parish: James Cadby, cloth worker; James Harris, carpenter; John Butterworth, cloth worker; John Savage, cloth worker; Samuel Tanner, cloth worker; Joseph Batten, cloth worker; William Wickham, cloth worker; and John Butcher, also a cloth worker. By far the biggest group, as has been said and can here be seen, were employees of Charles Wilkins in his Twerton woollen cloth mills.

The property under trust was described as a 'Chapel and Vestry room' erected on a plot which was 'bounded on or toward the east by a street or lane leading from the High Street of Twerton to the River Avon on or toward the south by the Poor House of Twerton aforesaid and on or toward the north and west by Ground belonging to the said Charles Wilkins'. Owning their own property through the legal process of charity trusteeship gave the Baptist community a greater security – and illustrates the thoughtful patronage of Wilkins for active and committed members of the community, and the welfare of members of his workforce. As important, the deed not only made provision for replacing deceased trustees from time to time, but also gave conditions about how and by whom the land could be used. The trustees were:

> Upon Trust to permit and suffer the said Chapel, Vestry rooms and premises to be used occupied and enjoyed as and for a place of public religious worship for the service of God by the society of Protestant Dissenters of the denomination of Particular or Calvinistic Baptists, maintaining the Congregational order of the churches and maintaining and acknowledging the Scriptural Doctrines of three equal Persons in the Godhead, Election,

---

[14] TBC, *Receipts and Vouchers*, 25 February 1830. Receipt for £1.0.0 ground rent from James Cadby for the year from 25 December 1829, signed William Daniel & Co.
[15] TBC, *Trust Deed*, 1 April 1830.

> Original sin, Redemption by Christ, Free justification by the imputed Righteousness of Christ, efficacious Grace in Regeneration, the moral law as a rule of life and conduct to all Believers, The final perseverance of saints, The Resurrection of the dead, The future judgement, The eternal happiness of the righteous and endless misery of the impenitent and practising Baptism by immersion to such only as are of years of understanding upon their own confession of repentance toward God and Faith in Our Lord Jesus Christ, now assembling in the said Chapel and all other persons who shall be hereafter united to the said Society and be in full communion therewith.

In other words, having been separated from Somerset Street to be an independent community in their own right, according to Baptist custom and practice, the trust deed further legally incorporated the community as a regular Particular Baptist church. The deed also gave the membership of the church on a two thirds majority the freedom to appoint and remove a minister or pastor without interference from the trustees, so long as that person acknowledged the doctrinal statement. Deacons could be appointed by a simple majority, and it was their responsibility to engage supplies for the pulpit if vacant for any reason. At a meeting on the first Wednesday in May male members were to elect a treasurer from among the deacons for the trust funds. The deacons were to collect and supply to the treasurer all contributions and subscriptions paid to support the public worship of God in the chapel; from which the treasurer could discharge ground rent, rates, taxes, insurance premiums, trustees and treasury expenses, pay any permanent minister, and meet any other legitimate costs. There was also provision for keeping full accounts and records of business transactions, and holding monthly general meetings and extraordinary meetings of church members. In effect the model of the mother church at Somerset Street was being duplicated in the new church at Twerton, adopting the normal customs and practices for the management of a Particular Baptist church.

Two letters survive with the copy of the deed, both addressed to Mr James Cadby at Charles Wilkins' factory in Twerton. Although undated, they provide further evidence, as R G Naish had so insisted and as we have seen earlier, that of the first appointed deacons it was James Cadby who took the leading administrative and management role in the church, acting as senior deacon and secretary:

> Sir
>
> Mr J G Smith will be ready to wait on Mr Wilkins either today or tomorrow and wishes you to appoint an hour with Mr W after 4 in the afternoon or if that will not do before 11 in the morning, Mr Smith to have the choice of either day. I should wish to have

the Lease despatched this week otherwise I fear Mr Smith will not be able to attend for a fortnight to come. As I presume you will not be able to send me an answer of the Bearer you must contrive to send someone in to my office to let me know how you have arranged. You had better write a note lest I should be out of the way.

I am Yours S

E. Tucker

Bath, 14 York St
Thursday

Sir

I forgot to say yesterday that it will be necessary for you to come in to attend with me before a Commissioner to acknowledge the Trust Deed before it can be enrolled. You will be otherwise in Town this Evening. I suppose when if you will call any time from 7 we will do the needful

Yours S

E Tucker

James Grant Smith of Westfield House, nephew of the elderly Opie Smith, was one of the trustees, as we have seen; and E Tucker was the solicitor acting on behalf of the parties.

At its monthly meeting on 7 April 1830, now properly constituted under a new trust deed, the Twerton church again considered enlarging the building onto the enlarged site, the size of the congregations and the extent of their activity having expanded sufficiently. This was overwhelmingly agreed; and James Cadby, John Wadham, John Butterworth, John Savage and James Harris were formed into a committee to manage the enlargement. They were permitted to borrow up to £60 and to pay interest to the donors. By end of the month £30 had been received from George Batchelor and £30 from Samuel Tanner, the agreed terms being four per cent interest, with six months notice for calling in the money. George Batchelor was closely connected with the Twerton Baptist community, although himself not a member of the church. The extensive construction work upon which they embarked would have involved closing the chapel for a number of weeks, but how many is not known.[16] James Cadby was still involved

---

[16] An interesting collection of receipts survive (TBC, *Receipts and Vouchers*. 29 March 1830 to 5 August 1830), mostly sewn together and unreadable, giving clues to the scale and cost of the operation: '800 Pantiles' £12.12.0; 'Part of Bill to Buy Lease, Trust Deeds, &c' £15.10.0; Mr Cadby's receipt for 'Red Deal' £1.12.6; a builders receipt for labour from Joseph Meiron, Carpenter, 21 April to 7 June, £200.0.10½; Mr Cadby's receipt for 'Red Deal', 'Pine' and 'Marble' £1.12.4; a receipt and bill to 'Mr Cadby' for building supplies £13.17.6; and on completion of the

in arranging supplies, as the correspondence shows, and perhaps they had been able to arrange a temporary meeting place in the same way that Baptists had first met together in the village in 1804, or perhaps there may have been a large enough room available at the mill. Cadby could certainly always be contacted by addressing letters to 'Mr Wilkins's Manufactory', as was the following message from a certain Mr Dear communicated through a friend:

> To Mr Cadby
>
> Mr Dear presents his kind regards & begs leave to say that he is disengaged for the next Sabbath & could supply Twerton chapel if desirable — The next two Sabbaths he is engaged —
> I thought it right to communicate this information on account of a call from one of the members of the Church some days ago.
>
> Prior P K Cogs
>
> April 15 1830

James Jackson, a frequent visitor to Twerton, was certainly aware both of the enlargement of the church and the difficulties involved in making arrangements, when he wrote to Cadby at the end of April:

> My Dr Sir,
>
> Perhaps it is best to omit a Sabbath or two. You will be kind enough to let me know when you wish my assistance and I am your humble servant.
>
> It will be very pleasant for you to commemorate the dying Love of a crucified Redeemer in the Holy Supper the First Sabbath after your enlargement and if you wish it I will give it the church unless you have some other minister in view.
>
> My kind regards to the friends — and Mrs. C. & family. The Lord be with your spirit.
>
> Affectionately Yrs
>
> J. Jackson
>
> Weston
> 31 April 1830

---

work Rev. Charles Davis's bill with receipt to 'Mr Cadby', dated 5 August, for '20 Chapel Candlesticks'. There are just one or two interesting accounts in the months and years following: 3s.6d 'Paid to Mr Jas. Harris for Sundry Jobs done at the Chapel' 7 November 1830; and ironmonger's receipt for 16s.10d 19 May 1831; and a painter's bill to 'Mr Cadby' dated 7 April 1834 for £1.6.6 which was settled on 18 April.

In the meantime there was still the task of finding preachers for the chapel in the new season when it was reopened. One reply addressed to James Cadby gives a salutary reminder that financial resources were very scarce and many local itinerant preachers were far from fully supported by their congregations, which were either too poor or too small, or otherwise even insensitive to their pastors' real needs. Many were employed, yet others suffered great hardship as they sought to serve the Lord and still provide for their families. If the congregation then needed to build a meeting house, it was essential to appeal to the wider church to raise the money. This was the case with the Baptist church at Corsham that had emerged from an Independent church under the leadership of Henry Webley. An account book records Henry Webley's 'begging expeditions' between 1828 and 1830,[17] and helps to explain the curious letter received by James Cadby at Twerton:

> Corsham May 20th 1830
>
> Sirs
>
> Mrs Webbley informed me that Last Evening she received a note from you inviting Mr Webbley to Twerton – I doubt not that he would have felt gratified in complying with your request but he has been out begging for some time & will not be home 'till next week.
>
> I am yours
>
> Mrs Hackman

The following Sunday, 23 May, the newly enlarged Baptist chapel in Twerton was opened. There were three services each with a sermon: James Jackson preached in the morning and afternoon, and Thomas Wallace in the evening. A total of £13.6d. was collected in total after the services towards reducing the debt. The cost of the enlargement and for making out the new deeds and lease came to £132.12s.1½d., considerably more than had been estimated. However there was now considerably more accommodation for the expanding church. For the deacons the ongoing responsibility of maintaining an adequate supply of preachers for the Sunday and the week night meeting continued. As popularity increased, so did the problems for James Cadby.

> My Dear Sir
>
> I consider it my duty to forward you a line, merely to state that, in consequence of my numerous and increasing engagements during the week, I shall be unable to preach at Twerton, as I have done, on the first Tuesday evening in the month; however, I shall be happy to take on Lord's day every month, or 6 weeks,

---

[17] *TBHS*, 1931, 236-237.

> if it be pleasing to the friends generally. I was thinking that such an arrangement would be more acceptable to the congregation, than an attendance once a month on a Tuesday. If, when you wish me to supply on the Sabbath, you would let me have a few days notice, I shall be obliged. I have always been pleased with the friends at Twerton, and if, at any period, I can serve them, by preaching an anniversary sermon, for the school, or chapel, I shall feel happy.
>
> With every mark of respect to yourself and family.
>
> I remn Yours truly
>
> Thomas Wallace
>
> Bath
> June 8. 1830

Another popular preacher at Twerton was James Evill. He had been brought up at Somerset Street Chapel as a member of the influential Evill family, from where he would have known well many of the Twerton members. In 1807, however, James Evill had moved with his wife to worship with the Independent congregation at Argyle Chapel, at which, as we have seen, Rev. William Jay was the influential minister. Early in 1831 Evill addressed a letter to 'Mr Cadby at Mr Wilkins Factory Twerton':

> Dear Sir
>
> I read your kind favour and the alteration is just what I wished and met my entire approbation, for it being, the ordinance of the Lord's Supper at Mr Jays the first Sabbath in the month, I found it very inconvenient the time being so that between their Service & yours, to be at Twerton in time. I therefore will (God willing) be with you the 2nd Sabbath in February the 13th day of the month with kind regard I am Yours sincerely
>
> Jas Evill.
>
> Bath
> 26th Jan 1831

The new year had started well, when on 16 January 1831 James and Mary Harris were accepted into membership by transfer from Phillips Norton. There was some consideration given to the fact that the church should now invite a permanent pastor and the suggested candidate was well known to the congregation. At the monthly meeting on 2 March it was agreed to arrange a special meeting when those not present before, having been 'spoken to', could attend. On 8 March the church decided unanimously to call James Jackson, 'one of our present supplies', to take on the pastoral care of the church. James Cadby was responsible for minuting the decision in the church book, and he included a copy of the letter sent to Jackson:

Twerton Nr Bath 10th March 1831

Dear Sir

Its with the greatest pleasure I have to present you with the unanimous and sincere wish of the members of our little church at Twerton that if it may be consistent with your views you will take the charge of our little Interest here and become our beloved Pastor but I feel this request is too great and that we are not worthy of your kind attention. I am fully aware that the Income of the House is but trifling and sure I am that this cannot tempt you nor can I conceive any one thing will cause you to accept of our week request but the Glory of your dear Saviour's Kingdom and the Love of Precious Souls in Twerton leaving the above to your serious consideration I remain dear Sir

Yours Affectionately

Jas Cadby

To Mr Jackson
Weston nr Bath

There is no reply recorded. Jackson did not accept the call to be minister at Twerton, although as a good friend of the church he continued to supply the pulpit on frequent occasions. The Twerton letters, in tandem with the surviving minute book, continue to tell the story of a busy and thriving church, which as we have seen was continually growing during this period. At the monthly meeting on 4 May, James Harris was unanimously elected deacon; and on Sunday 24 July the second baptising took place in the river Avon. John Vowels, William Baker, Solomon Slugg, John Bowering, William Fisher, Charlot Baker, Hannah Baily, Sarah Allen and Sarah Vowels were baptised in the Avon by Mr Dear of Bath in the morning, and received into membership in the afternoon.

The success of the church during this period is due in no small way to the commitment of members, friends, and visiting preachers; and the affection in which the fellowship at Twerton was generally held. It seems that in the Twerton Baptist church a community had evolved that held together well, but was also open enough to relate well to the wider communities around it. As we have seen throughout this study, community is important for a Baptist understanding of the church, and yet the nature and structure of that community has changed considerably. It is also true in Twerton that the benevolence and considerable financial support of Charles Wilkins, cloth manufacturer and owner of the Twerton mill at which, as we have said, Cadby and a number of the others were employed, played an important part in this regard – although Wilkins was himself an Anglican. This is significant for it raises the question as to why Wilkins should therefore be supportive of the Baptist community. A number of reasons are possible, other than this being an early act of ecumenism in an age before Dissenters were fully accepted by the established church. R G Naish discovered a note in the Twerton Parish Church records and adds his own comment on what it meant:

> '1846, March.— Old cottages by old poor house made over to the Baptists, who are said to have nearly 200 children in their Sabbath school and are greatly in need of a suitable schoolroom for their accommodation.'
>
> This looks like the representatives of the parish voting property to the Baptists for the religious education of the young. Note the phrases, "made over" and not Sunday but "Sabbath school." I find a surprising brotherhood among the differing denominations of old Twerton. There is no waning of it for a quarter of a century.[18]

What is not so surprising is that it is Naish who points this out, as we have already seen his socialist perspective on the story above. We have already seen the considerable influence of figures such as Opie Smith, James Grant Smith and James Evill in the church and as members of the Bath business community, and it may well be that this relationship extended to Wilkins, as strongly indicated in the following letter.

In the autumn of 1831 James Evill took it upon himself to contact Charles Wilkins concerning the Baptist meeting at Twerton:

> 5 Dartington Place Bath
>
> Dear Sir
>
> Having during my continuing in Business and since then having conferred you favours on my Son, I feel encouraged to take a liberty with you, which if too great I hope you will pardon.
>
> I feel an interest in the welfare of the inhabitants of Twerton and I cannot better discover it than to improve their morals & knowing that you have given proofs of your wish to do the same, by aiding the Cause of Religion (which is the only way to effect so desirable purpose), I send the enclosed for your perusal. Your liberality in granting a piece of ground & the improvement in the front of the little Chapel has been considered as no small evidence of your good wishes for its success & it is now the desire of those who attend not only to

---

[18] Naish, 1939, 24 November.

discharge the Debt, but also if possible to raise sufficient to erect a small Gallery for the Children who are instructed every Sunday by the persons capable of instructing them.

Not to intrude too much on your amiable time my request is, to entreat you & Mr Daniel will honour them by your contributing towards & kindly heading the subscriptions with your names, which I have left for that purpose & have taken the liberty of marking in pencil leaving the sum to your liberality.

As soon as I obtain this favour which I am very anxious to do — it is my intention to make application to many of my friends in Bath and elsewhere to add their names.

I have not informed Mr Cadby my intention of addressing you, but shall feel obliged if you will return the book to him who will convey it to me, without giving you the trouble. I cannot conclude without again hoping I shall not give offence by this application & beg leave to subscribe myself, with great respect. Your obed' friend

Jas Evill
formerly Jeweller in the Market place Bath

26 Sept 1831
Thursd' Morn'

The Rev W Jay has recently preached there & was much gratified by the attendance.

For James Evill, and the Baptist community he represented, the improvement of morals, the 'cause of religion', and the spreading of the gospel, were one and the same thing. In fact, as the 1817 Twerton Baptist Sunday School Annual Report had also made clear, there were other connections to be drawn. For the Baptists of Bath there was a direct relationship between the improvement of the lifestyle of the Twerton population, to which the Christian faith with its attendant religious and moral conversions were key, and the increased usefulness and productivity of the workforce. This fact would not have been lost on Charles Wilkins, as John Wroughton's study of 1972 uncovered.[19]

The manufactory of Charles Wilkins was renowned for its innovative medal winning cloth production, in which the prolific inventor Joseph Clissild Daniell of Limpley Stoke, also mentioned in the letter, was actively engaged. Kenneth Ponting writes:

> An interesting inventor, Jos. Clissild Daniell, lived at Limpley Stoke though all his trading career was spent with the important

---

[19] Wroughton, 1972, 5-20.

firm of Charles Wilkins at Twerton near Bath. Daniell has over 20 textile inventions to his name, two of which were especially important. He discovered that if woollen cloth is put into water and boiled for up to twelve hours, the finish becomes more permanent. Daniell was, in fact, doing the same as is done with the permanent setting of human hair. His process was known as roll-boiling and, later, potting.[20]

Furthermore, Wilkins offered good working conditions but was increasingly concerned about the behaviour of his workers. Especially he had noted the increased drunkenness of the young people in the village, as a result of new public houses opening within a short distance from the factory. He did his best to discourage this with a system of penalties for shoddy work and absenteeism, and by opening a school and reading room with moderately priced refreshments available – much as the Baptists had been doing among the community from their building at the top of Mill Lane. Indeed, as Wroughton discovered, from the 1830s attendance at public worship at least once on a Sunday was obligatory for all his employees. On the whole, though, through his influence and good conditions his workers were, according to the factory inspectors, distinguished by 'the character of being steady, sober, industrious and religious'.[21] It is evident that there was much general local concern for the ordinary people of Twerton, and their moral and spiritual state – and the participation of William Jay was also likely to encourage widespread support for this as he had a reputation amongst the middle classes and intelligentsia far beyond Bath.

It is a mark of the bonds within the community of the Baptist church in Twerton, however, that although they were as concerned about the effects of drunkenness on the moral and spiritual condition of the population, they were anything but swift in condemning James Tucker, whose name was still in the book as a member despite his request to be struck off in May 1829. The church took its time making a decision, which was made at the monthly meeting on 4 January 1832:

> Taking into consideration the conduct and disorderly walk of James Tucker the Church comes to a conclusion that he be no longer a Member of the Church, his beseting sin is drunkenness, which he has been oftimes reproved for, but still persists in the evil, which is a disgrace to the Christian Religion.

In the case of William Croomwell – husband of Martha Croomwell, who was a church member – the monthly meeting on 1 August 1832 agreed to address the issue by letter:

---

[20] Ponting, 1975, 27.
[21] Wroughton, 1972, 11-15.

> It is not with any degree of pleasure but rather a task in addressing you at this time, we wish to inform you of the disapproval of many of our friends seeing you in the Gallery on a Sabbath day sitting with those who are joining in the Praises of Allmighty God while at other times you are drinking getting drunk and Blaspheming his most holy name. Friend these things ought not to be and will you but turn it over in your own mind Conscience will say it ought not to be – We therefore wish when you do attend at the Chapel you will take your seat below stairs, and may the above hint enable you to see that you cannot serve God and Mamon.

The Twerton Baptist community took seriously the disciplined Christian lifestyle, but whereas its members were subject to its boundaries and expectations, when it came to those who were not members, such as William Croomwell, there was need to be more circumspect—although, as we see, in requesting him to behave in a more appropriate manner they did not miss the opportunity to issue a Gospel challenge.

It is apparent from his letter to Charles Wilkins that of all the frequent visitors to Twerton James Evill seems to have taken a particularly personal interest in the cause and its people. And on occasion he seems to have gone to great lengths to help find preachers. He wrote to James Cadby, again at his place of work:

> My Dear Friend
>
> I called upon Mr Eastman & find he is engaged but I have since seen Mr Wilkins who preaches at Marshfield, Colerne Hall & other places & who has promised to supply you on next Sabbath & will be with you on time. I have no doubt from what I have heard of his ability he will please the people with kind Jesus.
>
> I am Your servant
> Jas Evill
>
> Bath
> 13 Feb 1832

And another letter addressed to 'Mr Cadby At Mr Wilkins' manufacturer' reads:

> Saturday afternoon
> 21 Ap 1832
>
> Dear Sir
>
> I did not receive your letter until the above date. I am engaged the 29 Day & must therefore beg to alter my visit to Twerton the 2' Sabbath in May — & I should wish if possible it may be

so arranged that it may always be the 2nd Sabbath in the month. Hoping it will be no disappointment in not hearing before. I am Your servant

Jas Evill

I passed through Twerton about one March & looked hard to see if I could meet anyone I knew.

Whether James Cadby was slow to respond, or whether the letters crossed in the post, we shall never know. Nevertheless James Evill waited only two days before writing again, obviously in some hurry:

[AP23/1832]

Dear Sir

I shall feel much obliged to a reply to my note early tomorrow morning as I have an application to be at Bradford on the 2nd Sabbath in May, if you do not expect me on that day & they are waiting for my answer. I will endeavour to be with you on the 1st Sabbath being regular day — perhaps Mr Cott will give me a Crust of Bread and Cheese.

I remember you
Yours sincerely

Jas Evill   pray send early tomorrow that I may write by post.

The Twerton letters, alongside the corresponding sections of the church minute book, tell the story of a busy and active church community. They were still, however, considerably in debt from the cost of their new building. On 16 April 1832, after two years of waiting, George Batchelor received back the first £20 of his loan for the building extension. Whilst emphasising the growth of the congregation, it is also important to note that set backs were a normal part of life. John Wadham, with whom Cadby had worked so closely, died during 1831. The second member to depart was dismissed by letter of transfer to the Baptist church at Counterslip, Bristol, on 27 June 1832 – a significant number of letters concern such 'dismissals', the traditional Baptist term for letters of transfer of members between one church and another 'of the same faith and order'.

James Jackson had preached at Twerton on a regular basis for over a year when he informed the church during a Sunday service of his growing interest in the Baptist chapel in Thomas Street, off the London Road out of Bath to the east. He followed up his statement in person with a letter, again addressed to James Cadby at the Twerton Mills:

To my Christian Brethren at Twerton
My Dear Friends

On Sunday, I named you the probability of my not being able to visit you as usual if I engaged more permanently in Bath.

Now after a mature and prayerful consideration of all the circumstances of the Chapel in Thomas Street, I thought it my duty to give it a trial of a few months. What may be the future will of God concerning the cause there and of my own health I must leave entirely to him to determine.

In the use of your means as a church, I trust God will provide for you a respectable and useful supply. And should any circumstances arise that may lead me to believe it to be my Duty to drop this present connection — I would then resume my poor assistance with you — if that might be agreeable. I can assure you that the concern of Twerton lies very near my heart: and though I thus withdraw to supply another station, it is my wish if I can obtain a suitable supply, to come and break bread to you in the Lord's supper occasionally.

My Dear Brethren — see that you walk together in peace, and in love, Endeavouring to keep the unity of the spirit in the bond of peace — live in peace — he of one mind and the God of love and peace shall be with you.

Very respectfully your cordial well-wisher
James Jackson

P.S. I sincerely thank all of you, for every mark of action and kindness I have received from you. And I further beg to assure you whatever service I can at any time render you shall not lie wanting.

It will also afford me real pleasure at any time should my Brothers or Christian Sisters give me a call. I am a companion of those who fear God in his will. The Lord be with your spirits — Amen.

No 4 Prospect Place
Camden Place
25 May 1832

James Cadby recorded the church's reply in the minute book:

Twerton Nr Bath 29th May 1832

Dear Sir,

We received yours of the 25th and we humbly embrace the earliest opportunity to present to you the respectful thanks of our Brethren and Sisters the members of our little Church for all your kind services and Charitable assistance during the time you have supplied us and should it be convenient to you to administer the ordinance of the Lord's Supper to us on an occasion we shall feel very thankful, and we trust we shall be ever intresed in your prayers wishing you God Speed in your undertaking I remain with the greatest respect

Yours Affectionately

Jas Cadby
Jas Harris

As a result James Cadby had a regular gap in his pulpit supplies, and was soon engaged sending invitations to fill it. William Eacott received a letter during the following week, which gave him very short notice, and he replied accordingly:

Chapmanslade 7 June 1832

Very Dear Friend

I received your kind but unexpected letter Dated 5th and should have been happy to comply with your request Before the 29 But beeing out last Lord's Day — and to be at Warminster the 8 at Allington 15th and to be at Trowbridge between these two you will plainly see how I am situated, So God Willing I will come & see you once more hoping I shall see you in peace & prosperity & abounding in the Work of the Lord & that I may thro' your prayers Be brought in the fulness of the Gospel of Christ & until then May the Good Lord Bless preserve and keep you & Water you Every Moment with the Dew from above is the Desire of yours in the best Bonds

Wm Eacott

at the same time Tender my Kind Love to all friends & my Wife also joins me in Love to your selfe & Mrs Cadby & family.

Believing us to Remain yours Sincerely

W & J Eacott

James Jackson had agreed to return on occasion to break bread with the Twerton fellowship at the Lord's Supper. Evidently the invitation to administer the July ordinance was too soon after his departure, and he could not find a suitable supply. The Thomas Street congregation had experienced disturbance, and needed consistent ministry for a while, as indicated in Jackson's reply addressed to Cadby at Twerton Mills:

22 June 1832

My Dear Friend

It would have given me great pleasure to have been with you on the first day of July and to have participated with you in the Supper of our dying Lord: but I cannot obtain a suitable supply. My plan must be to engage before-hand a supply for Thomas Street and then give you timely notice of it, that it may as little as possible arrange the order of your supplies. How it may turn out with me in Thos. Street I know not. I think for the month it is perhaps as well as may be. My first congregation was 25 and I suppose we had on Sunday Evening Last 70 and upward which they say has not been the case for more than twelve months.

Will you present my respectful regards to the brethren to all the faithful in Christ Jesus.

Affectionately Yours

J J

No 4 Prospect Place
Camden Place
Bath

N.B. I am obliged to delay writing 'till now having just received Mr. Evill's negatives.

James Jackson's was not the only invitation to be turned down by James Evill in July. What distinguishes James Evill's correspondence from others' is his constant concern that if unable to fulfil an engagement it was the least he could do to obtain a replacement, even if his memory let him down on occasion:

Dear Sirs

An application has been made to me by my esteemed Pastor (Mr Jay) to supply the pulpit of Mr Gear of Bradford the Second Sabbath in August & today I have received a letter from Mr Gear making the same request. I am unwilling to alter your arrangements but I have seen Mr Wilkins who is going to London & he has kindly offered to supply my place on the 2nd Sabbath & I have engaged Mr _____ whose name I have forgotten who lives at Mr Griffiths in Stall Street to be with you on the first Sabbath in August. I will therefore if you are disengaged be with you on the Third Sabbath or come in again in my regular turn. I hope you will excuse this alteration but I really could not well refuse the application as I know it is to serve both Mr Jay and Mr Gear. You will be so kind to drop me a line by post when you fix for my coming. With kind rememberance to yourself & family & friends in general. I am Dearly Yours very Sincerely

Jas Evill

Bath
27 July 1832

I am going to Westbury Leigh tomorrow & shall return Monday when I hope to hear from you.

At the monthly meeting on 12 October 1832, the question of a permanent pastor was again discussed. There had been word that William Eacott was about to leave Chapmanslade, and so it was decided that this should be verified with him, before applying to him to become pastor. James Cadby however, in his characteristic humility, goes a little further in his letter:

Twerton Nr Bath 15 October 1832

Dear Sir,

I am requested to make known to you of a resolution passed at our Church meeting Friday evening the 12 October that on consideration of a report being made to us that you was moveable from Chapmanslade the members of our little Church resolved that I should write to you to know the particulars of such statement we feel very concerned about our little interest here Certainly we perceive a very wide door opened for usefulness and without a stated minister and the blessings of Allmighty God we know not how to accomplish it our friends as been making great inquirys amongst the members and also the hearers who they should prefer to be their Pastor and they cannot think of any one but Mr Eacott. I have been weighing the subject over in my own mind with respect to the support of a Minister here, the present Income of the House from the rents of the Pews will bring in about Thirty five Pounds an Anum which I must acknowledge is very little to support a Minister.

Dear Sir the above few lines will give you a sight of the friends mind and our circumstances and I should kindly thank you to lay the present case of our little intrest before your God and I trust our God and to give me your views on the subject as I would wish us and you to be directed by that hand who cannot err and is to good to be unkind and should you be directed so as to give us a favourable line that you are open to come amongst us you may expect to hear from us very soon.

To Wm Eacott   Jas Cadby.

Chapmanslade.

William Eacott was not leaving Chapmanslade and indeed he remained there until he moved to Southwick in 1840,[22] however he agreed to continue as an occasional supply preacher. At the monthly meeting on 7 November, John Hayter was elected deacon, one of his first tasks being to accompany James Harris to investigate a report of the 'trifeling and inconsistent walk & conduct of Jas Davis one of our members'. Church discipline continued to be a constant challenge, and it cannot be denied that with such a growing church the lack of a settled and dedicated pastor cannot have helped. Although in Baptist ecclesiology the presence of a minister is not necessary for a church's identity as a church, the value of a minister called by God to be its pastor is to be desired. Despite the difficulties attendant upon the deacons, who worked long hours and had their own families to support, the church continued to fill every Sunday, and there was the ongoing business of maintaining the school to attend to also. James Evill, however, was aware that their lack of a pastor had its practical advantages, as his letter shows:

> My Dear Friends
>
> It rejoices my heart to see the attendance at your place of worship & I hope it will continue. I cannot help at the same time grieve that any should be obliged to return for want of room. Could not Galleries be erected on the sides. I think the light might be derived from the Cieling & admit of more air — you know an increase of sittings would in time pay for the alterations & especially as you are at so little expense in providing for Minister. Do turn it over in your mind. Subscriptions at x per week would soon make a figure in your collection & Mr Jay will no doubt come & preach to make a collection towards the expenses, if not done it will perhaps be the means of another place being opened which will divide and separate, Think it seriously over & I will go to Mr Wilkins again.
>
> I have sent the Tune I promised to Mr Hayter which I hope they will sing next time I come & also "Leicester" which I much admire.
>
> I am now going to ask a favour at which I think I see you smiling but I wish you would get a few of the flocks that lie about your workshop & put them in a little bit of cloth no matter what the colour for a seat in the pulpit as I feel it rather hard and cold to my poor bones & I have no doubt others will be pleased with it. You need not be afraid of my going to sleep on that account, If any Expense I have no objections to defray it.

---

[22] Doel, 1890, 86-87.

With sincere regards

I am Yours Truely

Jas Evill

Bath
12 Nov 1832

What was not being paid out for a pastor would go towards the alterations, and James Evill would prevail upon his pastor and friend William Jay once more, and would be prepared to approach Charles Wilkins again too. James Evill's comfort was no doubt attended to without delay. In the meantime William Eacott's conscience was troubled, and he would have to put off using the new pulpit cushion until a more convenient time:

Chapmanslade Dec 20 1832

Dear Friend and Brother

with great reluctance I take my pen to write to you But a voice is on me & the Lord say if any Man vow let him keep his vow — that is I have promised that while I am permitted to be over any Church Never to be absent on Ordinance Days therefore though I made you promise of our Ordinance Day. Could you therefore for the Sake of peace have the goodness to alter my Day to the Second Sabbath in so doing you will Much oblige your unworthy friend W E and if convenient your silence will give consent. While for once I hope it will be for peace' sake and if impossible Send me a letter by post and I Must Break My vow also be as good as to inform friend Perce that Mr Hichcocks is Not coming to our Neighbourhood this Christmas and I hope that this unexpected letter will find you & your Dear Partner & your family in perfect health & all the church along Which the good Lord have called you to officiate & May the Gospel have that effect upon them to unGodly & worldly things Lost & to live safely & Godly in this presence would as to Me & Mine We are pretty well as to health But still find I am in the Wilderness & holding between two opinions waiting the small still voice saying this is the Way Walk in it for he has said I will Bring the Blind By a way they know not & also the inquiry who is a man you that heareth the Lord & Walketh in Darkness & hath No Light & My & My Wifes kind love to you & yours & to all friends & May the Lord Bless preserve & keep you & water you Every Moment with the Dew from above is the Desire of yours in the best Bonds

W Eacott

Of course James Cadby was only too willing to alter the engagement.

> Chapmanslade Dec 27 1832
>
> Dear Friend Cadby
>
> I feel thankful for your kindness for letting me off the 3 Sabbath & God Willing I will be with you on that Day & May My God and your God grant us to meet in the fulness of the Gospel of Christ and that I may Instrumently Water the souls of his Elect and I harmlessly confess this is my unfained Desire the good Lord knows & I Can confess that I am honestly sorry thus to trouble you with letters of a painful and Expensive Nature. But you May believe Me to Remain yours Sincerely in the Best Bonds
>
> W Eacott

The Twerton letters are full of such fascinating details that demonstrate the closeness of the relationship between those who visited Twerton and the Particular Baptist community there, indeed they illustrate well the depth of relationship between Calvinistic Baptists in the region that are not illustrated well by any other means. The preachers were committed to their task and to their people, often sacrificially and without personal gain.

Figure 34. Twerton Baptist Chapel, c1900

The early months of 1833 were once again encouraging, and George Batchelor received the final £10 of his loan. The highlight of the year was Sunday 23 June, when in the morning another 14 people were baptised in the river by William Eacott of Chapmanslade, assisted by Mr H T Crook. This was probably the Henry Crook who as a member at Somerset Street had preached at Twerton in the period 1815-17, and most likely on other occasions also. Subsequently Joseph Champion, William Baily, Henry Bowering, Thomas West, Henry Pattern, Richard Pattern, James Renolds, James Hibbard, John White, Elizabeth West, Mary Batten, Eliza Wheeler, Rhoda Cook and Mary Howe were received into membership in the afternoon. The issue of a settled pastor was still high on the agenda, for a fortnight later, on 3 July, a special meeting of 'both male & female' members was called to consider calling Henry Crook to the pastorate. Crook had been on probation for a month, but the meeting was less than unanimous in its support. Although Crook was notified of the result, he could not very well accept with only 26 in favour and 18 against his appointment. The following week, 9 July, a letter was sent to 'Mr Eavens' of Somerset Street. As we have seen, Evans had been appointed in 1832 by Somerset Street as assistant to the ageing John Paul Porter, after successfully preaching there on probation a year earlier. He had just tendered his resignation from Somerset Street, Porter having died the previous October, so he was invited to supply Twerton until such time as he could find another appointment. Whether he replied or whether he even occupied the pulpit we do not know. The monthly meeting on 4 September again turned its attentions to filling the pastorate permanently, evidently still keen to persuade William Eacott. It was agreed that in their letter they should reveal the strength of the vote:

> PS there was five of our members which was lawfully detained from the Church meeting which sent in their votes for you which would make 36 in favour & 12 against.

There is no record of a response from Eacott, although he did not accept, remaining at Chapmanslade for a further seven years. At a general meeting on 24 September the church agreed to invite a Mr Cox to supply the pulpit for one year:

> Twerton Nr Bath 25 Sepr 1833
>
> Kind Sir
>
> With respect to the subject under consideration at our Church meeting last evening it was considered advisable that Mr Cox should be invited to supply us for one year and then he would be able to see where and how the work would prosper in his hands and where we should be able to meet the demand in every way required of us this we have considered more for the satisfaction of Mr Cox than ourselves we do sincerely trust should Mr Cox be inclined to except of us which there was not

the least opposition against him in any way at our meeting we should live in his affection and him in ours and that he may be made instrumental in the hand of Allmighty God in doing much Good in this benighted village. Mr Coxs reply will be kindly received

I Remain Sincerely
& Affectionately with
kind regards

Jas Cadby

To Mr Cox
Mr Smiths
Westfield House, Bath

PS. We the undersigned do agree if Mr Cox accept the above invitation of becoming our Pastor to allow £40 for the year specefied

Jas Cadby
Jas Harris
Jn Hayter

Witness Jas Evill

This is the first reference to Cox or Cocks in the Twerton church records, whose name was variously spelt Cox or Cocks.[23] John Cocks was a friend of Opie Smith, in whose home at Westfield House he was temporarily living, and the two men had previously worked together in various West Country church planting activities including Crediton in Devon. There is no record of his preaching at Twerton prior to this, although presumably he had – no doubt brought to the attention of the church by Smith and Evill, who were anxious to see a settled pastorate as much as the Twerton members were.

The invitation to Cocks to become minister was accepted, yet there are early indications in the minute book that things might not have been as settled as they should be. John Hayter took the opportunity of the church members meeting on 2 October to submit his resignation without giving any reason.

Respected Friends

I avail myself of the present opportunity of resigning the Office of Deacon in this Church therefore am no longer your Humble Servant in that Capacity

Jn Hayter

---

[23] For Cocks' *Memoir* see *Baptist Manual*, 1851, 42-43.

Cocks' ministry began with a clean sweep. At his first monthly meeting with the church members he proposed five measures to carry the church forward, which were agreed to by the meeting. Firstly, preaching on the Sabbath would from now on be in the morning and evening services, not in the afternoon as before. Secondly, the afternoon service would become a 'prayer meeting', which would now contain only a short address by the minister. Previously the ordinance of the Lord's Supper was celebrated every second month, and so this was changed to the first Sabbath of each month. The final two measures affected week nights. In addition to the members meeting on the first Wednesday of the month, there would be 'a Deacons meeting with the Minister' on the Friday evening preceding the Lord's Supper. Another new meeting was introduced for the last Monday evening of each month, which would be for conversation and 'to lead them forward in the good old way', at which 'any of our members will be at liberty to attend on such occasions'.

Figure 35. Twerton Baptist Chapel, 1926

Before long the church was again busy working on enlarging its premises. James Evill had identified the problem of crowding, for the 'hearers' on a Sunday far outnumbered the members and their families, as was usually the case in Baptist churches at this time and as we have already noticed on previous occasions during the course of this study. Another £90 was borrowed from George Batchelor for 'erecting a new Gallery and other Necessary repairs to the Chapel', which he this time agreed to lend at four per cent interest with twelve months notice on calling in the money. There was already a gallery at the back of the chapel, so 'two new Gallerys' were erected on the sides. Together with altering the front of the chapel, and other necessary repairs, the total bill amounted to £113.5s.9d. The church minute book now has two pages removed, and there is no clue given as to the reason. The record continues with a record of the special church meeting that was called, as agreed, to consider extending John Cocks' pastorate after the end on his first probationary year. From the thirty two members gathered on 26 May 1834 the extended call was unanimous. Cocks was not present, which would be usual practice when considering matters such as this, so James Cadby wrote to him to explain the circumstances of the meeting and the wishes of the church:

> Baptist Chapel Twerton 27th May 1834
>
> Dear Sir
>
> I beg leave to hand you as under the particulars of our Church Meeting last evening when Thirty two members was Then present that on consideration of the time being drawing near which you consented to supply us we consider it advisable to adopt some plans whereby you may be more fully established amongst us and become the Pastor of our little Church and to take the full Charge over us after relating our intentions to all the friends then present we put it to a shew of hands when every hand was held up and all present appeared to be well Satisfied with your being solicited to comply with their request but there is one thing still needful and that is that some provision may be made by the way but I do not think that we can give you such an encouragement as we could wish respecting money matters I cant see under our present circumstances that we shall be able after other expenses is found to say that there will be more than £40 per anum for a Minister but we must leave it to your due consideration and prayer to the Great Head of the Church that our future steps may be directed by him is the sincere wish of your affectionate friend
>
> Jas Cadby.

John Cocks' reply does not survive, but the substance of it can be discerned from Cadby's reply a little over a week later. The stipend offered was considered to be inadequate for Cocks to accept. The church meeting therefore reconsidered and agreed to raise the offer from £40 to £50 a year, something they were clearly going to find difficult to do:

> Twerton Baptist Chapel 9th July 1834
>
> Dear Sir
>
> The twelve months for which you received an invitation being nearly expired we thought it proper to convene a Special Church

meeting for the purpose of inviting you to Settle with us as our Pastor, and as we have Sat under your Ministry with much pleasure and we hope profit we do now affectionately invite you to become our Pastor and we engage to raise towards your Support Fifty Pounds per year we regret the sum is so small but we trust by the Divine blessing upon your labours the time will arrive when the Sallary will be advanced Praying that the union may be affectionate lasting and attend with much Spiritual prosperity to our Souls and Glory to the Great Head of the Church

We remain Dr Sir
Yours Affectionately

Thos Avery	Jas Cadby
Wm Allen	Jas Harris
Jas Hibbard	Jn Butterworth
Jn Vowles	Jn Butcher
Mary Harris	Jas Taylor
Eliz Alderman	Jn Bowering
Martha Gane	Wm Baker
Sarah Cook	Thos West
Eliz West	Richd Pattern
Martha Needs	Jas Champion
Mary Howe	Wm Wickham
Rose Richards	Sam Tanner
Eliz Tanner	Jn Hayter
Sarah Allen	Jas Batten
Mary Hayter	Cht Baker
Eliz Taylor	Rhoda Cook
Mary Avery	Jane Jones
Martha Croomwell	Mary Batten
Jas Renolds	Thos Morrise
Maria Batten	Sarah Vowles
Maria Savage	Solomon Slugg
Geo Mitchell	

Very rarely in the letters are all the members names listed, but their inclusion on this occasion indicated the commitment of the whole community to the decision they had made. We have already encountered above each of the members named, with the exception of Thomas and Rebecca Morrise who had become members some time early in 1834. At the general meeting at which the above letter was signed John Hayter, who had resigned just a year earlier, and John Butterworth were elected deacons 'to assist Brother Cadby and Brother Harris'; and John Cocks' name was added to the membership roll. Up until this point James Cadby had acted as secretary or clerk to the Baptist church meeting at Twerton, and as such had signed minutes on the church's behalf. From now on the book was signed in the hand of John Cocks. Almost immediately church discipline was tightened, emphasising the strict nature of Twerton as a 'closed communion' church, and it was resolved:

> That if any of the members of this Church so absent themselves from the Lord's Table Three successive ordinance days, they shall be visited by two of the Deacons, to inquire into the cause of their absence, and make their report at the next monthly Church meeting. If the reasons assigned be not satisfactory, they shall be suspended for three months, at the expiration of which they shall acknowledge their fault & be restored: but, if they refuse to make such acknowledgement to the Church they shall be cut off.[24]

It was not long before the new disciplinary procedures were put into action. At the monthly meeting on 6 August 1834 Henry Bowering was suspended, and John Butterworth commissioned to visit him and warn him 'to be more stable & regular in future' or he 'shall be cut off from Church fellowship'. It was also decided that 'George Mitchell 'shall be suspended for 3 Months' because he had 'repeatedly been guilty of drunkenness'. The minister and deacons were assigned to 'inform him of it & admonish him to repent'. The next monthly meeting on 3 September heard John Butterworth's report, that Henry Bowering 'is satisfied with worshipping at the Church of England and has no desire to return to our communion; consequently, he no longer stands as a member with us.' In the membership roll it is recorded that Henry Bowering 'Left to join the Church Established by Law.' Although initially unclear what Henry Bowering's particular instability and irregularity were, it becomes clear that it was his attendance that was in question, rather than his behaviour. There had also been a clear shift in understanding from what we have already encountered at Somerset Street with the experience of Thomas Parsons. Parsons' right to leave membership on his own accord, without being dismissed, was challenged; whilst on this occasion at Twerton, Bowering is clearly permitted to leave on his own accord. Furthermore, moving to the 'Church Established by Law' is no longer a disciplinary offence—but then the balance of social, religious and economic relationships in the village needs to be taken into consideration, and indeed Charles Wilkins, the most generous of the patrons of the Baptist community, was, as we have seen, himself an Anglican.

At the 1 February monthly meeting the rule passed in the previous July was extended to allow a further three ordinance days before suspension: such members, it was agreed, 'shall receive censure in the name of the Church and be requested to fill their place at the Lord's Table in future'. This reflected a more

---

[24] TBC, *Minutes*.

generous spirit than had appeared in the earlier resolution. At the same time, James Harris resigned from the diaconate, and a vote of thanks to him was recorded. During the spring of 1835 Mary, Elijah, Sarah and Jemima Cocks, the minister's wife and family, were received into membership; as were William and Catherine Rudman, Mary Hayter and Edward Barnes. Later in the year Harriott Adlam, Ann Baynton, Clarissa Simpkins, Hannah Blagdon, Mary Colebrook, Sarah Spiller, Stephen and Cathrine Silcox and Mary Baynton became members, but the precise date is not recorded. All this time, as we have seen above in the graph of membership figures, the church was continuing to expand.

At the 29 April 1835 monthly meeting, however, resolutions were passed which marked the beginning of a painful, and mysterious, period in the church's life. Firstly it was resolved 'that a Church meeting be held the first Wednesday in every month of Males & Females: that the said meeting shall be made as much as possible a devotional meeting; and no subject shall be introduced but through the minister.' Whatever its motives, or however admirable its objectives, this was clearly a restriction to the principles of freedom for which the church had worked only seven years earlier. The Twerton Baptist community had only relatively recently been liberated from the control of the church at Somerset Street, and had been used to exercise the Baptist principle of the authority of the church members meeting at a time when it had no settled pastor. Furthermore, at this meeting it was resolved 'that as the following persons have acted contrary to Church order, & virtually separated themselves from our communion we do hereby declare that they no longer continue in Church fellowship with us.' The following names were then listed: William and Hannah Baily, Isaac and Priscilla Pearce, Samuel and Elizabeth Tanner, John and Sarah Vowles, John Bowering, Maria Savage, Eliza Wheeler, Joseph and Maria Batten, Joseph Champion, Henry Pattern, and Thomas Morrisse and his wife Rebecca. Comparing this list with the signatories John Cocks' letter of invitation and the Twerton membership roll, it can be seen how significant a number of the original members this excluded list represented. Why so many members had stopped attending is not recorded, although it seems clear that there was an issue regarding the authority of the minister. It is recorded that George Mitchel and William Fisher were then excluded from membership 'for immoral conduct', as was Grace Wilkins at the monthly meeting on 3 December.

Much of what happened subsequently is not recorded, and the minutes, loyally and faithfully maintained by James Cadby, remain silent. Cadby neatly copied a letter into the book, under the heading 'Resignation of Jn Cocks Pastor of Our Church':

> To the Baptist Church at Twerton
>
> In consequence of the many unpleasant things which have occured in the Church I have come to the conclusion of giveing up my charge over you I therefore inform you that I intend

resigning the Pastoral Office in four Months from the date hereof But I will not preach in the Chapel during that period.

John Cocks.

25th Decemr 1835

What these 'unpleasant things' were cannot with any certainty be surmised, although relationships between Cocks and the church that had committed itself sacrificially to his support, had irretrievably broken down. A special church meeting was swiftly arranged for 6 January 1836, where 'it was moved seconded and carried unanimously that the Revd John Cocks be no longer a Member of our Church', and Elijah, Sarah, Mary and Jemima Cocks were suspended for three months. It was recorded that 'The Church deeply regret the necessity for this measure but the reason of it are best known to the Parties hereby separated from us'. It was also resolved at this meeting to reinstate all the members 'unlawfully dismissed by the late Pastor', each one to receive 'an invitation to return and be received in full communion as before'. The resolutions were signed by James Cadby on behalf of the church. A further leaf was cut from the book at this point, possibly because Cadby had begun to record events that he would later feel were best left unwritten. This is of course speculation, but it demonstrates the care needed in reconstructing any story, and the problem when sources are lost or, as it would appear here, tampered with or altered. What we can be sure about is that here in the minute book we have James Cadby's record of how he believed the story should be remembered, and therefore in future retold.

Three days later the church received a note from Elijah, Sarah, Mary and Jemima Cocks, dismissing themselves from the church fellowship. John Cocks remained in Twerton, preaching to the congregation at the independent Prospect Chapel at the Bath end of the village. It is furthermore recorded that Elizabeth Alderman, one of the original members, 'Left to join Mr Cock's'. What is significant in all this is that it was established at Twerton that the church existed and could act independently of any minister. One of the constant tensions had always been between the authority of the church meeting and the authority of the minister. The Twerton Baptists desperately wanted a minister to be a part of the community, amongst them to guide, preach, teach, preside at the Lord's table, and to provide pastoral care, together all under the authority of Christ – in and of one mind. This they had not experienced from Somerset Street, nor had they experienced with their first minister, John Cocks; yet they knew it to be the ideal from the positive witness of the various itinerant preachers and neighbourhood ministers that visited Sunday by Sunday, and from their study and understanding of the New Testament church.

Happier days were approaching, however, and Cadby began his record of 1836 with a list of the members reunited with the church in Christian fellowship on 17 January: Samuel Tanner, Isaac Pearce, Thomas Morrise, Samuel Batten,

William Baily, John Vowels, John Bowering, Joseph Champion, Elizabeth Tanner, Priscilla Pearce, Rebecca Morrise, Hannah Baily, Sarah Vowles, Maria Batten, Maria Savage, Eliza Wheeler, Sarah Allen, John Biggs, Sarah White and Henry Crook. The last three names were not listed earlier, and added to the membership roll at the latest entry. Furthermore it was resolved 'that our Brethren Isaac Pearce & Thomas Morrise be United as Deacons in Union with the Brethren James Cadby Jn Hayter & Jn Butterworth.' The whole proceeding was witnessed and signed by James Jackson, their loyal friend from Thomas Street Chapel, who had been present to chair and minister to them at their meeting.

The first experience of the Twerton Baptist community with their own pastor was not a long or happy one. It is therefore unsurprising that in the official records there is very little reference to the circumstances leading to the appointment of Joseph Rodway of Bradford on Avon to the pastorate. He was invited by letter on 8 August, and offered a salary of £50 per annum. Again, being part of the wider network of Baptist churches on the Bath and West Wiltshire border, it is possible that Mr Rodway was known to the Twerton congregation and had previously supplied the pulpit or had come on recommendation. However, Rodway's arrival as minister at Twerton did not herald the end of the John Cocks episode. At the monthly meeting on 2 November it was resolved:

> that as John Cocks has in his possession three Stools and Baptizeing Gowns which forms a part of the property of our Church — that the said John Cocks be immediately applied to for such property and if not speedily returned to us legal steps are to be taken to recover it

A letter was duly written by James Cadby to put into action the wishes of the church:

> Twerton 3d Novemr 1836
>
> To John Cocks
>
> We the Undersigned having received full power and duly authorized at our last Church Meeting 2d Novemr 1836 do make a full demand of the property you hold of ours that is three long Stools and two Baptizeing Gowns and we do further inform you that if you do not make a Speede surrender of the above to us being our property we shall Immediately take legal Steps to recover the same
>
> Jas Cadby   } Deacons
> John Butterworth

This was effective, for in red ink in the same hand the church book reads, 'John Cocks attended to the above, the following day 4th Novemr, by returning the Stools & Gowns to us according to our demand'. There then follow a further two pages which had been written on but cut from the book, after which the record is silent for seven years. To summarise the church's situation, it was growing in number of worshippers, the Sunday school was bursting at the seams, and the members were in debt from their building projects and commitments to their minister's stipend. The main drift in the church's life can be surmised from the fact that by the end of 1837, the date at which this study ends, necessity demanded a printed appeal on their behalf:

> The Case of the Baptist Church, Twerton, Somerset.
>
> There was a small Chapel built in this Village for the worship of Almighty God about the year 1808, when it was supplied by different Ministers for many years; and, we trust, the Word was made useful to many souls: the Congregation increasing, it was found necessary to enlarge the chapel; and, having found a piece of land given for the purpose, it was done, which cost £132.12s.9d.
>
> In the year 1830, we were formed into a Church, consisting of thirty members; to whom the ordinances have been administered regularly.
>
> Having a Sabbath School, our place of worship again became too strait for us, so that we were obliged to erect side galleries, which, with other alterations, cost £113.5s.9d., the whole sum being £245.18s.9d.; towards which have been collected and subscribed, principally by ourselves, £125.18s.6d.: so that we are now in arrears £120, towards the liquidation of which we have a weekly subscription. We are in great want of a Schoolroom, as we have upwards of 130 Children in our Sabbath School: we expect we could erect a Schoolroom for about £150.
>
> Under these pressing circumstances, we apply to the friends of the dear Redeemer for assistance; not doubting but they will come forward to our help.
>
> We are a poor people, all obliged to labour for our bread; and can do but little for our Pastor, but hope, in time, to do more. Every trifle will be thankfully received.
>
> Joseph Rodway. Pastor
> James Cadby,
> John Hayter,
> Thos. Morris,
> Isaac Pearce, Deacons.

"I have much pleasure in adding my signature to the above testimony respecting the Baptist Meeting-House at Twerton.
"William Pechey, Bath."

"So have I.
"James Jackson, Bath."

"As deserving a Case as any ever submitted to the Religious Public: may brother Rodway meet with great success in begging for it! This is the prayer of
"P. Cater, Bath."

"Having taken a deep interest in the Cause at Twerton from my first coming to Bath, and having been intimately acquainted with its history during that period; and, moreover, having the greatest respect for its present Pastor; I have no ordinary pleasure in recommending this Case to the best patronage of the Christian Public.
"John Jackson, Bath."

"The Case at Twerton has been known to me for more than twenty-eight years; it is, therefore, with pleasure I join the brethren in recommending this Case to the attention and kindness of the Christian Public.
"John Owen, Bath."

"I cordially join with the above in recommending the Case at Twerton to the friends of the dear Redeemer.
"Joseph Seymour, Bradford."

"Having a full conviction that this Case is an interesting one, and well knowing Mr. Rodway, I have great pleasure in recommending his intended application to the liberality of the Religious Public.
"William Gear, Bradford."

"I readily unite with my brethren in recommending this Case.
"Wm. Jay, Bath."

The above appeal was issued by the church at the beginning of 1838. The text was written in a small notebook which had previously been circulated, to which the noted sponsors added their messages of support, and finally there followed details of the amounts promised by churches and individuals. The book itself travelled widely, particularly in the Bath and West Wiltshire area, and printed copies of the appeal were circulated. By this time the church was in considerable debt, still owing the £120 balance on their previous enlargement venture, and faithfully seeking to extend the Lord's work in the neighbourhood by building a permanent schoolroom.

Bath Baptists approaching 1837

We began our study with the suggestion from Joseph Belcher's statistical tables published in the *Baptist Magazine* that something significant was happening in Bath, and that there was an underlying story that needed to be recovered to explain the growth in Baptist church life.[25] Our study has focused on accounts of the Baptist community at Somerset Street[26] and the later community at Twerton as best illustrating the remarkable way Baptists engaged with the Gospel and with their community during the period 1714 to 1837. Yet in Belcher's tables for 1831 and 1835 there are six Bath congregations listed, in addition to the congregation at Twerton. The first listed is the Somerset Street community, with John Paul Porter as its pastor in 1831. Subsequent to Porter's death and the departure of Shem Evans soon afterwards, there followed the short pastorates of John Jackson recorded here in 1835 and William Peachey, who had taught at the Bristol Academy.[27] Philip Cater's name against the second church listed indicates that this is the Baptist community at York Street, which we have also encountered earlier in this study, and for which Cater has been an important source for the narrative. The third church in the 1835 list has Owen Clarke as its pastor, and is clearly the group that separated from Somerset Street during the crisis of 1828. When Porter and the others regained control of the Somerset Street building, Clarke and his supporters continued meeting in Corn Street for a while until their lease expired in 1836, when they moved to Wood Street behind the Lower Bristol Road.[28] This congregation later gave birth in 1839 to Providence Chapel on the Lower Bristol Road, and a splinter group from Providence in 1849 moved into the vacated Ebenezer Chapel in Widcombe. This is the chapel that made such a profound impression on John Haddon, as recorded in the introduction to this study.

The fourth Bath Baptist congregation in the 1835 list had John Chalker as its minister and met at Thomas Street. Chalker had been dismissed from membership at Somerset Street on 11 April 1830 to be Thomas Street's first minister.[29] This was the church that Opie Smith had contributed £100 towards its construction. The *Baptist Magazine* informs us that in the autumn of 1830 'a new Baptist Chapel was opened in Thomas Street, Walcot, Bath, when the Rev. J. Chalker was ordained as pastor of the church collected in that place.'[30]

---

[25] See Figure 4.
[26] Formerly Garrard or Gerrard Street.
[27] Attryde & Moore, 1972, 3. The comment by Attryde & Moore that 'Two very short pastorates followed, but the names of the men concerned do not appear in the records' can now be amended. Jackson's name appears in the *Baptist Magazine* tables and Peachey signed the returns to the Registrar General in 1837.
[28] Parker, 1975, 7. Subsequently in 1841 Owen Clarke left Bath to work full time for the British and Foreign Temperance Society for whom he had been agent for some time. *Baptist Magazine*, 1859, 235.
[29] SSBC, *Minutes*, 11 April 1830.
[30] *Baptist Magazine*, 1830, xxii, 395.

Whether Chalker was actually still present at the church in 1835 is unclear, for it is Thomas Street that James Jackson feels a particular responsibility for, as we discovered in his correspondence with Twerton. In the third decade of the nineteenth century, as the period of this study draws to its end, it is clear that a change had been taking place. Although preaching stations were established as a result of itinerant preachers being sent out into the outlying districts such as at Twerton, and new churches were being formed either in an unplanned fashion or out of conflict within the existing community such as at York Street, it would now seem that there was also an increasingly clear mission strategy in place – such diversity again emphasising the now fragmented nature of Baptist life in Bath. Thomas Street was clearly part of the strategic concern of Baptists in the region around Bath, as the *Baptist Magazine* explained:

> The population of the neighbourhood being very considerable, and the places of worship few, it is hoped that the blessing of God will attend the establishment of this place, and that the light of divine truth may be diffused abroad among many who have hitherto sat in darkness and the shadow of death.[31]

Despite these hopes and prayers Thomas Street struggled to maintain a witness in Walcot and had closed well before mid-century. By the 1880s the four hundred seat chapel in Thomas Street was being used as a chapel of ease by the Anglican parish of Walcot.[32]

The fifth Bath Baptist church was according to the 1835 list pastored by William Clarke, who is known to have been a Scotch Baptist. They met in a large room rented in a house at 2 Chandos Buildings from around 1826, when Clarke is reported to have settled in Bath, and are still recorded as meeting in 1851.[33] William Clarke described the 160 strong congregation as 'Holding no name but Christian: Denominated "Baptists"'.[34] This turn of phrase reflects the way that Clarke is also represented in the story of the Scotch Baptists, who had isolated congregations in cities throughout England, and were informally associated with their Scottish roots by correspondence and are characterised as an 'argumentative' connexion.[35] Their presence in Bath in the 1830s reflects an earlier period in the Bath Baptist community that we have already encountered, for amongst Scotch Baptists 'there was something of a prejudice against a trained ministry'.[36] William Clarke added his contribution to the controversy from Bath, and the significance of this is highlighted in a recent study by Brian Talbot.[37] Talbot argues that the causes of much of the division and disunity

---

[31] Ibid.
[32] Silvester, 1888, 20.
[33] *Religious Census*, 1851. Original Returns.
[34] Ibid.
[35] Meek & Murray, 1988, 38.
[36] Ibid, 43.
[37] Talbot, 2003, 65-6.

amongst Scotch Baptists were the personality clashes and controversial views of many of its scattered leadership:

> Other tensions were caused by eccentric individuals, such as William Clark from Bath. He led a controversy over the use of Bible commentaries and theological books, both in his own congregation and in the connexion. He claimed that it was man's wisdom that was the cause of all the troubles in the church.[38]

Figure 36. Thomas Street Chapel

---

[38] Ibid, 65. The *Baptist Magazine* and *Religious Census* show Clarke's name spelt with an 'e', whereas Brian Talbot spells it without. It is clear that they all refer to the same person.

Clarke pursued the controversial theme, supported by sixteen members of his congregation, in a correspondence with James Everson of Monmouth which lasted several years. Talbot cites letters from 1827 to 1830, and points out the irony that as a classics teacher Clarke is himself employing human argument and texts in making his elongated case.

The sixth and final Bath Baptist congregation listed in the 1835 statistics is more of a mystery. Associated with S Saniger as minister in 1831, there is uncertainty about which congregation this refers to. There were certainly other Baptist congregations emerging at this time in the city, such that the total indeed exceeds the six listed in the *Baptist Magazine*. From 1829 to mid-century Meyler's *The Original Bath Guide* announces that 'A small Chapel has also been opened for divine service in Hetling-court, by some of the seceders from the Baptist congregation in Somerset-street.'[39] Indeed the Somerset Street minutes for 8 May 1828 records the dismissal of four members 'to the new formed Church in Hetling Court'. These were times of great confusion, and membership numbers fell dramatically, often with no reason recorded. Chandos Buildings and Hetling Court are adjacent, so these references in the guides and minute book may be to the same Scotch Baptist congregation. Furthermore, as we have seen above, the York Street secession initially met in Hetling House for a short while in 1828 before moving to York Street. Hetling House, now Abbey House, is at the other end of Hetling Court from the Hetling Pump Room. The reality is that there was a profusion of public meeting rooms in the vicinity, so the true picture may never appear. Amongst the other possibilities within this period would be the Union Chapel, formed on Combe Down in 1814, as a joint mission between the Baptists at Somerset Street and the Independents at Argyle Chapel but 'intended for those holding doctrines published in London in 1689.'[40]

Furthermore, as we have seen from John Haddon's description above, a further group met in the former Freemason's Hall in York Street. Led by William Morshead, formerly the assistant minister of St Mary's Chapel, Queen Square – one of Bath's leading proprietary chapels – the Masonic Hall Chapel congregation began in a flurry of controversy. In 1832 Morshead had published a tract entitled *Is the Church of England Apostate? Being a Christian Minister's Protest on Leaving That Establishment* in which he renounced Anglican doctrine and practice, maintaining his own ignorance of the truth at his ordination and his need to leave its membership.[41] Rev. James R Page answered Morshead's complaints in *Anatomy of The Rev. Wm. Morshead's "Christian Minister's Protest," Entitled "Is the Church of England Apostate?"*, published later the same year, but his efforts were swiftly rebutted by Morshead in *The Apostasy of the Church of England Not Disproved by The Rev. R. Page's Anatomy of a "Christian Minister's Protest."*

---

[39] *The Original Bath Guide*, 1829, 83.
[40] Owens, 1909, 26. The reference is to the 1689 *Baptist Confession*. The lease for the chapel was signed by both John Paul Porter and William Jay.
[41] Morshead, 1832, 13.

Figure 37. Former Bethesda Chapel, York Street

Amidst the controversy there were, amongst other critical accusations, charges made that Morshead had become Baptist and his church was a Baptist church. This impression clearly stuck, and the story communicated through Haddon and others. This confusion was clearly compounded by the empty Masonic building being acquired as an independent Bethesda Chapel by John Wallinger in 1842 – again, not Baptist – and the other pre-existing Baptist Chapel being located nearby at the other end of York Street. In a brief undated pamphlet William Morshead had previously sought to set the record straight:

> The various mistakes and false reports that have long been abroad respecting this place have led to the publication of the following short account of what has been done, and is now doing here...But it was not so clear to others as we would ourselves have made it, that in leaving one error, we had not gone into the opposite extreme; that though seceders, we were not political Dissenters; though attached to the study of unfulfilled prophecy, we were not Irvingites; though (with few exceptions) baptized on a profession of faith, we were not Baptists.[42]

Thus according to their own testimony, there never was a Baptist community meeting at the Freemason's Hall prior to its purchase by the Society of Friends – but, rather, two distinctly different independent congregations.

---

[42] Morshead, c.1832. *Some Account of the Worship and Preaching at the Freemason's Hall, Bath.*

Chapter 7: Conclusion

This study has been a beginning at setting the record straight, and to demonstrate the importance and significance of the Baptist community within the history of Bath. The story in 1837 is that there were considerably more Baptists in Bath than the statistics would suggest and much of this story remains untold. No reference, for example, has been made in this study to the united chapel opened in 1808 at Combe Hay and run in cooperation with the Independent congregation at Argyle Chapel and the Countess of Huntingdon Chapel congregation in the Vineyards;[1] nor to the Baptist chapel at Limpley Stoke opened in 1816 on the encouragement of Opie Smith of Bath and George Head of Bradford on Avon a year earlier.[2] Furthermore, James Jackson, who we have seen in connection with Twerton and Thomas Street, was busy during this period planning to plant a new Baptist community at Bathford. He had purchased the land in 1827, and at his own expense built the chapel which was opened in 1839 and in which he preached until his death in 1853.[3] As the numerous private houses licensed for religious activities also help to demonstrate,[4] there is an underlying untold story of a significant Baptist presence.

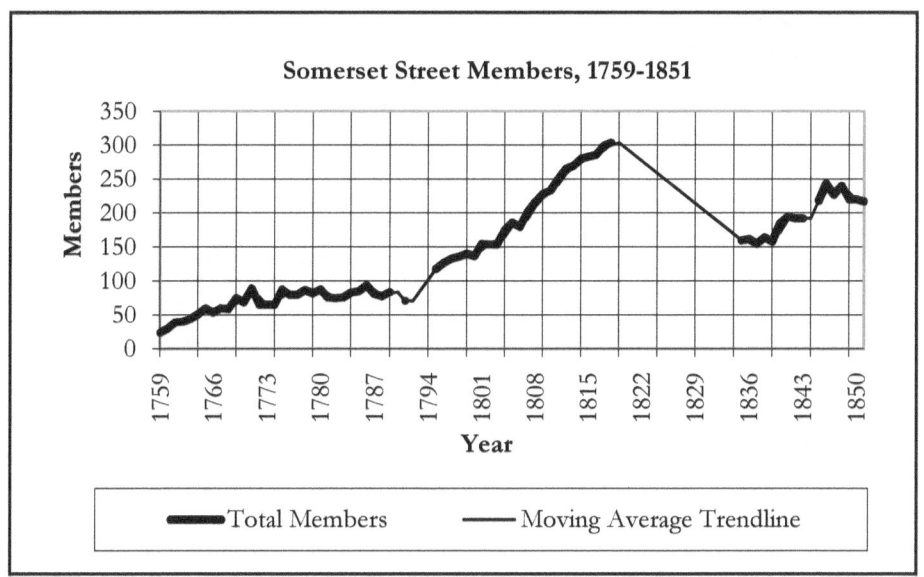

Figure 38. Somerset Street Members, 1759-1851.

---

[1] *Baptist Magazine*, 1808, i, 38.
[2] Ibid, 1822, xiv, 161.
[3] Laurence, 1985, 23-4.
[4] SRO. Q/RRW 1, D/D/RM. *Dissenters' Certificates*.

The main story has been that of the Baptist community meeting at Somerset Street and **Figure 38** summaries the growth that we have seen exhibited, an expected growth chart but with its own local explanation in the characters of two different ministers and the theology they lived by. The turmoil that we have noted around 1790 and in the late second and early third decades of the nineteenth century are clearly apparent and reflected in the levels of recorded membership, but it is significant that growth continues from 1834 onwards. Furthermore, when from 1837 the Somerset Street figures are added to the membership numbers of other Bath Baptist churches, it can be seen that not only does the growth continue, but in the wider community the number of Baptist members more than doubles in the period between 1816 and 1846.

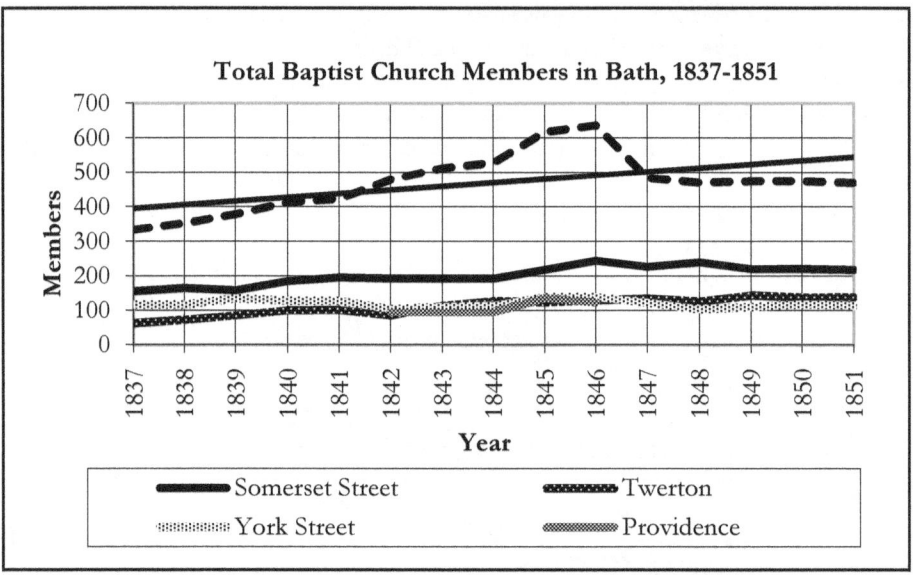

Figure 39. Total Baptist Church Members in Bath, 1837-1851

This is shown in **Figure 39**, although because the record is not consistent, and there are no records at all for some churches, the numbers shown must be on the low side. The continuation of this growth trend can further be seen when all the statistics quoted thus far are consolidated into one series of graphs. **Figure 40** summarises the total recorded number of Bath Baptist members from 1766 to 1851. **Figure 41** shows the growing population of the city of Bath for the same period of time, allowing a comparison to be made. **Figure 42** provides a comparison, giving the number of members as a percentage of the population, and demonstrates how significant the growth rate really was.

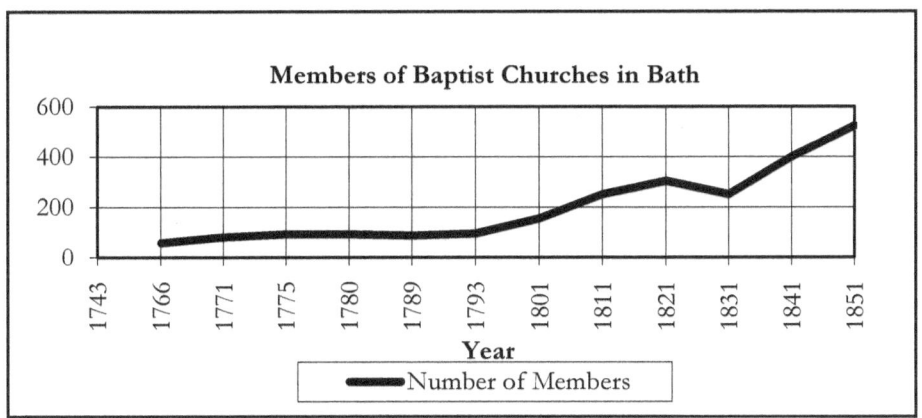

Figure 40. Members of Baptist Churches in Bath.

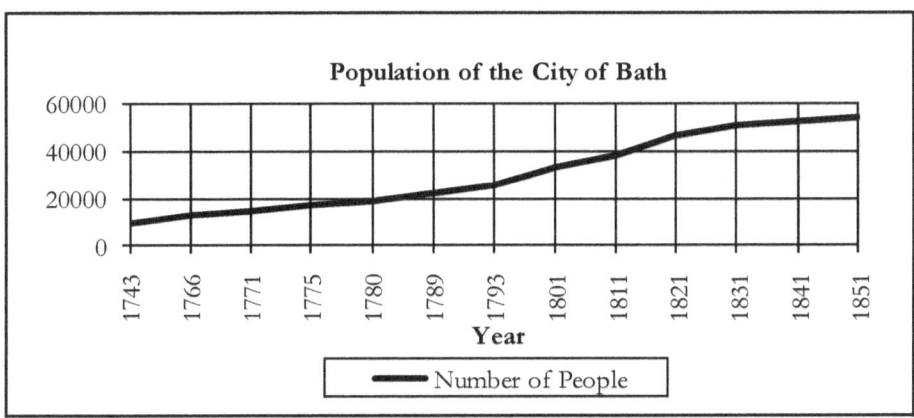

Figure 41. Population of the City of Bath.

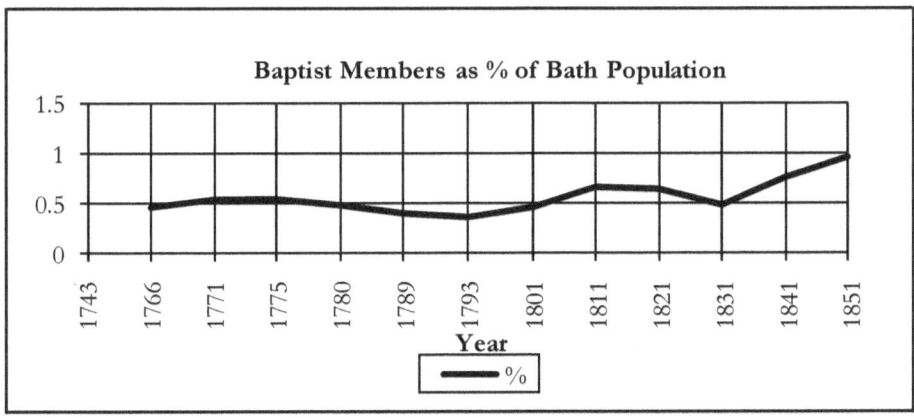

Figure 42. Baptist Members as % of Bath Population.

A question with which this study has been engaged throughout, and which it is appropriate to return to one last time is whether Bath Baptists, as Nonconformists, were engaged in the cultural life of their society in a way that would satisfy Matthew Arnold's criticism. In one sense Arnold's rebukes are not easily answered, as they are based on an ingrained familial prejudice that is evident also in the work of Thomas Arnold. In *Principles of Church Reform* Thomas Arnold argued for the destruction of Dissent, albeit peaceably:

> These principles I believe to be irrefragable; that a Church Establishment is essential to the well-being of the nation; that the existence of Dissent impairs the usefulness of an Establishment always, and now, from peculiar circumstances, threatens its destruction; and that to extinguish Dissent by persecution being both wicked and impossible, there remains the true, but hitherto untried way, to extinguish it by comprehension; that different tribes should act together as it were in one army, and under one command, yet should each retain arms and manner of fighting with which habit has made them most familiar.[5]

Nevertheless there have been 'improving' engagements witnessed within this study, such as assistance given for the poor, or the focus on education; and even those engagements tending towards 'perfection', such as engagement in the arts and sciences, and in poetry. Most remarkable in this way has been Robert Parsons himself, able to engage as carver mason in the purely decorative arts based on classical imagery, of which surely Arnold would have approved, whilst maintaining a Calvinistic faith that encouraged disengagement to a large degree. Where Parsons was successful was in his ability to separate worldly and spiritual concerns, and to transform the worldly in the process.

This has been the study of a local Baptist community existing in a remarkable context. In Chapter One we were introduced to the 'long eighteenth century', which at times it must have seemed, and some of the clues indicating the worthwhile pursuit of the Baptist story, from Belcher's tables of statistics to glimpses of the ways previous historians have appreciated or neglected the Baptist contribution. Something remarkable was happening in Bath during the period that is significant enough to explore. In Chapter Two we were introduced to the Western Baptist Association background, and the dual origin of the Bath Baptists from the Haycombe congregation and from among the Presbyterians was considered as a starting point for the story. The subject of Chapter Three was Robert Parsons, first Baptist minister in the city of Bath, and the church community gathered in the city. It has been possible to compile a significantly more substantial biographical account of Parsons' life and career as stone-mason carver than has previously been attempted, and this demonstrates

---

[5] Arnold, 1845, 259.

his particular contribution not only within the Baptist community but also in the surrounding culture of Georgian England. Despite Walter Wilson's analysis that the discipline of the church was based around the Parsons' own strict principles and character, we have rather seen that the tightly ordered Baptist community was governed as much by its mutually agreed covenant as the personality of its pastor. The way that worked out in practice was a moderate strict Calvinism. Chapter Four outlined some of the intellectual and spiritual issues which began to challenge the nature of the Baptist community, and that would eventually herald a change and transformation into a more fragmented Baptist community in Bath at the beginning of the nineteenth century. The correspondence and publications of both Robert and Thomas Parsons highlight a tension over the place of education and learning in the preparation of Christian ministers, and just as the father would contribute to a wider discussion of an educated ministry, so the son would enter the public arena as a significant early defender of Christian pacifism amongst other concerns. An increasingly open and diverse community was the mark of the next phase in the Bath Baptist community's life, and Chapter Five focused on this from the perspective of the new community being formed at Twerton, the growth of the Somerset Street congregation under the leadership of John Paul Porter, and the substantial contribution of Opie Smith to the story of Bath Baptists – as well as his substantial economic contribution to the city. Opie Smith's name had been associated with many West Country Baptist churches although very little has previously been known about his life – this study has demonstrated the possibility of compiling a more substantial biography in due course, and the value of this in further bringing Bath Baptist history to a wider contemporary audience. During the course of the first two decades of the nineteenth century the increased fragmentation of the Somerset Street church had caused deep wounds that needed a period of consolidation before continued growth would happen – as we have seen, this was made possible as the remaining church retreated into the protection of its foundation covenant document. In Chapter Six we saw the Baptist community planted in Twerton take on its own life and identity in relationship with the wider Baptist community around it. The story of the Twerton Baptists can be told because of the survival of an important collection of letters, a substantial collection with the potential to take the story further up to the middle of the century, letters which provide a window into the practical workings of a Baptist community in the 1820s and 30s. As the year 1837 approached, a thriving yet diverse Baptist community was apparent in Bath. Originally one Baptist community, there were now six or seven independently identifiable congregations.

We began our study with images of Bath as a place of pleasure and vice, and noted the tensions this raised for serious Christian visitors and residents. By the end of our period, Bath had largely become a place of genteel residence and a commercial centre – in which Bath Baptists were equally engaged. Frederick

Trestrail visited Bath in 1823. The young Trestrail would later train for Baptist ministry at the Academy in Bristol and would become amongst other things the Secretary of the Baptist Missionary Society, but in 1823 he was accompanying a friend who was planning to set up gas production in Falmouth and was visiting the gasworks at Bath and Bristol as part of his preparation. Having spent time in Bristol, the first time Trestrail had seen the city to which he would later move, the friends travelled by stage coach the short distance to Bath, 'and one wondered that cities so near in position could be so unlike in character.' Trestrail wrote in his reminiscences:

> Pultney Street, with the Sidney Gardens at the end, seemed to me then about the finest that could be imagined. Bath was at this time the resort of wealth and fashion, and one saw a class of persons little known or seen before. I was surprised to observe so many elderly people, evidently suffering from various maladies, and who, by dint of dress, false teeth, false hair, and rouge, were trying to cheat others, and perhaps themselves, into the belief that they were still robust and young. I distinctly remember that the spectacle struck me as a sad and mournful one.[6]

Clearly the fashionable company had long since moved on to other resorts. Nevertheless, Bath was still a place to visit, although also clearly an uncomfortable place to stay in for any length of time.

During the nineteenth century Bath Baptists continued to consolidate their influence in the structures of the city. In 1872 the Somerset Street part of the by now fragmented Bath Baptist community moved from Somerset Street to new purpose built premises in Manvers Street, where they remain today. Its progress as explored in this study was by no means always smooth, and that would continue to be true after 1837 and even beyond the move to Manvers Street. Nineteenth-century Baptists were becoming increasingly influential in the local business and political communities, through a process of 'mutual improvement' and other means.[7] This steadily increased through the nineteenth and into the twentieth centuries.[8] Through the early decades of the twentieth century there was a growing body of local opinion which suggested that Manvers Street's interests were indeed too influential in the local political sphere, as a section from the satirical cartoon published in the local press in 1935, **Figure 43**, illustrates.[9] For some decades the Manvers Street Baptist Church deacons'

---

[6] Trestrail, nd, 5.
[7] Chandler, 2003.
[8] Bush, 1934. Alderman Bush's reminiscences are full of anecdotes and stories from his long experience at both Manvers Street and in the wider community.
[9] *Bath and Wilts Chronicle and Herald*, Wednesday 16 January 1935.

meeting was referred to locally, and not always affectionately, as the 'Bath City Council in prayer'.[10]

Figure 43. The Living Giants of Manvers Street, 1935.

In Twerton, too, the Baptist community continued to improve the lives of the villagers with whom it was in contact. The church was influential in the woollen mills for some considerable time after the death of Charles Wilkins. Matthew Arnold had suggested that Nonconformity and industry were an unsuccessful combination:

> I remember a Nonconformist manufacturer, in a town of the Midland counties, telling me that when he first came there, some years ago, the place had no Dissenters; but he had opened an Independent chapel in it, and now Church and Dissent were pretty equally divided, with sharp contests between them.[11]

In 1907 an aging John Kempton wrote a letter from Paulton to his friends at Twerton where he had been minister and school teacher forty-five years earlier. In it he reminisces about old times, but commends the church on its continuing good relationships in the village. Of Mr Carr, then owner of the woollen mills, Kempton writes:

---

[10] Local reminiscence heard on several occasions in the past from senior members at Manvers Street. See also Chandler, 2003.
[11] Arnold, 1869, xxxiii.

> I remember after tea …we marched about 360 children up to Mr Carr's house who was very kind to us and to me in particular for beside giving a subscription of £15 to the S. School he gave me £15 annually for the day school.

Furthermore, of the Anglican priest in the village, Kempton continues:

> One thing I missed when coming to Paulton was the presence and kindness of the clergyman the Rev. G Buckle. I never failed to show my colours and yet he was like a brother to me and both he and Mr Davis the church schoolmaster contributed to a testimonial when I left.

The Particular Baptist and the Anglican priest, friends and brothers for ever. But Matthew Arnold had presumably not visited Twerton.

On one level any consideration of church history is a theological or confessional task. Haddon Willmer, a Baptist theologian, has argued,

> The church is a community of faith only within the constant practice of critical reflection on its history. This reflection is not a way of leaving faith behind, but is an action of faith seeking understanding for fuller obedience. The church seeks to know itself by examining the way it has come to the present moment. The church takes responsibility for the way it is and, for that, it needs to understand its own history as the history of the gospel within the history of the world. Church history is a means of churchly self-monitoring, which helps it to navigate through the times given to it.[12]

Sometimes, also, exploring a church's history can be a matter of justice or integrity. The history of the Bath Baptist community between 1714 and 1837 is an interesting and important one, that really has not been well served in the past, and the significance of which has been substantially lost. It is hoped that this present study will have gone some way towards beginning the process of restoring the history of the important cultural, social and religious contribution that Bath Baptists made to the life of Georgian Bath.

---

[12] Willmer, 2002, 209.

Bibliography

Abbreviations:

AL	Angus Library, Regent's Park College Oxford
BBC	Bristol Baptist College
BBCB	Broadmead Baptist Church, Bristol
BCL	Bath Central Library
BL	British Library
BRL	Bristol Reference Library
BRO	Bath Record Office
CRBC	Cairn's Road Baptist Church, Bristol.
DWL	Dr Williams's Library, London
IGI	International Genealogical Index
MSBC	Manvers Street Baptist Church, Bath
OPBC	Oldfield Park Baptist Church, Bath
SRO	Somerset Record Office, Taunton
SSBC	Somerset Street Baptist Church (now MSBC)
TBC	Twerton Baptist Church, Bath
TNA	The National Archives (formerly PRO)

A) Primary Sources

Manuscript Sources:

—— *A Narrative of the Proceedings of the General Assembly, 1689-82.* Manuscript and published editions bound together. AL.

—— *Gifford's Remains.* Manuscript collection of letters and other items from the collection of Andrew Gifford and others. BBC.

Argyle Independent Chapel, Bath. *Baptismal Registers, 1783-1854; Burial Registers, 1790-1888; Monumental Inscriptions.* Transcribed by Sheena M Carter, 2002. CD-ROM.

Bath & Wells Diocese Dissenters Certificates. SRO, D/D/RM.

Bath Central Library. *Local History Collection.* Collections of numerous papers, plans, photographs, relating to the history of Bath. BCL.

Bath City Records Office. *Miscellaneous.* Collections of deeds, legal documents and records relating to Bath and its environs. BRO.

Broadmead Baptist Church. *Minutes.* BBCB.

Deverell F W R and Bush S L. c1950. *The History of Manvers Street.* Manuscript for presentation at the Manvers Street Guild. MSBC.

City of Bath. *Quarter Sessions Books.* BRO.

County of Somerset. *Registrar General's Returns. 1852. Dissenting Places in Somerset Licensed 1688-1851.* SRO, Q/RRW 1.

Gay, Richard. nd. *Sermon, late seventeenth century*. ms. AL.
Godwin, Benjamin. 1839-59. *Letters*. Autobiographical Correspondence written to his son John Godwin. MS. AL.
Gore Langton Deeds, 1550-1788. DD/GL 63, SRO. Deeds and other documents relating to property in Englishcombe.
Merritt, John Silas. nd. *A Complete History of Old King Street Baptist Church, Bristol, 1640-1890*. MS. CRBC.
Mean, Joseph. 1798. *Collections Biographical Historical and Miscellaneous relating to the History of Dissenting Churches of the Congregational, Presbyterian Antipaedobaptist Denominations in England and Wales*. ms, L6/15 f.525-527, DWL.
Old King Street Baptist Church, Bristol. *Minutes*. CRBC.
Parsons, Robert. 1763. *Letter to Western Baptist Association*. BBC.
Parsons, Thomas. c.1770. *A Collection of Vases, Terms, &c. by Thomas Parsons, Carver, Bath*. 38:18, BCL.
Reeves Collection of letters and other items belonging to John Saffery in Salisbury (Sarum). AL
Reeves Private Collection of letters and other items from members of the Gay family at Haycombe, Bath. AL.
Root, Jane. *Shedule of Bath Deeds*. Bath Archaeological Trust. BRO.
Russ, Elsie A. 1925-1959a. *Bath Reference Library Local Index*. BCL.
Russ, Elsie A. 1925-1959b. *Biographical Reference Book for Bath Celebrities*. ms, typescript. BCL.
Somerset Street Baptist Church. *Accounts*. MSBC.
Somerset Street Baptist Church. *Birth and Burial Registers*. RG4/1790, TNA.
Somerset Street Baptist Church. *Minutes*. MSBC.
Somerset Street Baptist Church. *Proceedings in the Singing Gallery, 1814-1844*. MSBC.
Somerset Street Baptist Church. *Sunday School Records*. MSBC.
Steele Papers: Collection of letters and other items belonging to the Steele family donated by H Steele-Smith. AL
Thomas, Joshua. c.1795. *The History of the Baptist Churches in Wales*. ms, BBC.
Thompson, Josiah. c.1770 [1774]. *Protestant Dissenting Congregations*. ms, iv, 38.10 f.172, DWL.
Twerton Baptist Church. 1814-1874. *Account Books*. BRO.
Twerton Baptist Church. 1816-1853. *Correspondence*. BRO.
Twerton Baptist Church. 1817. *Sunday School Annual Report*. TBC.
Twerton Baptist Church. 1825-1905. *Receipts and Vouchers*. BRO.
Twerton Baptist Church. 1828-1879. *Minutes*. OPBC.
Twerton Baptist Church. 1830. *Trust Deed*. copy, BRO.
Western Baptist Association Records 1733-1809. ms, G98a. BBC.
Willway, Irene. 1967. *History of Manvers Street Baptist Church*. Manuscript. MSBC.
Wilson, Walter. no date. *Account of Various Congregations*. ms, i, 63.I.1. ff.98-101. DWL.

York Street Baptist Chapel. 1828-1859. *Membership Roll*. MSBC.

Unpublished Correspondence:
Davis, John P S. 1987-1991. *Correspondence with Author*.
Holland, Elizabeth A. 1997. *Correspondence with Author*.
Smith, Connie. *Correspondence with Author*.
Wilson, Ellie. 1948. *Correspondence with F.W.R. Deverell*.

Printed Sources:

Bath Guides & Directories:
────── *Bath and Bristol Guide*.
────── *Gibb's Bath Visitant*.
────── *Historic and Local New Bath Guide*.
────── *New Bath Guide*.
────── *Original Bath Guide*.

Journals, Magazines & Newspapers:
────── *Baptist Annual Register*.
────── *Baptist Handbook*.
────── *Baptist Magazine*.
────── *Baptist Manual*.
────── *Baptist Quarterly*.
────── *Bath and Cheltenham Gazette*.
────── *Bath and Wilts Chronicle*.
────── *Bath and Wilts Chronicle & Herald*.
────── *Bath Chronicle*.
────── *Bath Journal*.
────── *Evangelical Magazine*.
────── *Gentleman's Magazine*.
────── *Transactions of the Baptist Historical Society*.

────── 1791. *Remarks on a Printed Letter (Lately Published) and Addressed to the Members of the Baptist Society, Meeting in Gerrard Street, Bath, By Mr. Thomas Parsons*. Bath.
────── 1794. *The Second Year's State of the Casualty-Hospital in the City of Bath, with an Alphabetical List of Subscribers and Benefactors, for the Year 1794*. Bath.
────── 1846. *Remarks on a Letter Addressed by a Church of the Baptist Denomination, meeting in York Street Chapel, Bath, to one of its Seceding Members*. Bath.
Anstey, Christopher. 1766. *The New Bath Guide*. 1970 edition, Bath, Adam & Dart. With an introduction by Kenneth G Ponting.
Bristol Association Circular Letters 1824-1851. BBC.
Carey, William. 1792. *An Enquiry into the Obligations of Christians, to use Means for the Conversion of the Heathens*. Leicester. 1991 edition. Didcot, BMS.

Carey, William. 1793-1833. *Journal and Selected Letters*. Collected and Edited by Terry G Carter. 2000. Macon Georgia, Smyth & Helwys Publishing Inc.

Cater, Philip. 1831. *The Fall of a Great Man: A Sermon, Occasioned by the Death of the Rev. Robert Hall, A.M., Preached in the Baptist Chapel, York Street, Bath.* Bath.

Cater, Philip. 1836. *An Address to the Members of the Church and Congregation meeting in York Street Chapel, Bath.* Bath.

Cater, Philip. 1839. *Trials of Young Men in Business. A Sermon Preached at York-Street Chapel, Bath.* Bath.

Cater, Philip. 1859. *The Difficulties of a Baptist Minister; with a Farewell Sermon, preached in York Street Chapel, Bath.* Bath.

Collier, Thomas. 1652. *Pulpit-Guard Routed.* BBC.

Collier, Thomas. 1676. *An Additional Word to the Body of Divinity.* BBC.

Collier, Thomas. 1677. *A Brief and True Narrative of the unrighteous dealings with Thomas Collier.* DWL.

Court of Chancery. 1829. *The Case of the Baptist Church, Bath.* BBC, BCL & MSBC. Legal documents and proceedings as published by both parties to the case.

Coxe, Nehemiah. 1677. *Vindiciae Veritatis, Or A Confutation of the Heresies and Gross Errours Asserted by Thomas Collier in his Additional Word to his Body of Divinity.*

Edwards, Thomas. 1646. *Gangraena.* London. 1977 edn. The Rota and the University of Exeter; repr. 1998.

Falconer, Thomas. 1804. *A Letter to the Rev. Richard Warner.* Bath.

Fuller, Andrew. *The Complete Works of the Rev. Andrew Fuller.* (3 vols). ed. Fuller, Andrew Gunton; rev. Belcher, Joseph; 1845 edn. repr. Harrisonburg, Virginia: Sprinkle Publications, 1988.

Gadsby, J. 1870. *A Memoir of the Late Mr William Gadsby, for Thirty-Eight Years Pastor of the Baptist Chapel, Rochdale Road, Manchester.* 1990 edn, with new type-set and chapter divisions. Welsh Tract Publications, Salisbury, Maryland.

Gadsby, William. 1884. *Sermons.* compiled by J Gadsby. 1991 edn. Harpenden, Gospel Standard Trust Publications.

George, Timothy and George, Denise. (eds). 1996. *Baptist Confessions, Covenants, and Catechisms.* Nashville, Tennessee: Broadman & Holman Publishers.

Gill, John. 1735-8. *The Cause of God and Truth in Four Parts.* 1855 edn. repr. Paris, Arkansas: The Baptist Standard Bearer Inc, 2000.

Gill, John. 1769. *A Body of Doctrinal Divinity; or A System of Evangelical Truths, Deduced from the Sacred Scriptures.* 1839 edn. repr. Paris, Arkansas: The Baptist Standard Bearer Inc, 2000.

Gill, John. 1770. *A Body of Practical Divinity; or A System of Practical Truths, Deduced from the Sacred Scriptures.* 1839 edn. repr. Paris, Arkansas: The Baptist Standard Bearer Inc, 2000.

Gill, John. nd. *The Collected Writings of John Gill.* CD-ROM. © 2000 Ages

Software Inc.

Graves, Richard. 1773. *The Spiritual Quixote or The Summer Ramble of Mr Geoffrey Wildgoose*. 1967 edition. Oxford University Press.

Hall, Robert. 1846. *The Miscellaneous Works and Remains*. London.

Jay, William. 1809. *The Memoirs of the Life and Character of the Late Rev. Cornelius Winter*. London.

Jay, William. 1833. *The Christian: A Sermon Delivered at the Interment of Mrs Marianna Head, in the Baptist Meeting, Bradford, March 1, 1832*. Bath.

Jay, William. 1854. *The Autobiography of William Jay*. Edited by Redford, George and James, John Angell. 1974 edition, Edinburgh, Banner of Truth Trust.

Lumpkin, William L. (Ed). 1959. *Baptist Confessions of Faith*. 1969 edn. Valley Forge, Judson Press.

Manvers Street Baptist Church. 1912. *Manvers Street Sunday School Centenary Record*. June, 1912.

Morshead, William. 1832. *Is the Church of England Apostate? Being a Christian Minister's Protest*. Bath.

Morshead, William. 1832. *The Apostacy of the Church of England Not Disproved by The Rev. R. Page's Anatomy of a "Christian Minister's Protest."* Bath.

Morshead, William. c.1832. *Christian Worship at the Masonic Hall, York Street*. Bath.

Morshead, William. c.1832. *Some Account of the Worship and Preaching at the Freemason's Hall, Bath*. Bath.

Page, James R. 1832. *Anatomy of The Rev. Wm. Morshead's "Christian Minister's Protest," Entitled "Is the Church of England Apostate?"* Bath.

Parsons, Robert. 1745. *Advertisement*. 1879c13(15), BL.

Parsons, Robert. (attrib.) 1772. *A Letter to the Rev. Mr. Fletcher, of Madely, on the Differences Subsisting between him and the Hon. and Rev. Mr. Shirley*. Bath.

Parsons, Robert. 1774. *Abilities for the Ministry of the Gospel from God alone. A Discourse on 2 Corinthians iii. 6. Delivered to the Baptist Congregation Meeting in Bath in June, 1774*. Bath. BCL.

Parsons, Thomas. 1791. *To the Members of the Baptist Society Meeting in Gerrard-Street, Bath*. BCL.

Parsons, Thomas. 1799. *Effusions of Paternal Affection, on the Death of a Lovely Daughter*. Bath.

Parsons, Thomas. 1800. *Letters to a Member of the British Parliament, on the Absurdity of Popular Prejudices*. Bath.

Parsons, Thomas. 1804. *Christianity, a System of Peace: A Letter to the Rev. Thomas Falconer; in which a Vindication of the Subject of the Rev. Richard Warner's Sermon, entitled "War Inconsistent with Christianity," is Attempted*. Bath.

Parsons, Thomas. 1804. *A Second Letter to the Rev. Thomas Falconer; in which The Arguments adduced in Support of Defensive War are examined; and a Further Vindication of the Subject of the Rev. Richard Warner's Sermon, is Attempted*. Bath.

Parsons, Thomas. (attrib.) 1808. *High Church Claims Exposed, and the Protestant*

Dissenters and Methodists Vindicated: or Free Remarks on a Pamphlet Entitled 'Strictures on Subjects chiefly related to the Established Religion and the Clergy, In Two Letters to his Patron, from A Country Clergyman' In a Letter to the Author. Bath.

Rippon, John. 1790-1802. *Baptist Annual Register.* London.

Rippon, John. 1838. *A Brief Memoir of the Life and Writings of the Late Rev. John Gill, D.D.* Reprinted from Dr. Gill's *Exposition of the Bible* published posthumously. repr. Harrisonburg, Virginia: Sprinkle Publications, 1992.

Skinner, John. 1797. *West Country Tour: Diary of an excursion through Somerset, Devon and Cornwall.* 1985, edited and introduced by Roger Jones. Bradford on Avon, Ex Libris Press.

Skinner, John. 1803-1834. *Journal of a Somerset Rector: Parochial Affairs of the Parish of Camerton.* 1971, edited by Howard and Peter Coombs. Weston-super-Mare, Kingsmead Press.

Steele, Anne. 1760. *Hymns.* 1967, edited by J R Broome. London, Gospel Standard Baptist Trust.

Thomas, Sarah. 1994. *The Secret Diary of Sarah Thomas 1860-1865.* Edited by June Lewis. Moreton-in-March, The Windrush Press.

Warburton, John. 1857. *Mercies of a Covenant God, being An Account of Some of the Lord's Dealings in Providence and Grace with John Warburton, Minister of the Gospel, Trowbridge.* 1964, edited by Geoffrey Williams. London, The Evangelical Library.

Warner, Richard. 1804. *War Inconsistent with Christianity: A Fast-Sermon.* Bath.

Watts, Isaac. 1707. *Hymns and Spiritual Songs.* London, John Lawrence.

Wesley, John. 1735-1790. *Journal.* (4 vols). 1906 edition. London, J M Dent & Sons.

Western Baptist Association Circular Letters 1752-1853. BBC.

Western Baptist Association Fund Appeal Letter 1775. BBC.

White, B R. 1971-1974. *Association Records of the Particular Baptists of England, Wales and Ireland to 1660.* Three Parts, with Index 1977. London, Baptist Historical Society.

Whitefield, George. *Journals.* 1960 edition, London, Banner of Truth.

Wood, John. 1745. *A Description of the Exchange of Bristol.* Bath.

Wood, John. 1765. *A Description of Bath.* 1969 edition, Bath, Kingsmead Press.

Young, C M and Handcock, W D. (eds). 1956. *English Historical Documents.* xii(i) 1833-1874. 1964 edition, London, Eyre & Spottiswoode.

B) Secondary Sources

Published Articles:

―――― 1931. 'Collecting for a Chapel.' *Baptist Quarterly.* v, no.5, 236-237.

Bates, E Ralph. 1981. 'Eighteenth-Century Chalices in Bath Methodism.'

Proceedings of the Wesley Historical Society. xliii, part 2, 29-30.
Bates, E Ralph. 1983. 'Wesley's Property Deed for Bath.' *Proceedings of the Wesley Historical Society.* xliv, part 2, 25-35.
Birch, Kerry J. 1997a. 'Baptist Burial Grounds in Bath.' *Baptist Quarterly.* xxxvii, no.1, 20-32.
Birch, Kerry J. 1998. 'Richard Gay of Haycombe: An exploration of a story and its influence on local Baptist family and community history.' *Baptist Quarterly.* xxxvii, no.8, 367-385.
Bone, Mike. 2000. 'The Rise and Fall of Bath's Breweries: 1736-1960.' *Bath History.* Bath, Millstream Books. viii, 106-133.
Bush, Sydney W. 1934. 'Reminiscences.' *Manvers Street Magazine.* This occasional series of articles only survives because they were collected together in a scrapbook. The last is dated September 1934. MSBC.
Clews, Stephen. 1994. 'Banking in Bath in the Reign of George III.' *Bath History.* Bath, Millstream Books. v, 104-124.
Clipsham, Ernest F. 1963-4. 'Andrew Fuller and Fullerism.' *Baptist Quarterly.* xx, nos.3-6; 99-114, 146-154, 214-225, 268-276.
Copson, Stephen. 1997. 'Anatomy of a Dispute Between Thomas Collier and Thomas Hall.' *Bible, History and Ministry: Essays for L G Champion on his Ninetieth Birthday.* Bristol, Baptist College. 107-121.
Davis, Graham. 1986. 'Entertainments in Georgian Bath: Gambling and Vice.' *Bath History.* Gloucester, Alan Sutton Publishing Ltd. i, 1-26.
Fawcett, Trevor. 1990. 'Eighteenth-Century Shops and the Luxury Trade.' *Bath History.* Gloucester, Alan Sutton Publishing Ltd. iii, 49-75.
Fleming-Williams, Ian. 1986. 'Introduction.' *The Barkers of Bath.* Bath City Council, Museums Service. Catalogue of an Exhibition at the Victoria Art Gallery, Bath, 17 May to 28 June 1986.
George, Timothy. 2001. 'John Gill.' in *Theologians of the Baptist Tradition.* eds. George, Timothy and Dockery, David S. Nashville, Tennessee: Broadman & Holman Publishers. 11-33.
Hayden, Roger. 1999. 'The Contribution of Bernard Foskett.' *Pilgrim Pathways: Essays in Baptist History in Honour of B R White.* Macon, Mercer University Press. 189-206.
Jeremy, David J. 1967. 'The Social Decline of Bath.' *History Today.* xvii, 242-249.
Keevil, A J. 2000. 'Barrack(s) Farm, Wellsway, Bath: The Estate and Its Holders.' *Bath History.* Bath, Millstream Books. viii, 27-55.
Kirkby, Arthur H. 1954. 'Andrew Fuller – Evangelical Calvinist.' *Baptist Quarterly.* xv, no.5, 195-202.
Langley, Arthur S. 'Baptist Ministers in England about 1750 AD.' *Transactions of the Baptist Historical Society.* vi, 1918-1919, 138-162.
Lovegrove, Deryck W. 1980. 'Particular Baptist Itinerant Preachers during the late 18th and early 19th Centuries.' *Baptist Quarterly. Xxviii.* 127-141.
Manco, Jean. 1988. 'The Cross Bath.' *Bath History.* Gloucester, Alan Sutton Publishing Ltd. ii, 49-84.

Morgan, Kenneth. 1994. 'The John Evans List of Dissenting Congregations and Ministers in Bristol, 1715-29.' *Reformation and Revival in Eighteenth-Century Bristol*. Barry, Jonathan and Morgan, Kenneth. (eds). Bristol Record Society. 63-73.

Meek, D E and Murray D B. 1988. 'The Early Nineteenth Century.' Bebbington, D W. (ed). *The Baptists in Scotland: A History*. Glasgow, Baptist Union of Scotland. 26-47.

Naish, R G. 1934. 'Early History of West Twerton Baptist Church.' *Bath and Wilts Chronicle and Herald*. An article on 6 July followed by a series of eight articles between 24 August and 5 September. Other articles on the History of Twerton appeared in the years up to 1939.

Neale, R S. 1964. 'The Industries of the City of Bath in the First Half of the Nineteenth Century.' *Proceedings of the Somerset Archaeological and Natural History Society*. cviii, 132-144.

Nettles, Tom J. 1997. 'John Gill and the Evangelical Awakening.' *The Life and Thought of John Gill (1697-1771): A Tercentennial Appreciation*. Haykin, Michael A G. (ed). Leiden, New York and Koln: Brill.

Phillips, Paul T. 1973. 'The Religious Side of Victorian Bath, 1830-1870.' *Social History*. vi, 224-40.

Price, S J. 'The Centenary of the Baptist Building Fund.' *Baptist Quarterly*. iii, 276.

Price, S J. 'The Early Years of the Baptist Union III.' *Baptist Quarterly*. iv, 171.

Pugh, R B. 1959 'Chartism in Somerset and Wiltshire.' *Chartist Studies*. Briggs, A. (ed). London, Macmillan.

Reeves, Marjorie. nd. 'Protestant Nonconformity.' *The Victoria History of the Counties of England: A History of Wiltshire*. iii, 99-149.

Reeves, Marjorie. 1999. 'Literary women in eighteenth-century Nonconformist circles.' Shaw, Jane and Kreider, Alan. (eds). *Culture and the Nonconformist Tradition*. Cardiff, University of Wales Press.

Richey, Russell E. 1973. 'English Baptists and Eighteenth-Century Dissent.' *Foundations*. xvi. No.4, 347-354.

Roberts, Phil. 2001. 'Andrew Fuller.' in *Theologians of the Baptist Tradition*. eds. George, Timothy and Dockery, David S. Nashville, Tennessee: Broadman & Holman Publishers. 34-51..

Sloman, Susan. 2007. 'An eighteenth-century stonecarver's diary identified: Eight months in the life of Thomas Parsons (1744-1813) of Bath.' *The British Art Journal*. vii. No.3, 4-13.

Torrens, Hugh. 1978. 'Geological Communication in the Bath area in the last half of the eighteenth century.' Jordanova, L J and Porter, Roy S. (eds). 1979. *Images of the Earth: Essays in the History of the Environmental Sciences*. British Society for the History of Science, Monograph 1, 215-247.

Torrens, Hugh. 1983. 'Letter to Editor.' *Geological Curator*. iii. no.7, 421, with reference to iii. no.6, 386.

West, W M S. 1980. 'Baptists and Statements of Faith.' *Expository Times*. vol.91, no.8, 228-233.

West, W M S. 1984. 'Methodists and Baptists in Eighteenth Century Bristol.' *Proceedings of the Wesley Historical Society.* xliv, part 6, 157-167.

White, B R. 1968. 'The Doctrine of the Church in the Particular Baptist Confession of 1644.' *Journal of Theological Studies.* New Series. XIX, 2, October 1968.

Whitley, W T. 1916. 'Association Life till 1815.' *Transactions of the Baptist Historical Society.* v (1916-1917), 19-34, 196.

Whitley, W T. 1920. 'An Index to Notable Baptists, Whose Careers began within the British Empire before 1850.' *Transactions of the Baptist Historical Society.* vii (1920-1921), 182-239.

Whitley, W T. 1932. (attrib.) 'Bath.' *Baptist Quarterly.* Iv. 279.

Willmer, Haddon. 2002. 'Writing Local Church History.' *Ecumenism and History: Studies in Honour of John H. Y. Briggs.* Anthony R. Cross (ed). Carlisle, Paternoster Press. 208-224.

Published Studies:

———— 1844-1848. *History of the Churches.* Bridgwater, Western Baptist Association. Published in 5 parts along with the Circular Letters.

———— 1928. *One Hundred Years: The Centenary Story of Oldfield Park Baptist Church, Bath, 1828-1928.* Bath, Oldfield Park Baptist Church.

———— 1950. *Old King Street Baptist Church, Bristol, Tercentenary Souvenir.* Bristol, Old King Street Baptist Church.

———— 1978. *How Firm a Foundation: Twerton Baptist Church and Oldfield Park Baptist Church Ter-Jubilee 1828-1928.* Bath, Twerton and Oldfield Park Baptist Churches.

Arnold, Thomas. 1845. *Miscellaneous Works.* London, Fellowes.

Arnold, Matthew. 1869. *Culture and Anarchy.* 1994 edition. Yale University Press.

Bebbington, D W. 1989. *Evangelicalism in Modern Britain: A History from the 1730s to the 1980s.* London, Unwin Hyman Ltd.

Borsay, Anne. 1999. *Medicine and Charity in Georgian Bath: A Social History of the General Infirmary, c.1739-1830.* Aldershot, Ashgate Publishing Ltd.

Borsay, Peter. 2000. *The Image of Georgian Bath, 1700-2000: Towns, Heritage, and History.* Oxford University Press.

Boyce, Benjamin. 1967. *The Benevolent Man - A Life of Ralph Allen of Bath.* Harvard University Press.

Brackney, William H. 1999. *Historical Dictionary of the Baptists.* Lanham, Maryland, and London; Scarecrow Press.

Brackney, W H; Fiddes, Paul S; and Briggs, John H Y. (eds). 1999. *Pilgrim Pathways: Essays in Baptist History in Honour of B. R. White.* Georgia USA, Mercer University Press.

Brewer, John. 1997. *The Pleasures of the Imagination: English Culture in the Eighteenth Century.* London, HarperCollins.

Briggs, J H Y. 1994. *The English Baptists of the Nineteenth Century.* Didcot, The

Baptist Historical Society.
Brock, Peter. 1972. *Pacifism in Europe to 1914*. Princeton University Press.
Broome, J R. (ed). 1967. *Hymns by Anne Steele*. London, Gospel Standard Baptist Trust.
Broome, J R. 1996. *John Warburton, Servant of a Covenant God.* Harpenden, Gospel Standard Trust Publications.
Brown, Raymond. 1986. *The English Baptists of the Eighteenth Century*. London, The Baptist Historical Society.
Buchanan, R A and Cossons, Neil. 1969. *The Industrial Archaeology of the Bristol Region*. Newton Abbot, David & Charles.
Carey, S Pearce. 1923. *William Carey 1761-1843.* London, Hodder and Stoughton Ltd.
Carlile, John C. 1905. *The Story of the English Baptists.* London.
Carter, Terry G. (ed.) 2000. *The Journal and Selected Letters of William Carey*. Georgia, Smyth & Helwys Publishing.
Cater, Philip. 1834. *Memoirs of the Life and Character of the Late Rev. John Paul Porter.* Bath.
Champion, L G. 1961. *Farthing Rushlight: The Story of Andrew Gifford 1700-1784*. London, The Carey Kingsgate Press.
Chandler, Eric. 2003. *Improving Baptists: The Mutual Improvement Society at Manvers Street Baptist Church*. Bath, Open House Publications.
Chandler, J H. 1985. *Wiltshire Dissenters' Meeting House Certificates and Registrations 1689-1852*. Devizes, Wiltshire Record Society.
Chapman, Mike. 1996. *A Guide to the Estates of Ralph Allen around Bath, Based on his map in the Bath Record Office*. Bath, Survey of Old Bath.
Chapman, Mike. 1997. *An Historical Guide to the Ham and Southgate Area of Bath*. Bath, Survey of Old Bath.
Chapman, Mike; Hawkes, John and Holland, Elizabeth. 1998. *The J. Charlton Map of Lyncombe and Widcombe 1799*. Bath, Survey of Old Bath.
Chapman, Mike and Holland, Elizabeth. 2000. *Bath Guildhall and its Neighbourhood: 800 Years of Local Government*. Bath, Survey of Old Bath.
Chapman, Mike and Holland, Elizabeth. 2001. *"Bimbery" and the South-Western Baths of Bath*. Bath, Survey of Old Bath.
Clarke, Gillian. 1987. *Prior Park: A Complete Landscape*. Bath, Millstream Books.
Clarke, Philip and Lyn. 1977. *The Baptist Church at Chipping Sodbury: Its Story through Four Centuries*. Chipping Sodbury Baptist Church.
Cliff, Philip B. 1986. *The Rise and Development of the Sunday School Movement in England 1780-1980*. Nutfield, Redhill, Surrey, National Christian Education Council.
Coard, Peter. 1972. *Vanishing Bath*. Bath, Kingsmead Press.
Collinson, John. 1791. *The History and Antiquities of the County of Somerset*. Reprinted, Gloucester, Alan Sutton Publishing Ltd, 1983.
Cottle, Basil. 1987. *Joseph Cottle of Bristol*. Bristol Branch of the Historical Association.

Cowherd, Raymond G. 1956. *The Politics of English Dissent.* London, Epworth Press.
Cox, F. A. 1842, *History of the Baptist Missionary Society.* (2 vols). London.
Cragg, Gerald R. 1960. *The Church and the Age of Reason 1648-1789.* 1970 edition. Harmondsworth, Penguin Books Ltd.
Crofts, Bruce. (ed). 1990. *At Satan's Throne: The Story of Methodism in Bath.* Bristol, White Tree Books - an imprint of Redcliffe Press Ltd.
Cryer, Neville. 1978. *Bibles Across the World.* London, Mowbray.
Currie, Robert; Gilbert, Alan and Horsley, Lee. 1977. *Churches and Churchgoers: Patterns of Church Growth in the British Isles Since 1700.* Oxford, Clarendon Press.
Davis, Graham and Bonsall, Penny. 1996. *Bath: A New History.* Keele University Press.
Davis, Graham and Bonsall, Penny. 2006. *A History of Bath – Image and Reality.* Lancaster, Carnegie Publishing Ltd.
Davis, John P S. 1991. *Antique Garden Ornament: 300 years of creativity: Artists, manufacturers & materials.* Woodbridge, Antique Collector's Club.
Davis, Sally. 1984. *John Palmer and the Mailcoach Era.* Bath Postal Museum.
Day, Joan. 1973. *Bristol Brass: The History of the Industry.* Newton Abbot, David & Charles.
Dictionary of Evangelical Biography. 1995. Donald M. Lewis (ed). Oxford, Blackwell Publishers Ltd.
Dix, Kenneth. 2001. *Strict and Particular – English Strict and Particular Baptists in the Nineteenth Century.* Didcot, The Baptist Historical Society for The Strict Baptist Historical Society.
Doel, William. 1890. *Twenty Golden Candlesticks! or A History of Baptist Nonconformity in Western Wiltshire.* Trowbridge and London.
Durnbaugh, Donald F. 1968. *The Believers' Church: The History and Character of Radical Protestantism.* 1985 edn. Scottdale, Herald Press.
Ede, Mary. 1989. *The Chapel in Argyle Street, Bath 1789-1989.* Bath, Central United Reformed Church.
Ella, George M. 1994. *William Huntington: Pastor of Providence.* Darlington, Evangelical Press.
Ella, George M. 1995. *John Gill and the Cause of God and Truth.* Eggleston, Co. Durham, Go Publications.
Ella, George M. 1996. *Law and Gospel in the Theology of Andrew Fuller.* Eggleston, Co. Durham, Go Publications.
Ella, George M. 1997. *John Gill and Justification from Eternity: A Tercentenary Appreciation 1697-1997.* Eggleston, Co. Durham, Go Publications.
Evill, William. 1904. *Rambling Records of a Long and Busy Life.* London, Printed for Private Circulation.
Fawcett, Trevor. 1995. *Voices of Eighteenth-Century Bath - An anthology of contemporary texts illustrating events, daily life and attitudes at Britain's leading Georgian spa.* Bath, Ruton.

Fawcett, Trevor. 1998. *Bath Entertain'd – Amusements, Recreations and Gambling at the 18th-Century Spa*. Bath, Ruton.
Fawcett, Trevor. 2001. *Bath Administer'd – Corporation Affairs at the 18th-Century Spa*. Bath, Ruton.
Fawcett, Trevor. 2002. *Bath Commercialis'd – Shops, Trades and Market at the 18th-Century Spa*. Bath, Ruton.
Fuller, J G. 1840. *The Rise and Progress of Dissent in Bristol; Chiefly in Relation to the Broadmead Church: With Brief Accounts of The Church Meeting in King Street, and of The Community of Friends. Including Notices of the Early History of Castle Green, Bridge Street, and Lewin's Mead*. Bristol.
Fuller, J G. 1842. *A Memoir of the Rev. Thomas Roberts, M.A. Pastor of The Baptist Church, in King Street, Bristol: With an Enlarged History of the Church, from the Earliest Recorded Period, to the Present Time*. Bristol.
Fuller, J G. 1843. *A Brief History of the Western Association, from its Commencement, about the middle of the seventeenth century, to its division into four smaller ones – the Bristol, the Western, the Southern, and the South Western – in 1823*. Bristol.
Gadd, David. 1971. *Georgian Summer: Bath in the Eighteenth Century*. 1977 edn. Bradford-on-Avon, Moonraker Press.
George, Timothy. 1991. *Faithful Witness: The Life and Mission of William Carey*. Leicester, Inter-Varsity Press.
Gilbert, Alan D. 1976. *Religion and Society in Industrial England: Church, Chapel and Social Change 1740-1914*. London, Longman Group Ltd.
Goldsmith, Oliver. 1762. *The Life of Richard Nash*.
Grenz, Stanley J. 1994. *Theology for the Community of God*. Carlisle, Paternoster Press.
Grenz, Stanley J. 1998. *Created for Community: Connecting Christian Belief with Christian Living*. Grand Rapids, Baker Books.
Gunnis, Rupert. 1951. *Dictionary of British Sculptors 1660-1851*. Second revised edition. London, The Abbey Library.
Haddon, John. 1982. *Portrait of Bath*. London, Robert Hale Ltd.
Hall, C Sidney and Mowvley, Harry. 1991. *Tradition and Challenge: The Story of Broadmead Baptist Church, Bristol from 1685 to 1991*. Bristol, Broadmead Baptist Church.
Hart, Gerald S. 1987. *Ministry 200: The Story of Pill Union Church*. Bristol, Pill Union Church.
Hayden, Roger. (ed) 1974. *The Record of a Church of Christ in Bristol, 1640-87*. Bristol Record Society.
Hayden, Roger. 2005. *English Baptist History and Heritage*. Second edition. Didcot, Baptist Union of Great Britain.
Haykin, Michael A G. 1994. *One Heart and One Soul: John Sutcliff of Olney, his friends and his times*. Darlington, Evangelical Press.
Haykin, Michael A G. (ed). 1997. *The Life and Thought of John Gill (1697-1771): A Tercentennial Appreciation*. Leiden, New York and Koln, Brill.
Haykin, Michael A G. (ed). 1998. *The British Particular Baptists 1638-1910*. Vol 1.

Springfield, Missouri, Particular Baptist Press.
Haykin, Michael A G. (ed). 2000. *The British Particular Baptists 1638-1910*. Vol 2. Springfield, Missouri, Particular Baptist Press.
Haykin, Michael A G. (ed). 2003. *The British Particular Baptists 1638-1910*. Vol 3. Springfield, Missouri, Particular Baptist Press.
Haykin, Michael A G. (ed). 2004. *'At the Pure Fountain of Thy Word': Andrew Fuller as an Apologist*. Carlisle, Paternoster Press.
Hembry, Phyllis. 1990. *The English Spa 1590-1815: A Social History*. London, The Athlone Press.
Hill, Mary K. 1989. *Bath and the Eighteenth Century Novel*. Bath University Press.
Holland, Elizabeth. 1992. *The Kingston Estate Within the Walled City of Bath*. Bath, Survey of Old Bath.
Horne, C Silvester. 1903. *A Popular History of the Free Churches*. London.
Hutchings, Victoria. 2005. *Messrs Hoare Bankers: A History of the Hoare Banking Dynasty*. London, Constable & Robinson Ltd.
Inglis, K. S. 1963. *Churches and the Working Classes in Victorian England*. London, Routledge and Kegan Paul.
Isaac, Peter. 2000. *A History of Evangelical Christianity in Cornwall*. Printed for the author by W E C Press, Gerrard's Cross.
Ivimey, Joseph. 1811-30. *History of the English Baptists*. (4 vols). London, Published by the Author.
Jackman, Douglas. 1953. *Baptists in the West Country*. Dorchester, The Western Baptist Association.
Kelly, Alison. 1990. *Mrs Coade's Stone*. Upton-upon-Severn, The Self Publishing Association Ltd.
Kember, Ian. 1998. *Silver Street: A Baptist Chapel and Its Town. The Early Years 1814-1851*. Taunton Baptist Church.
Lees-Milne, James. 1962. *The Earls of Creation: Five Great Patrons of Eighteenth-Century Art*. 1986 Edition, London, Century Hutchinson Ltd in association with the National Trust.
Leitch, Russell. 1985. *The History of Keynsham Baptist Church*. Keynsham Baptist Church.
Little, Brian. 1980. *Bath Portrait: The Story of Bath*. Bristol, Burleigh Press.
Little, Peter R. 1995. *A History of Twerton*. Privately printed.
Lovegrove, Deryck W. 1988. *Established Church, Sectarian People: Itinerancy and the Transformation of English Dissent, 1780-1830*. Cambridge University Press.
Lumpkin, William L. (ed). 1959. *Baptist Confessions of Faith*. 1969 edn. Valley Forge, Judson Press.
Machin, G I T. 1977. *Politics and the Churches in Great Britain, 1832-1868*. Oxford University Press.
Manco, Jean. 1995. *The Parish of Englishcombe: A History*. Bath, Englishcombe Parish Council.
Manley, Ken R. 2004. *'Redeeming Love Proclaim' – John Rippon and the Baptists*. Carlisle, Paternoster Press.

Mann, J de L. 1971. *The Cloth Industry in the West of England from 1640 to 1880*. Oxford University Press.
Manning, Bernard Lord. 1942. *The Hymns of Wesley and Watts*. London, Epworth Press. Reissued 1988.
Manning, Bernard Lord. 1952. *The Protestant Dissenting Deputies*. Cambridge University Press.
McLaughlin, David and Gray, Michael. 1989. *Bath in Camera 1849-1861, Early Rare Photographs, Calotypes by The Rev. Francis Lockey LLD 1796-1869*. Bath, Monmouth Calotype & London, Dirk Nishen Publishing.
McGlothlin, W J. 1911. *Baptist Confessions of Faith*. Philadelphia, American Baptist Publication Society.
Meyler, T S. 1823. *The Original Bath Guide*. Bath.
Mitchell, Brigitte and Penrose, Hubert. 1983. *Letters from Bath 1766-1767 by the Rev. John Penrose*. Gloucester, Alan Sutton Publishing Ltd.
Moon, Norman. 1979. *Education for Ministry: Bristol Baptist College 1679-1979*. Bristol Baptist College.
Morden, Peter J. 2003. *Offering Christ to the World: Andrew Fuller (1754-1815) and the Revival of Eighteenth Century Particular Baptist Life*. Carlisle, Paternoster Press.
Murch, Jerom. 1835. *A History of the Presbyterian and General Baptist Churches in the West of England*. London, R. Hunter.
National Trust. 1985. *Bath Assembly Rooms*. Guide. Bath, National Trust.
Naylor, Peter. 1992. *Picking up a Pin for the Lord: English Particular Baptists from 1688 to the Early Nineteenth Century*. London, Grace Publications.
Neale, R S. 1981. *Bath: A Social History 1680-1850 or A Valley of Pleasure, yet a Sink of Iniquity*. London, Routledge & Kegan Paul.
Nettles, Thomas J. 1986. *By His Grace and for His Glory: A Historical, Theological, and Practical Study of the Doctrines of Grace in Baptist Life*. Grand Rapids, Baker Book House. 2002 edn. Lake Charles, Louisiana, Cor Meum Tibi.
Oliver, Robert W. 1968. *The Chapels of Wiltshire and The West*. Volume 5 of *The Strict Baptist Chapels of England*. London, The Fauconbery Press for the Strict Baptist Historical Society.
Oliver, Robert W. 1989. *Baptists in Bradford on Avon*. Bradford on Avon, Old Baptist Chapel.
Oliver, Robert W. 2006. *History of the English Calvinistic Baptists 1771-1892*. Edinburgh, The Banner of Truth Trust.
Owens, Nield. 1909. *Union Chapel, Combe Down: Its History and Progress*. Bath, Union Chapel.
Parker, Grace M. 1975. *Widcombe Baptist Church: The First 150 Years*. Bath, Widcombe Baptist Church.
Parkinson, Louis C. 1908. *Praise and Progress, being a Brief History and Account of The Present Word at Manvers Street Baptist Church, Bath*. Bath, Manvers Street Baptist Church.
Payne, Ernest A. 1944. *The Free Church Tradition in the Life of England*. London,

SCM Press Ltd.
Payne, Ernest A. 1959. *The Baptist Union*. London, The Baptist Union.
Peach, R E M. 1893. *Street-lore of Bath: A Record of Changes in the Highways and Byways of the City*. Bath and London.
Pitt, Graeme. 1987. *A Better Chance: The fortunes of a colonial pilgrim in Australia*. Adelaide, South Australia.
Pollock, John. 1977. *Wilberforce*. 1982 edition. Tring, Lion Publishing.
Ponting, Kenneth G. 1971. *The Woollen Industry of South-west England*. New York, Augustus M Kelley Publishers.
Ponting, Kenneth G. 1975. *Wool & Water: Bradford-on-Avon and the River Frome*. Bradford-on-Avon, Moonraker Press.
Ramsbottom, B A. 2003. *William Gadsby*. Harpenden, Gospel Standard Trust Publications.
Reeves, Marjorie and Morrison, Jean. (Eds). 1989. *The Diaries of Jeffery Whitaker Schoolmaster of Bratton, 1739-1741*. Trowbridge, Wiltshire Record Society.
Reeves, Marjorie. 1997. *Pursuing the Muses: Female Education and Nonconformist Culture 1700-1900*. Leicester University Press.
Rogers, Kenneth H. 1976. *Wiltshire and Somerset Woolen Mills*. Edington, Pasold Research Fund Ltd.
Rogers, Kenneth H. 1986. *Warp and Weft: The Somerset and Wiltshire woollen industry*. Buckingham, Barracuda Books.
Rosman, Doreen M. 1984. *Evangelicals and Culture*. 1992 reprint. Aldershot, Gregg Revivals.
Rosman, Doreen. 2003. *The Evolution of the English Churches 1500-2000*. Cambridge University Press.
Rouse, Marylynn. 2000. *The Life of John Newton by Richard Cecil*. Fearn, Christian Focus Publications.
Rupp, Ernest Gorden. 1986. *Religion in England 1688-1791*. Oxford University Press.
Scott, Maurice. 1993. *Discovering Widcombe and Lyncombe, Bath*. Bath, Widcombe Association. Revised 2nd edition.
Sell, Alan. 1982. *The Great Debate: Calvinism, Arminianism and Salvation*. Worthing, H E Walter Ltd.
Shaw, Ian J. 2002. *High Calvinism in Action. Calvinism and the City. Manchester and London, 1810-1860*. Oxford University Press.
Shaw, Jane and Kreider, Alan. (eds). 1999. *Culture and the Nonconformist Tradition*. Cardiff, University of Wales Press.
Shorney, David. 1996. *Protestant Nonconformity and Roman Catholicism: A guide to sources in the Public Record Office*. London, PRO Publications.
Silvester, James. 1888. *The Parish Church of Walcot, Bath: Its History and Associations*. Bath.
Sitwell, Edith. 1932. *Bath*. London, Faber & Faber.
Skeats, Herbert S and Miall, Charles S. 1891. *History of the Free Churches of England 1688-1891*. London, Alexander & Shepheard.

Sparkes, Douglas C. 1996. *Pensions – Provision for Retired and Disabled Ministers*. Didcot, The Baptist Historical Society.

Stone, Barbara G. 1973. *Bath Millennium: The Christian Movement 973-1973*. Bath, Ebdons.

Stott, Anne. 2003. *Hannah More: The First Victorian*. Oxford University Press.

Swaine, Stephen Albert. 1884. *Faithful Men; Or, Memorials of Bristol Baptist College, And Some Of Its Most Distinguished Alumni*. London, Alexander & Shepheard.

Talbot, Brian R. 2003. *The Search for a Common Identity: The Origins of the Baptist Union of Scotland 1800-1870*. Carlisle, Paternoster Press.

Thompson, David. 1885. *"A Book of Remembrance;" or A Short History of the Baptist Churches in North Devon*. London, Alexander & Shepheard.

Toon, Peter. 1967. *The Emergence of Hyper-Calvinism in English Nonconformity 1689-1765*. London, The Olive Tree.

Trestrail, Frederick. no date. *Reminiscences of College Life in Bristol*. London, E Marlborough & Co.

Turner, A J. 1977. *Science and Music in Eighteenth Century Bath*. An Exhibition in the Holborne of Menstrie Museum, Bath, 22 September to 29 December 1977, catalogued by A J Turner with the assistance of I D Woodfield and contributions by H S Torrens. Bath, Holborne of Menstrie Museum.

Turner, J. 1872. *The Bath Sunday-Schools: Their Rise and Progress*. Bath, Bath Sunday School Union.

Tyte, William. 1898. *History of Lyncombe and Widcombe with Recollections of the Parish in the Thirties*. Bath, Bath Chronicle Office.

Tyte, William. 1903. *Bath in the Eighteenth Century: Its Progress and Life Described*. Reprinted, with Additions, from the *Bath and County Graphic*. Bath, Bath Chronicle Office

Underdown, David. 1992. *Fire From Heaven*. London, HarperCollins.

Underwood, A C. 1947. *A History of the English Baptists*. London, Kingsgate Press.

Urdank, Albion M. 1990. *Religion and Society in a Cotswold Vale 1780-1865*. Berkeley and Los Angeles, University of California Press.

Walton, Robert C. 1946. *The Gathered Community*. London, Carey Press.

Ward, W R. 1972. *Religion and Society in England 1790-1850*. London, B T Batsford Ltd.

Wassell, David. 1862. *Doing Good: A Brief Memoir of the late Mr George Cox of Bath*. Bath, Somerset Street Baptist Church.

Watts, Michael R. 1978. *The Dissenters: From the Reformation to the French Revolution*. Volume I. Oxford University Press.

Watts, Michael R. 1995. *The Dissenters: The Expansion of Evangelical Nonconformity*. Volume II. Oxford University Press.

Watts, Michael R. 1996. *The Chapel and The Nation: Nonconformity and the Local Historian*. London, The Historical Association.

Welch, Edwin. 1995. *Spiritual Pilgrim: A reassessment of the life of the Countess of Huntingdon.* Cardiff, University of Wales Press.
White, B R. 1996. *The English Baptists of the Seventeenth Century.* 2nd Edn. Didcot, The Baptist Historical Society.
Whitley, W T. 1916-1922. *A Baptist Bibliography.* (2 vols). Compiled for the Baptist Union of Great Britain and Ireland. London, The Kingsgate Press.
Whitley, W T. 1923a. *A History of the British Baptists.* London, Charles Griffin & Company, Ltd.
Whitley, W T. 1923b. *The Story of the Western Baptists.* Torquay, Devon & Cornwall and Western Baptist Associations.
Whitley, W T. 1930. *Calvinism and Evangelicalism in England especially in Baptist Circles.* London, The Kingsgate Press.
Williams, Thomas Minns. 1955. *A Short History of Old King Street Baptist Church, Bristol.* Bristol, Old King Street Baptist Church.
Williams, W J and Stoddart, D M. 1978. *Bath—Some Encounters With Science.* Bath, Kingsmead Press.
Wroughton, John. (Ed) 1972. *Bath in the Age of Reform.* Bath, Morgan Books.

C) Unpublished Studies

Birch, Kerry J. 1997b. *Richard Gay of Haycombe: an exploration of a story and its influence on local Baptist family and church history.* Bristol Baptist College Dissertation for BA Honours degree of the University of Bristol.
Chambers, R F. no date. *Where Heated Waters Spring: The Story of the Strict Baptist Chapels of Bath.* ms. BCL.
Hancock, Noel Paul. 1991. *The Life and Work of the Reverend Benjamin Godwin: A Baptist response to the Oxford Movement.* Thesis for the degree of Master of Philosophy of the University of Nottingham.
Hayden, Roger. 1991. *Evangelical Calvinism among Eighteenth Century British Baptists with particular reference to Bernard Foskett, Hugh and Caleb Evans and the Bristol Baptist Academy, 1690-1791.* PhD Thesis, Keele University.
Land, Richard Dale. 1979. *Doctrinal Controversies of English Particular Baptists (1644-1691) as illustrated by the Career and Writings of Thomas Collier.* DPhil Thesis, University of Oxford.
Neale, R S. 1963. *Economic Conditions & Working Class Movements in the City of Bath, 1800-1850.* Thesis for the degree of Master of Arts of the University of Bristol.
Oliver, Robert W. *The Emergence of a Strict and Particular Baptist Community among the English Calvinistic Baptists 1770-1850.* CNAA PhD Thesis, London Bible College.
Smith, Karen Elizabeth. 1986. *The Community and the Believer: A Study of Calvinistic Baptist Spirituality in Some Towns and Villages of Hampshire and the Borders of Wiltshire, c. 1730-1830.* DPhil Thesis, University of Oxford.

www.ingramcontent.com/pod-product-compliance
Lightning Source LLC
Chambersburg PA
CBHW021838220426
43663CB00005B/298